Practical Software Estimation

Infosys Press

Infosys Press seeks to develop and publish a series of pragmatic books on software engineering and information technologies, both current and emerging. Leveraging Infosys's extensive global experience helping clients to implement technologies successfully, each book distills critical lessons learned and shows how to apply them in a real-world, enterprise setting. Readers will find throughout this open-ended and broad-ranging series a wealth of practical insights, specific guidance, and informative examples not readily available elsewhere.

✦✦ Addison-Wesley
www.awprofessional.com

Infosys®
www.infosys.com

Infosys®

Practical Software Estimation

Function Point Methods for Insourced and Outsourced Projects

M. A. Parthasarathy

Foreword by N. R. Narayana Murthy
Chairman and Chief Mentor
Infosys Technologies Ltd.

✦ Addison-Wesley

Upper Saddle River, NJ • Boston • Indianapolis • San Francisco
New York • Toronto • Montreal • London • Munich • Paris • Madrid
Capetown • Sydney • Tokyo • Singapore • Mexico City

Many of the designations used by manufacturers and sellers to distinguish their products are claimed as trademarks. Where those designations appear in this book, and the publisher was aware of a trademark claim, the designations have been printed with initial capital letters or in all capitals.

This document contains material, which has been extracted from the International Function Point Users Group (IFPUG) *4.2 Counting Practices Manual*. It is reproduced in this document with the permission of IFPUG (http://www.ifpug.org). The International Function Point Users Group (IFPUG) is a not-for-profit, member run, user group. The IFPUG mission is to be a recognized leader in promoting and encouraging the effective management of application software development and maintenance activities using Function Point Analysis and other software measurement techniques. For more information contact IFPUG at http://www.ifpug.org, or e-mail ifpug@ifpug.org, or phone (USA) 609-799-4900, or fax 609-799-7032.

The author and publisher have taken care in the preparation of this book, but make no expressed or implied warranty of any kind and assume no responsibility for errors or omissions. No liability is assumed for incidental or consequential damages in connection with or arising out of the use of the information or programs contained herein.

The publisher offers excellent discounts on this book when ordered in quantity for bulk purchases or special sales, which may include electronic versions and/or custom covers and content particular to your business, training goals, marketing focus, and branding interests. For more information, please contact U.S. Corporate and Government Sales, (800) 382-3419, corpsales@pearsontechgroup.com.

For sales outside the United States, please contact International Sales, international@pearsoned.com.

This Book Is Safari Enabled

The Safari® Enabled icon on the cover of your favorite technology book means the book is available through Safari Bookshelf. When you buy this book, you get free access to the online edition for 45 days.

Safari Bookshelf is an electronic reference library that lets you easily search thousands of technical books, find code samples, download chapters, and access technical information whenever and wherever you need it.

To gain 45-day Safari Enabled access to this book:

- Go to http://www.awprofessional.com/safarienabled

- Complete the brief registration form

- Enter the coupon code W2G8-LHVF-XVZQ-XWFQ-B9GX

If you have difficulty registering on Safari Bookshelf or accessing the online edition, please e-mail customer-service @safaribooksonline.com.

Visit us on the Web: www.awprofessional.com

Library of Congress Cataloging-in-Publication Data

Parthasarathy, M. A.
  Practical software estimation : function point methods for insourced and outsourced projects / M. A. Parthasarathy.
    p. cm.
  Includes bibliographical references and index.
  ISBN 0-321-43910-4 (pbk. : alk. paper)
  1. Computer software—Development. 2. Computer software—Development—Estimates. I. Title.

  QA76.76.D47P356 2007
  005.3—dc22

                                                                    2006036476

ISBN 0-321-43910-4

Text printed in the United States on recycled paper at Courier in Stoughton, Massachusetts.

First printing, February 2007

To

My son, Aravind, and my wife, Rama,
who kept pushing me to complete this book.

My father, Tiru Narayan, and my mother, Padma,
for grooming me to be worthy of many achievements!

My fellow Infoscions,
for providing me the platform to learn and share.

CONTENTS

FIGURES

TABLES

FOREWORD

In order to derive continuous improvement in the software engineering process, it is essential to measure and control the process. Good software estimation methodologies ensure process predictability and clarity on timelines. Accurate estimation benefits several stakeholders and results in

- Better profitability
- Better employee morale
- Higher customer satisfaction

In situations where the end customer is not very conversant with software engineering or the nuances of programming, estimation gives credibility to the software engineering process, and helps the service provider gain respect from the customer. Superior estimation methodologies lead to optimal utilization of inputs and improve the quality of the end product, both of which result in higher satisfaction levels. In essence, a process-driven objective estimation, which eliminates the person dependency, is a competitive advantage for the organization that implements it.

Despite considerable effort and costs having gone into research on improving the accuracy of software estimation, the results have been far from satisfactory. Estimation accuracy has varied from as low as 5% to as high as 350%! There are a number of reasons for such a high degree of variation in estimations, including inadequate scope capture, lack of appropriate technical skills, and poor project execution techniques.

Heads of large IT organizations continue to be tormented by one of the most difficult facets of managing IT business: controlling their budgets. Estimates that cover costs towards discretionary and non-discretionary expenses, including operational and infrastructure costs, have always been a source of dispute and ambiguity. Unlike hard facts and figures available in manufacturing industry, there are many gray areas in the software industry that have yet to be ironed out.

This book attempts to address many of the gray areas in the software project execution process. M. A. Parthasarathy of Infosys has used his vast experience in project execution in writing this book. Starting from a very basic explanation of the ingredients of a typical estimation activity, he proceeds to remove some of the basic misconceptions about software estimation.

In a truly "flat world" scenario today, there is a compelling need for IT organizations to bring together an international global workforce where people from different countries and cultures come together to produce world-class services and products, resulting in many complexities in software project execution. In this context, it is very important to have process driven effort and cost estimation methodologies.

Software professionals and managers will find this book insightful and lucidly written, providing an analytical approach to estimation methodologies.

N. R. Narayana Murthy
Chairman and Chief Mentor
Infosys Technologies Ltd.
Bangalore

PREFACE

I never imagined that writing a book would be such an exhausting but exciting experience. Originally I only had a mental picture of how the book would evolve, with certain key aspects of software estimation I intended to write down. But as the chapters unfolded one after another, the thoughts poured out more freely. The difficult part was organizing the thoughts into a structured way of presentation, adding tables and diagrams to enhance the enumeration, and tying up other loose ends to make the whole discussion complete in all respects (almost all). I hope I have been successful in doing this.

Although I had fairly deep knowledge and experience in software estimation techniques from my early years as an IT professional, it was at Infosys that I had the extraordinary experience of doing a deep dive into a huge variety of estimation-related interactions. Having personally trained more than 500 software professionals at Infosys on Function Points and other estimations methods, the amount of knowledge I acquired during these sessions was huge. Added to this was the visibility I gained as an estimation expert, which brought another storehouse of enriched knowledge. This enrichment happened through a regular stream of queries and issues that the project managers, programmers, and architects brought to me. Analyzing and solving these issues was exciting, although challenging. But the biggest benefit was to me, that of improving my estimation skills. Every situation was unique and needed interpretation and application of a variant of standard estimation methods.

IT professionals who have been working with large outsourcing organizations similar to Infosys across the globe have likely experienced a fairly wide variety of project execution situations during their service. The experience takes various forms, including project execution, technical challenges, customer interactions, testing and debugging issues, and to some extent estimation-related challenges. I have been quite fortunate to have received the maximum experience of estimation-related challenges across a wide variety of projects, either directly or through issues and challenges posed to me by project teams. It is this experience that I have hoped to put together in the form of this book and share with a global community of IT professionals.

Quite frequently I have seen IT professionals in need of assistance to arrive at a good estimation figure for a complex or unique project. I have tried to provide that assistance, realistically and practically, throughout this book. I would receive the ultimate satisfaction from knowing that IT professionals have been able to resolve the majority of estimation-related issues through the examples and instruction in this book!

Layout of Chapters

Having been actively involved in software project management and software estimation-related activities for a long time, direct interaction with software project managers, architects, and programmers was among the many benefits I received. The layout of the chapters of this book has been designed to start with general software estimation topics, including an introduction to basic estimation concepts, followed by a discussion of the function point estimation method and, finally, in later chapters, coverage of a variety of other software project estimation needs.

Chapter 1, "Introduction," has been written as an introduction to estimation concepts for project managers and programmers who have had very little exposure to estimation principles and the ingredients that constitute estimation. This chapter broadly covers basic aspects of how estimations are done in different project execution situations and how these estimates can be refined through continuous improvement cycles.

Chapter 2, "Role of Estimation in Software Projects," takes you forward toward establishing a link between estimation and software project execution. The intention is to explain various complexities of software projects and show how estimates also need to be customized accordingly. Complexities include project execution lifecycle models, technology platform variations, and project size. Project managers with previous project execution and basic estimation related exposure can skip this chapter.

Chapter 3, "A Study of Function Point Analysis," takes you through the various aspects of the IFPUG Function Point Analysis (FPA) method. The FPA method is discussed in full detail here, including discussion on how to identify attributes of the various components of the FPA method. IT professionals who do not have a good knowledge of IFPUG FPA method should definitely read this chapter in detail.

Chapters 4 and 5 cover "Data Functions" and "Transactional Functions" extensively. For IT practitioners, it is essential that a mapping of the FPA estimation method is provided to the actual software project execution process. These chapters provide the detailed mapping along with extensive examples from real software project situations. If you have gone through Chapter 3, it is advisable to read Chapters 4 and 5 also.

Chapter 6, "General System Characteristics," has been especially written to delve into the most critical and complex part of the IFPUG FPA method. Estimators have often experienced difficulty in making the right judgment of the correct level of impact (degree of influence) of each of the 14 general system characteristic (GSC) parameters. An effort to map the GSCs to the software architecture and its performance parameters have been made here. This chapter should be very interesting to serious estimators.

Chapter 7, "Size, Effort, and Scheduling of Projects," has been put together to help understand the process of converting the software size, as discovered in earlier chapters, to effort and schedule. Criticality of certain software project execution environment including productivity of the team, resource loading, and use of tools has been used as important input to derive project effort and schedule. All estimators, managers, and even programmers should definitely go through this chapter.

Chapter 8, "Estimation Flavors," exposes you to some of the practical estimation-related problems encountered during actual project execution. Typical estimation methods provide us with basic estimation processes that are usable in software development projects and sometimes in maintenance projects. But this is not the total reality in an IT organization environment. There are a host of other project execution varieties including migration, reengineering, porting, and more. This chapter picks up a few such popular software projects and maps the standard estimation method (IFPUG FPA) to the situations.

Chapter 9, "A Sense of Where You Are," addresses the dynamic project execution situations and how estimates are required to be revisited at every milestone stage. It explains how the information about the executed part of the project can be effectively analyzed and utilized to predict the remaining project execution effort and duration.

Chapter 10, "Tips, Tricks, and Traps," brings to you a variety of complexities that occur during project execution situations and provides possible solutions on how to tackle these situations. This chapter will be very handy to estimators who face many complex project execution scenarios.

Chapter 11, "Insourcing versus Outsourcing," discusses various aspects of project execution that are unique to situations when the project is executed through insourcing as against the situation when the project is executed through an outsourcing vendor. The focus is on the way estimates are impacted by insourcing and outsourcing situations.

Chapter 12, "Key Factors in Software Contracts," will be of great interest to managers and software professionals involved in preparing software contracts. Popular contracting models involving fixed price, time, and material are discussed with respect to impact on estimation process. Also discussed are certain project execution lifecycle models that have a direct impact on estimations.

Chapter 13, "Project Estimation and Costing," takes you further from project sizing and effort estimations to converting them into actual costs. Discussions on aspects of resource loading based on project execution phases, technical complexities, and its impact on overall costs will help you understand some of the flavors of project costing.

Chapter 14, "Other Estimation Methods," is an important chapter for estimators and managers who are keen to know more about additional popular estimation methods (other than the function point method). This chapter discusses aspects of how various estimation methods are modeled based on heuristic and parametric approaches. Brief discussions on a few estimation methods, including Delphi method, COCOMO II, and COSMIC-FFP, are covered.

Chapter 15, "Estimation Tools," gives you key tips on features you should look for while selecting estimating tools for procurement. A comprehensive list of popular tools available in the market, along with a brief discussion on each tool's features, is provided.

Chapter 16, "Estimation Case Study," is perhaps one of the most important chapters for all serious software professionals, estimators, and managers. The first case study in this chapter extensively covers details of the estimation process for typical development projects. Also provided is a case study on estimation for executing an enhancement request in a maintenance project.

With the intention of providing ready-to-use formats for easy and quick counting of Function Point parameters like data and transaction functions, I have provided sample tables in Appendixes A and B.

Bangalore, 2007

ACKNOWLEDGMENTS

Throughout the journey of writing this book—and in a few situations before, which actually led to the writing of this book—a number of well-wishers have helped me. In no particular order, I would like to place on record my heartfelt thanks to all of them.

For initiating the idea of writing a book on estimation and continually reminding me to act on it, I would like to thank many of my close friends, in particular, my colleagues S. V. Subrahmanya and Shubha V. One person acted as my guide and mentor, always carefully listening to my radical ideas on software estimations and many other IT related topics: Srinath Batni. Srinath always participated actively in my thought processes and in fact refined and improved upon the ideas on several occasions. My thanks to Srinath for all the support and contributions.

My heartfelt thanks to Narayana N. R. Murthy, Nandan M. Nilekani, Kris Gopalakrishnan, Shibulal and K. Dinesh, founders of Infosys, for providing me with the opportunity to validate and develop some of my estimation-related initiatives. The insight and thought leadership demonstrated by them on many software estimation related processes have immensely helped me mature as an estimation expert.

I would like to thank the reviewers of this book for having gone through the pain of careful evaluation of the contents. My thanks to Frank Parth, Paul Below, Jim Brosseau, Joseph M. Tarrani, and U. Maitland. The review comments I received from these professional reviewers have greatly improved the quality of the book's contents.

I want to make a special mention of my colleagues from our own Infosys internal estimation core group, ESTEEM (Estimation Enterprise Model), who provided me with opportunities to explore ideas, come up with improved solutions to estimation-related problems, and much more. I would like to convey my appreciation to Dinesh Ganesan, Aman Kumar Singhal, Milind V. Badkundri, and Siddharth Sawhney (all from the ESTEEM team) for taking time off from their busy schedules to review the manuscript and provide invaluable suggestions.

Deependra Moitra and his team provided me with the much-needed guidance and assistance to establish the relationship with the publishers of this book. Special thanks to Pandurangan A. G., for facilitating the Foreword by N. R. Narayana Murthy. Vijayaraghavan T. S., Aarathi Chellappa, and Kanupriya Sindhu helped me with corporate clearances. My thanks to them.

The ever-encouraging support and guidance provided to me by my publishers have greatly helped me to keep moving forward with the difficult chapters of the book. I would like to mention my special appreciation to Peter Gordon and Kim Boedigheimer of Addison-Wesley for this. It was only when the manuscript reached the copyediting stage that I realized how bad my grammar and sentence formation capabilities were. Many thanks to Katherine Murray for going through every sentence of the manuscript painstakingly and polishing the contents. My thanks to Tyrrell Albaugh and her team for facilitating production-related activities.

My daily carpooling to the office has brought its own extra benefits. Not only was I able to try out many of my "great" ideas about estimation and software engineering in general and get appropriate answers (not always palatable!), but I was also gently but consistently pushed to complete the book at the earliest possible date, in the larger interest of the software developer community across the globe. For all this and much more, I would like to thank Dr. Ravindra Muthya Pranesha.

Bangalore, 2007

CHAPTER 1

Introduction

What Is Software Estimation?

Estimation: It is the mark of an instructed mind to rest satisfied with the degree of precision which the nature of a subject requires, and not to seek exactness where an approximation may suffice.
—Aristotle, 330 BC

Estimation is a frequently occurring phenomenon in our everyday lives. When we leave home for the office in the morning, we roughly estimate the time it will take to reach the office. When we plan to make a business analysis presentation in a meeting, we estimate the time it will take to complete the presentation, perhaps including time for questions and answers as well. A building contractor estimates the schedule and cost required to construct a building according to specific requirements. The driver of a car moving at a specific speed encounters an object crossing the road and instantly estimates the time it will take the car to reach the point of intersection and then corrects the speed accordingly. In all these everyday situations, the estimating activity happens sometimes consciously and sometimes subconsciously. It remains for the user to determine the level of estimation accuracy needed, based on the criticality of the activity itself. Above all, the process of estimation itself is refined iteratively in each of the preceding situations, based on historic data or past experience.

The parameters that define estimation vary depending upon the activity being estimated. Activities could be cost, resources (for example, materials), manpower, and equipment. Other parameters could be elapsed time, schedule, or other similar attributes. The key parameter common to all situations is experience. Whatever the method of estimation, the differentiating factor between a good and bad estimate is the experience of the estimator in arriving at the right mix of the parameters and their attributes. Organizations that are established in implementing quality practices like ISO 9002 and/or SEI/CMMI [1] document individual experiences as best practices and make them available to other estimators across the organization. Basically *the environment in which the activity is being executed* defines the estimation parameters. Typically, we would not be able to correlate and compare the estimations for two different categories of activities. For example, the time required to travel a certain distance in a certain traffic environment cannot be compared with the time taken to complete the construction of a building.

The Dream Project

Sunil was completely shattered. He was totally exhausted, both physically and mentally. He felt his career as a software professional was doomed. After toiling for almost nine months on one of the most grueling software project assignments he had ever had, the project itself was scrapped by the customer. He was totally at a loss to imagine what had gone wrong.

Although the project started nine months ago, to Sunil it seemed just a few weeks ago. Sunil was a lucky project manager indeed; he had been selected to lead a very prestigious software project. Almost all the components of the project seemed to be right. The project was being executed for one of the company's largest customers. The customer team was tech savvy. The technology was state-of-the-art. The application being developed was expected to bring a dramatic increase in business for the customer, based on some very innovative thinking by the business users. Above all, Sunil felt confident this would be a successful project due to the excellent environment in which he was working. His manager was a very good senior software professional, and the team members were well skilled in the technology on which the application was being developed. All the required tools and other development environment were in place.

Sunil's team followed all the processes needed in good software project execution. The requirements were done with due diligence and after a couple of thorough reviews, the customer signed off on the project. The design was carefully done, keeping both function and performance in view. The team included good developers and the code generated was of good quality. Early tests of some of the modules showed good results. Everything seemed to be going fine, Sunil recalled.

Of course there were a few hiccups on the way, but Sunil thought he addressed them quite well. Although there were a few slippages in the schedule, Sunil was confident of recovering. But now, as he recalled the events that happened during the early days, he wondered whether he really did a good job of fixing the issues and the connected risks. Did he fail to recognize the early warnings? He remembered each of these situations quite vividly:

Project Kick-Off: Immediately after the customer signed off on the big contract for the project, Sunil decided to do a detailed evaluation of the scope first including derived effort and schedule estimations. He brought a couple of senior team members and did an effort estimation based on the past experience of delivering similar projects. They had not previously sized a project of this magnitude; however, they had completed smaller projects and thought they would be able to do an extrapolation and arrive at a good guesstimate for the current project. They quickly realized that it was indeed a very large project. After several rounds of deliberations, it was decided to fix the delivery schedule at 15 months with an average team size of 30 members. The team was aware that the customer had a tight deadline and any further extension of schedule might not be allowed.

Schedule Renegotiation: During discussions with the customer on project execution strategy, team members realized that the customer was quite inflexible on the 10-month delivery schedule agreed upon during contract negotiations. Sunil had no option but to return to the drawing board and recalculate the project schedule and the related impact on other project delivery aspects. They had to do several review rounds to arrive at the best possible project execution plan. The reduction of schedule by 30 percent (from 15 months to 10 months) had a direct impact on the average team size, increasing it by a whopping 50 percent (from 30 members to 45 members). In order to reach this timeframe, they also reduced the buffer that had been built in earlier. As a result, all the phases of the software project were very tightly planned with little scope left to maneuver slippages.

Requirements Phase: During the requirements gathering phase, the scope was reviewed with the business users. The business users pointed out that due to recent changes in government regulations, the software application required specific changes in order to comply with the new regulations. This also meant changing the functional workflow of activities. Sunil's team included all the relevant changes and did a quick re-estimation. The overall effort had gone up by another 6 percent. Once again, a negotiation with the customer to increase the schedule was denied. The result was an increase in team size by another three members. Sunil was worried about the possible impact and increased risk but was confident his team would deliver.

Design Phase: The first serious signs of problems surfaced during design phase. The software was being developed on the Java platform. The technology vendor had recently introduced a new product that would dramatically change the way the business workflow could be manipulated directly by the end users. Although the product was a boon to the users, it meant two significant deviations to the project team: the team had to learn and understand features of the new product, and the team would need to invest additional effort to include the new product into the revised architecture of the software application. Overall, the effort went up again. Sunil's team was rightly worried this time. The size of the project was ballooning, but the end date of delivery was not allowed to change.

Project Progress Review: Sunil felt it was time to escalate the situation to his manager internally. His manager decided to do a complete review of the project status. Another surprise was soon to be discovered. The project had already slipped by two weeks. The late changes in project scope and the last-minute changes due to the addition of the new product had made their impact on schedule slippage. This situation was further aggravated when it was discovered that the new product was still in beta and had quite a number of bugs that needed to be removed by the vendor. By now the team size had grown to 50 members and it was looking almost impossible to meet the 10-month schedule.

Build Phase: During the coding stage, one of the key senior members fell ill and had to take two weeks leave. Two other developers decided to quit, thus adding salt to the wound. The early schedule slippage had a crunching impact on the time provisioned for the coding (build) phase. Despite Herculean efforts, the team found it impossible to meet the original deadline. Sunil had no other option but to go back to the customer to negotiate more time.

During discussions with the customer, the critical nature of the whole project emerged. The business users had planned strategically for this project to be ready in 10 months in order to meet a possible window of business opportunity that would last only a few months. Missing the deadline would mean a loss of business opportunity. The chances of similar opportunity occurring in the near future were almost nonexistent. Sunil was a depressed project manager when he returned from the meeting with the customer. The project team met to discuss the situation. Many enthusiastic younger team members felt there still was a last chance to meet the deadline if everyone pitched in with extra effort. The team decided to work extended work hours and weekends. There was an air of expectation and things seemed to improve.

But not for long. During early tests, serious performance issues were detected. Inconsistencies in coding standards followed by different groups within the project team were also found. This again was a setback that had a direct impact on delivery schedule. It was now impossible to meet the deadline under any circumstances. After internal deliberations with the team and Sunil's manager, it was decided to convey the sad news to the customer. The only option was to extend the delivery schedule by three months. The customer was aghast at the proposal. The matter was escalated to higher management and after a couple of rounds of senior level meetings it was decided by the customer to scrap the project.

What really did go wrong?

For a detailed solution to this project problem, please refer to Chapter 9, "A Sense of Where You Are."

Ingredients of a Good Estimation

Unless all the key ingredients of estimation are identified and assessed thoroughly, the process of estimation itself will be incomplete and in many situations, the end result will not be of much use. The key elements are discussed here.

Activity Scope

The important key element that forms the basis of estimation is the scope of the activity being estimated. *Scope* is a very loose term and will take different shapes in different situations. For example, if you were constructing a building, the scope would probably be the square feet of area being built. If you were traveling between two locations, the scope would be the distance in miles. If you intend to build a wardrobe for your bedroom, the scope would again be the area in square feet. If you are building a software application, the scope could be the size of the software in terms of functionality that it delivers or in terms of lines of code delivered. If you are making a business presentation to your customer, the scope could be the content that you intend to cover in order to make a good sales pitch. For a sportsperson who is practicing hard to win a 100-meter race, the scope would be the exact 100 meters the person needs to cover.

Work Environment

The environment in which the activity is being executed makes a huge impact on the overall estimation. While driving a compact car in the U.S., I could cover 10 miles in 12 minutes on Highway 101 in California. But it takes 45 minutes to drive seven miles on a similar highway between Madiwala and Electronic City in Bangalore, India. Likewise, it would be as tough to drive on the main streets of New York as it is easy to drive around the Parliament House in New Delhi. Obviously there is a big difference in environment between these situations. In this sense, *environment* refers to the layout of roads, traffic rules, and the people who follow (or do not follow) traffic regulations. It also refers to the capacity of the roads, which can handle a certain density of traffic. In another example, I could be constructing a building of a certain size in a crowded locality of a city or I could be constructing the same building in a jungle area. In the first case, there would be severe restrictions on movement of material and equipment, and in the second case, quite a

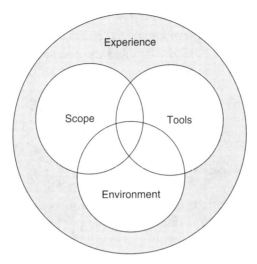

Figure 1.1 *Estimation ingredients.*

bit of effort would go first into clearing the jungle and then making long trips (for the material and for me) to the site on regular basis. Environment topics could range from weather conditions to political interference. They all play a crucial role in the final estimation. Figure 1.1 shows the various ingredients of estimation.

Consistency

Historic data, the competency of the team that executes the activity, and best practices developed over the years derive the estimation of time and hence the schedule for the activity to be delivered. Despite the repetition of similar sets of activities involved in completing a particular assignment, each new attempt is different in some way from previous one. Teams encounter new obstructions, issues, and hurdles, which may or may not have occurred in the previous occasion. It is these iterations that make a person or a team "experienced." And by carefully recording and analyzing the experiences, you can add immense value to the final estimation. In software parlance, the rate of delivery of a unit of work is better known as *productivity*.

Usage of Tools

Tools that are used to execute an activity play a significant role in defining the effort and the time taken to complete the activity. Tools can take different forms, shapes, and sizes depending upon the type of activity. The tool could be the type of car used for traveling between two locations, the construction equipment used for constructing a building, the sports gear used by the athletes, or the utility of other software tools used by the software developer. Effective use of tools has a major impact on productivity.

Learning from Past Experience

The popular definition of an expert, "One who has learned from past mistakes," has much relevance when you have a need for improving a defined process through multiple and continuous iterations. Fortunately, you need not learn everything from your past mistakes; you also can learn from others' mistakes, provided you have a well-defined process to record experiences and mistakes, and devise corrective actions. Each of the iterations of the improvement cycle will consist of the following:

- Define/refine the execution model
- Estimate required parameters based on the execution model
- Implement the defined model
- Continuously monitor during execution
- Measure key parameters of output generated (metrics)
- Analyze metrics, find the area of improvement, and refine the execution model

In each of these iteration cycles, the original estimation at the beginning of the cycle will be validated at the end of the cycle and based on the data collected, the estimation will be refined.

Software Project Estimation

Is estimation for a software development activity different from other estimations? I would say it is similar to any other estimation activity if you know the key parameters required to do an estimation—for example, scope, environment, experience, and tools. Figure 1.2 enumerates the two sides of the same coin. The three ingredients (scope, tools, and environment) are shown in two different contexts: general engineering and software engineering. In both situations, the contribution of all three ingredients is equally significant and plays an important role in arriving at final project execution estimates.

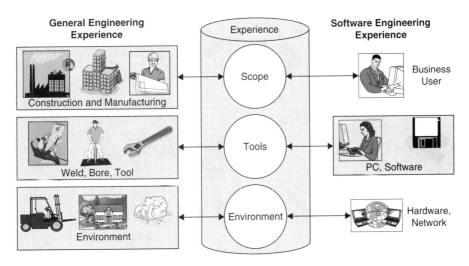

Figure 1.2 *Estimation ingredients—comparison.*

Project Scope

Software developers do realize that it is extremely difficult to capture accurately the scope of a given software project. A wide variety of ingredients make a software system complete. Here are just a few:

- Business functionality addressed through the application system
- The various modules of the application
- The platform, language, and database used
- Tools used as part of the application
- Performance and other execution capacity attributes of the system
- Interface with other systems in the environment

Although the number of methods used to capture the scope of the components of a software system have evolved over the last few decades, almost none of them can size the scope with precision. In software terms, the scope is equated with the *size* of the software system. The size has been defined in different units of measurement, such as Lines of Code (LOC), Function Points (FP), number of programs, and number of objects. Some of the popular software estimation models that have been developed by experts include

- Function Point Analysis Method [2]
- Mark II Function Points [3]

- COCOMO II Model [4]
- Feature Points [5]
- Object Points [6]
- COSMIC-FFP Method [7]
- Delphi Method [8]
- Use Case Points [9]
- Others (See Chapter 14, "Other Estimation Methods.")

Software Environment

A software system needs the right environment to exist and perform in much the same way a fish needs water to live. Most software systems are designed and developed for a particular target environment. Sometimes a variant of the software does execute in similar environments, which have basically originated from a common basic environment. For example, a software system developed for UNIX version 9.4 is likely to work with UNIX version 10.0, and with very few changes, it may work on the Linux operating system as well. But it is very unlikely for a software system developed on a mainframe operating system to work without changes on a Microsoft Windows operating system. There are many such parameters that define the environment in which a software system was developed and as a result, the software system can work only in certain target environments. Some of the key parameters that define the software environment are

- Operating system (including the version)
- Technology platform
- Programming language
- File system
- Database system (if applicable)
- Interfaces to other environments (if applicable)
- Hardware
- Communication system (if applicable)
- Architecture of the application system
- Performance and other scalability expectations from the software system

Developing a software system based on the environment in which the system is expected to execute has a considerable impact on the estimated effort. In situations where the same software system needs to execute in multiple types of environment, the effort to develop such a feature further adds to the overall effort.

Team Experience

Competency of the developers of the project team is a key factor that impacts the effort required to deliver the software system. Experience gained by developers while delivering software development projects helps enhance the competency of individuals as well as the team. Given the same software project scope, different teams may use different levels of effort. Some of the key aspects that define the competency of a developer team are

- Ability to understand clearly the scope
- Technical expertise on the development platform
- Project management expertise
- Quality procedures and processes
- Software testing skills

Software Development Tools

A wide variety of tools available in the market helps the developer in a variety of ways and forms. Some of the popular tools are

- Design tools
- Build tools
- Tools to review code according to standards
- Online documentation
- Tools to develop repeatable test scenarios
- Configuration tools

Each tool helps in some portion of the software development lifecycle. The benefits of using tools vary. The tools could help you adopt formal designing or coding practices, prepare documentation, configure the development environment, or facilitate easy testing of individual modules or programs. Directly or indirectly, the final benefit of using a tool is that it helps you complete the activity faster, thus saving development time.

The capability of the project team to deliver measurable outputs at a unit rate is termed **productivity.** For example, if the measurable output of the project is in function points count and the unit of time is hours, the productivity can be described in function points per hour. Experience, environment, and tools are all components of productivity.

Continuous Improvement Cycle

No two software projects are ever the same.
Even if the same project is redone!

Every new software project is a unique experience to the team. I'm sure that software project execution teams will agree with me whether they are part of the internal "Information Systems" department of an organization or they are from an external "Outsourcing" organization, and no matter how many software projects they have executed.

Parameters other than scope, environment, experience, and tools change the way project execution takes place. For example:

- *User* (customer): The adage, "The customer is king," fits very aptly into a software project contract. From concept to commissioning, as the project execution lifecycle progresses, so does the user's conceptual image of the end product. Steve McConnell [11] has observed: "… software development is a process of gradual refinement. You begin with a fuzzy picture of what you want to build and then spend the rest of the project trying to bring that picture into clearer focus." At times the user has only a conceptual image of the product at the start and as time progresses, the image gets refined until the user is almost sure of what he or she wants. And by this time, the software project is almost nearing its end. With the user in this state of mind, imagine the uncertainty the development team would have to manage.

- *Technology:* Upgrades in technology are not uncommon during the project execution lifecycle, particularly if the project is of long duration. And it may be possible that the user has the inclination to adopt the latest technology. If this happens, it has a direct impact on the project execution process and, as a result, the estimation, effort, and schedule.

A good software project execution team understands these fluctuating aspects of project execution and builds a certain amount of flexibility into their execution model.

The estimation effectiveness shown in Figure 1.3 improves with each iteration of project execution. As a process, the learning during each

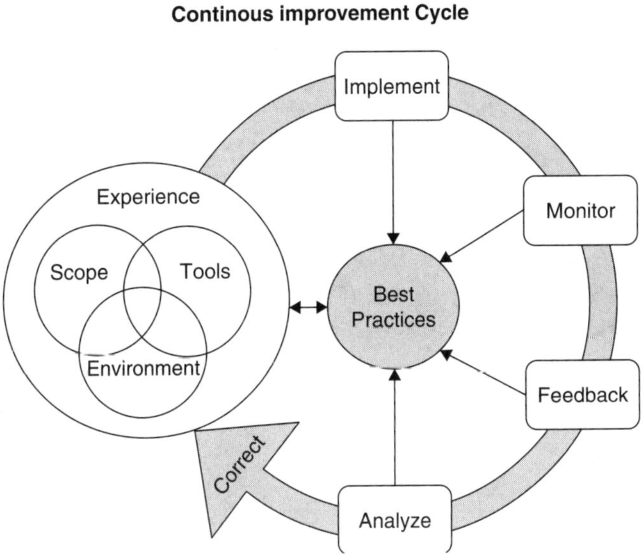

Continous improvement Cycle

Figure 1.3 *Estimation effectiveness.*

cycle is extracted during the cycle and converted into best practices. The measure and analyze processes help in identifying the shortcomings as well as the best practices that happened during a particular cycle. Based on these findings, a corrective action is applied before the next cycle of project execution.

Why Software Is "Soft"

Have you ever wondered who originally gave the name "software" to applications that were developed using a set of programs in a particular language, and why? Maybe the name originated because the end product was not actually visible to the user and only the effect of the "software" could be experienced. Maybe the name came from the fact that software is malleable enough to be modified, stretched, tinkered with, and purified through fire (destructive testing). The end product could look better and better as it passed through these iterations. Let's look at some of the serious aspects of the *soft* issue here.

Consider a typical software project execution lifecycle. In almost every phase of project execution, the *soft* part of the software being developed causes significant impact on the clear understanding of scope, quality, effort, and finally the schedule of delivery itself. Here are a few parameters to consider:

User: Put yourself in the shoes of the user. You can almost never say with absolute confidence that the scope defined by you, as captured by the project team, is final and that barring a few minor changes there will not be any significant changes in scope as the project progresses. As the user, you know this but confidently ask the project team to proceed with requirements definition. This often happens in project situations, due at least in part to a lax attitude by the stakeholders. The software being *soft* does play a significant role here. The killer assumption you (as the user) make here is that as the software project continues with construction, there exists ample opportunity to modify the scope at any time. The modification could happen even during the acceptance phase!

Designer: As much the user banks on the software being *soft*, the designer also carries the same assumption forward. The design is completed to the extent possible, based on the scope provided by the user, and passed on to the developer team. The understanding is that when additional (or balance) scope is provided, the designer returns to the design document and makes appropriate changes. "But this will mean rework," cries the developer. No problem; the software is *soft* and can be modified.

Developer: The developer team bears the brunt of the entire chain of reactions due to incomplete scope and incomplete design all because of the fact that software is *soft*. This is almost the last phase of project execution before test and acceptance happens. The developer team cannot pass the buck any further. Every small change in scope has a rippling and ballooning effect on the design, build, and test phases. Because of this, the quality, effort, and schedule of the project take a hit. All because software is *soft*.

How does this impact the estimation of the project? It is obvious that impact is huge!

On the other hand, if I compare *soft* with *hard*, there are clear differences in the way *hard* things are produced. For example, imagine a television manufacturing factory. If you look at an assembly line in the shop that rolls out a particular model of TV, you might be amazed to see the way the shape of the final product slowly builds as it moves along the assembly line. You would also notice that each and every component of the TV belongs in a specific place and it fits perfectly! Why? Someone in the manufacturing design office has taken extreme care to ensure that each and every assembly and subassembly has been carefully crafted to fit. Also planned well in advance are the workflow arrangements—what needs to come in what order and how the parts are tested. Imagine what would happen if you apply the same rules to *soft* products. Can the manufacturer afford to design a circuit board that is in its early stage of draft design and let it go into production? Can the LCD panel of the TV tube or the outer frame of the TV case go into production without the rest of the components being designed to fit perfectly with each other? The daily losses would be huge and the lack of fit among the components would almost turn the set into junk.

But it is *not* so with *soft* products!

Why Software Estimation?

A true professional always plans his or her project meticulously before the actual execution of the work begins. Effort estimation of individual activities is a key input to any good planning process. A building contractor must have a good handle on various activities in different phases of the project with near accurate estimates of resources, material, equipment, costs, etc., in order to be able to monitor and execute the project within a given time schedule. Of course, the customer for whom the building is being constructed must have an estimate of the amount of financing needed for milestone payments. Also as the project execution moves toward the final stages, the re-estimation needs become more frequent and critical. Disruptions in the building construction activities due to reasons like unplanned absenteeism of labor or delay in supply of critical construction material may force the project manager to reassess the impact on project schedules. In order to reschedule the project, it is necessary to re-estimate some of the activities.

Metrics—Past, Present, and Future

Those who cannot remember the past are condemned to repeat it!
—Santayana

Several well-documented analysis reports [10] highlight key factors responsible for failures of software projects, with bad estimation being a major contributor. Going a step further, there are several known reasons for estimations to be bad. These reasons include

- Ignoring past/historic data
- Optimism and bias in estimations
- Uncertainty of requirements
- Non-estimation
- Management pressure
- Unskilled estimators
- Budget constraints

Each of these factors, either individually or in combination, causes bad estimations. Enabling estimators through formal training and mentoring does help, but the training needs to be complemented with a well-defined process to formally collect metrics on past data. If implemented, the development team can now successfully *bat the googlies bowled* (a cricket term) sometimes by the management in the form of budget constraints and unreasonable delivery schedules.

The ISO and the SEI organizations have well-defined processes to collate metrics, and analyze and suggest improvements to a project execution activity. Estimation plays a significant role in defining and capturing metrics as per the ISO and SEI/CMMI recommendations. There are various estimation units that include Lines of Code (LOC), Function Points (FP), and Actual Effort (Person Hours), which can be effectively utilized as a yardstick to measure the size of a software application (these units of measurement are discussed in detail in later chapters). These yardsticks provide a critical reference baseline to rationalize the actual results of the software project execution process across multiple projects. For example, the productivity of the development team is defined as Function Points per Person Month (FP/PM) and sometimes as Person Hours per Function Point. The Defects Density that the development team generates is measured in terms of Defects per 1000 FP (there are other units of measure, too). Organizations that are able to implement effectively the ISO or SEI/CMMI processes find these measuring yardsticks of immense value. They help measure various project execution parameters across a wide variety of technology platforms, business functions, and even competency of the development teams in an "apples to apples" situation. Here are some of the key benefits of using a metrics collection process in an organization:

- *Past* project execution metrics help in assessing and analyzing the capabilities, strengths, and weakness of the processes, domain, and technology skills as well as the project execution methods deployed across the organization.

- Past experience also shows that as the project execution starts nearing the end stage, the testing and bug fixes activities increase. Typically the programmers in the project team would be under tremendous pressure to manage several activities simultaneously. These activities include completion of ongoing modules, testing the completed modules, and fixing the bugs reported on the tested modules. With the fast-approaching project delivery date, the pressure mounts exponentially, quite often leading to more mistakes. Metrics on these operational issues should be used to fine-tune estimations for similar projects.

- *Present* project execution metrics help in measuring, mentoring, and monitoring the ongoing projects in different lifecycle stages of execution. Comparing them with past metrics helps quick correction and fine-tuning, thus improving the probability of delivering the project on time, within cost, and with quality parameters.

- *Future* needs are those set as targets for achievement in the next six to 12 months. These targets could include improvement of productivity by 5 percent or a reduction in defect density by 10 percent. Once again, good estimation methods with defined units of measurement help in clear definition of future plans.

Estimation Dilemma!

Larry was clearly in a frustrated mood. Despite having the assistance of a good technology expert and couple of senior developers from his team, Larry was unable to pin down the exact development effort that the team needed in order to be able to deliver the project on time.

Just a week ago his manager, Peter, asked Larry to take this new project. The organization was losing considerable revenue because of fraudulent medical insurance claims. In the recent management meeting, it was decided to develop an application that could collate, analyze, and detect possible fraudulent cases well in advance. Peter was given the responsibility to put together a team and deliver this application. Larry had a record of successful project delivery and because this project was critical, his selection was an obvious choice. Larry was given just two days to come up with a project execution plan. Of course, the elapsed time to deliver was decided by the management well in advance. Larry had four months to do this.

Larry had enthusiastically started working on the project execution plan. He arranged a meeting time with a couple of subject matter experts, and obtained the allocation of a trusted technology expert and a couple of senior developers. The team went through an elaborate requirements-capturing process and also a high-level architecture definition of the application. At the end of the second day, Larry had in front of him a fairly well-defined scope. In order to obtain multiple approaches to effort estimations, Larry asked the technology expert and the developers to come up with their estimations separately. As a seasoned project manager, Larry worked on his own estimations. When Larry and his team compared the three estimates, the differences were too high to be in the comfort zone. The lowest and the highest estimates differed by more than 100 percent. Absolute lack of any process to collate and analyze historic data added to the woes of Larry's team. They had no backup support to depend on.

A classical case of lack of estimation capabilities in the organization was staring Larry in the face!

Importance of Estimation

As discussed in the beginning of this chapter, one of the critical factors that determine the success of your project involves how well you are able to estimate the parameters that control the project execution itself. Accurate estimates are as critical to software projects as they are to projects in manufacturing, construction, and similar professions.

Bad estimations or no estimations can lead to situations where the success of the project itself is at risk. Here are a few examples:

- Software projects have a notorious tendency of leaning toward failure if not handled with utmost diligence. Even published reports show success rates of software projects as quite low. Bad estimations are among the major causes for project failures.
- The process of estimation should encompass all the activities that consume effort and provide sufficient contingency for other risk factors that might derail the project. The risk factors include
  - Inconsistent or incomplete project scope definition
  - Competency of the project team resources
  - Complex business rules and algorithms
  - Unexpected change in technology environment
- Project management depends heavily on your anticipating the slippage in the project execution process well in advance and making appropriate corrections. Effort estimates for individual activities and a constant check on deviations in these efforts are critical inputs to good project management practices.

Estimation—Who and How

Software estimation is an art. As such, it requires an estimator to have artistic capability. Each estimator paints his or her own style of estimation picture—some artists follow traditional art forms and others develop their own techniques. No matter what an estimator's style, some of the key stakeholders who need estimates include

- The business folks
- The end user
- The sponsor
- The subject matter experts (SME)
- The project manager
- The developer
- The IT management
- The outsourcing vendor (if involved)

The Business Folks: Without the business people, a software project does not exist, more-or-less. You may have all the other stakeholders you need to execute the project but without a business need it is next to impossible to kick start the project. The business envisions a new business opportunity that exists in the near future. In order to be able to reach and take advantage of the new business opportunity, the business team debates and visualizes the need for their IT group to enhance and provide new business functionality in their application systems. Thus the need for a fresh software project is born. But if you are wondering about the link between business and software estimation, the answer is the time-to-market that is given to the developer team. The clear mandate that is given to the project sponsor is this: No matter what effort and resources are required, you have to deliver by a given time! Any delay beyond that certain stretch of time may result in the whole project becoming inconsequential. The business need may not exist after that point.

The End User: Equally important are the end users. They are the most difficult community of all the stakeholders, and sometimes they are also the business folks themselves. Most end users are typically senior employees of the organization. Having seen several generations of system changes, they are the most difficult to satisfy with further changes to application usage patterns. As such, they need to be involved in key project planning activities from the start. The project delivery schedule is the key area of interest to end users because that determines when they need to start getting acclimatized to the new functionalities in the upgraded applications.

The Sponsor: Being the sponsor of the project brings clear responsibility on two fronts: budget versus expenses, where the sponsor needs to keep a tight check on the costs incurred against the deliveries, and the time schedule the sponsor has promised to the end users (business folks). Without a good handle on estimates of cost and effort, and, as a result, the schedule, it would be impossible for the sponsor to manage these important commitments. The cost estimates also are useful in making a build-or-buy decision while evaluating COTS (Common Off The Shelf) products.

The Subject Matter Experts (SME): Similar to the end user, the SMEs need to plan their participation in advance. The project schedule that is based on estimated effort would highlight the periods of participation by SMEs.

The Project Manager: Project management, among other essential ingredients, is one of the critical factors needed in order for a software project to be successful. Meticulous planning, continuous monitoring, and applying corrective factors at the appropriate time are the traits of a successful project manager. Estimation of size, and hence the effort, is a major input to project management process. Tom DeMarco [12] has observed, "Estimating is at the very heart of the difficulty we have in controlling software projects." It is not enough if a project manager does the estimation once in the beginning of the project. Re-estimation activity at the completion of every milestone of the project is absolutely essential. We will discuss this in detail in subsequent chapters. Change in scope during project execution is a common phenomenon, better known as *scope creep*. A project manager will need a good estimation model to size the scope creep and arrive at the increase in overall effort, change in schedule, and costs based on the actual impact on the project deliverables due to scope creep.

The Developer: As important as it is to other stakeholders to be aware of estimation needs of various activities of the project, it is equally essential that the developer team have a good understanding of the estimated effort that has been calculated for each of the design or coding activities assigned to them. A true developer will understand the effort allotted to the assigned activity and will continuously check to ensure the target is met.

The IT Management: The responsibility for managing all IT-related activities within the organization remains with the IT group. For them, the main focus is to develop and deliver the project on time and within budget. Also of interest to the IT group are the maintenance costs when the application goes live (Total Cost of Ownership). The estimated effort and hence the schedule and cost would be key inputs.

The Outsourcing Vendor: Quite frequently the software projects are outsourced to external vendors. The vendor prepares estimations based on the skills and competency he or she has in domain and technology areas.

If we look holistically at the complete scenario of a software project execution, the single most important aim that emerges is the successful delivery of the project that meets the scope, is within the budgeted costs, delivered on time, and of good quality. The business user is ultimately the last and the main person to be impacted if there is any slip in the schedule or in the quality of the product delivered.

Conclusion

Estimation is an art of approximation and an activity that is done before the product has even started to take shape. It is natural that measurement of such an activity is never 100 percent perfect. Given that the estimation of an activity is dependent on four major factors—scope, environment, experience, and tools—it is evident that if you improve the confidence in predicting the outcome of these factors, it helps in improving the accuracy of estimation.

Understanding the process of estimation in software projects is not enough by itself; it is equally critical that you understand how to apply the estimation knowledge appropriately to different situations during the lifecycle phases of the project execution. And while applying the estimation methods, you also need to take care to implement the necessary corrective steps in order to bring the project back on the track. This is experience! You could follow all instructions as written in this book, but bringing the right mixture of the process and methods comes only by experience.

Boehm and Fairley [13] have highlighted the significance of being aware of the context in which estimations are being done in their article "Software Estimation Perspectives." They make the following points:

• It is best to understand the background of an estimate before you use it.

• It is best to orient your estimation approach to the use you're going to make of the estimate.

I will attempt to explain all of these complexities as well as the ambiguities of the process of estimation throughout the rest of this book. Let's explore together the various nuances of software estimation in the coming chapters.

References

1. The Capability Maturity Model Integrations (CMMI) was developed by the Software Engineering Institute (SEI), Carnegie Mellon University. www.sei.cmu.edu/cmmi

2. The Function Point Analysis method was developed by Allan Albrecht and is now maintained by International Function Point Users Group. www.ifpug.org

3. Symons, Charles. *Software Sizing and Estimating: Mark II Function Points* (Function Point Analysis), John Wiley & Sons, 1991.

4. Boehm, Barry W. *Software Engineering Economics,* Prentice Hall, 1981. http://sunset.usc.edu/research/COCOMOII/index.html

5. Feature Points developed by Capers Jones of Software Productivity Inc. is a variant of IFPUG Function Point Analysis. www.spr.com/products/feature.shtm

6. Banker, R., R. Kauffman, and R. Kumar. "An Empirical Test of Object-Based Output Measurement Metrics in a Computer Aided Software Engineering (CASE) Environment," *Journal of Management Information System*, 1994.

7. COSMIC-FFP, version 2.0. Copyright © 1999. The Common Software Measurement International Consortium (COSMIC). www.cosmicon.com

8. Delphi Method was originally developed by the Rand Corporation (1948) and improved into Wideband Delphi Method by Barry W. Boehm and colleagues in the 1970s.

9. Schneider, Geri, and Jason Winters. *Applying Use Cases—A Practical Guide*. Addison-Wesley, 1998.

10. The Standish Group International, Inc. *The Chaos Report*. 1995.

11. McConnell, Steve. *Rapid Development*. Microsoft Press, 1996.

12. DeMarco, Tom. *Controlling Software Projects*. Englewood Cliffs, NJ: Prentice Hall, 1982.

13. Boehm, Barry W., and Richard E. Fairley. "Software Estimation Perspectives." *IEEE Software*. November/December, 2000.

Other Interesting Reading Material

McConnell, Steve. "What Is an Estimate," in *Software Estimation—Demystifying the Black Art*. Microsoft Press, 2006. Pp. 3–14.

CHAPTER 2

Role of Estimation in Software Projects

Software Projects and Estimation

Managing software projects successfully requires a combination of skill, training, and experience. Whatever the business need that the project is addressing, structured and planned project execution is of paramount importance. Software projects are very different from traditional projects such as constructing a building or a steel plant or landing a rocket on the moon. In most construction projects, you can see the progress of work being done. In software projects, until the coded modules are sent to test it is impossible to determine how much real progress is being made. Even after the programmer claims the module is completed, the testing and integration efforts may show problems that will require extensive redesign and recoding.

In any field, a well-defined project will contain the following attributes:

- Goal to be achieved
- Resources required
- Behavioral parameters (quality and performance)
- Costs involved
- Timeframe to complete

A good project management process is necessary to bind these attributes and make a successful delivery of the end product. The process encompasses certain key ingredients that include

- Developing a good project execution plan
- Converting the goal into a well-structured requirement specification
- Dividing the project into well-defined phases
- Allocating the right resources to the right job
- Working out the cost of project execution
- Delivering the project within the overall timeframe

At the heart of each software project is a key element: *scope*. In a broad sense, scope encompasses the entire set of activities that are necessary for a software project to be executed successfully. Scope includes software development, deployment, enabling users, and procuring and setting up the appropriate hardware. But specific to a software application development project, scope is limited to the business and technical functionalities that will be delivered through the software. Every other attribute, including effort, resources, schedule, and cost, are derivates of scope. A project may have a set of sub projects to be delivered; each sub-project will have its own scope; and the overall project scope will be a sum of the scope of all its sub-projects plus other overheads. Transforming the scope into effort and other related parameters is the art of estimation.

Estimation touches almost every aspect of software project execution. This chapter explores the execution aspects of a typical software project in a bit more detail and establishes the importance of estimation in each of the project lifecycle phases. The three phases are the project budget approval phase, the project contract phase, and project execution phase.

Project Budget Approval Phase

In large organizations, often the need for a new software project is conceived to meet business needs of the organization. But before the approval to go ahead is given, the core management deliberates various aspects of the project, including the budget to be allocated. This budget includes not just the cost of project execution but also all other related costs like infrastructure, operational, and maintenance costs. Because this is the conceptual stage of the project, the functional scope of the software application is still very hazy. In this situation, arriving at an estimated cost for the project is quite difficult. Typically a ballpark budgetary figure is calculated, based on a reference to software with similar functionalities executed in the recent past. Sometimes it is a total "gut feel" estimate.

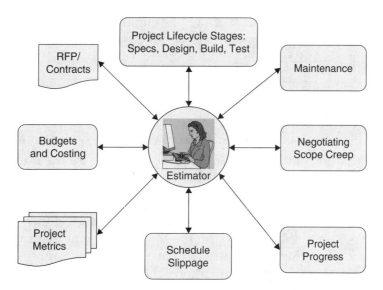

Figure 2.1 *Role of estimation.*

The role of estimation here is quite complex but critical at the same time. It's complex because the information related to the business functionality the software application needs is in an incubation stage. The business users as well as the IT folks are yet to deliberate the complete details of the scope. As such the details available are very high-level details. The role of estimation (Figure 2.1) is critical because the estimated figure drives the budget to be allocated, and if this figure is beyond allowable limits, the project itself might not be approved. For most projects, estimates during this phase are expected to be very rough estimates. Budget estimates to ±30% are usually sufficient. (*Note:* This means that at this stage when estimates are still being budgeted based on ambiguous information, the estimated figures could vary between +30% to –30% of actual numbers.)

Project Contract Phase

Having obtained the budget approval from management, the sponsor of the project now works toward getting the project executed. The sponsor has a couple of options: assign the project to the internal IT group, invite external vendors to submit a bid through an RFP (request for proposal); or maybe do a combination of both.

At this stage, it is essential that the estimation of the project cost is done with due diligence and that the figure is accurate. Other indirect expenses—including infrastructure, retraining the user community, and operational expenses—are also estimated. Certain risks that the sponsor might face include

- The sum total of project execution costs and all other indirect costs might exceed the budget amount allocated.
- Upon floating an RFP and processing the bids, it might turn out that even the lowest bidder's figures exceed the budget amount.
- It is not uncommon for the management to revise the budget figures (downwards) due to business pressures.

If the project is budget driven, the sponsor has no other option but to go back to the drawing board and rework the scope of the project so as to fit the expenses within the budget. The task will become even more difficult because cutting the scope will require appropriate approval from the business users. In certain situations, the sponsor may decide to execute a separate requirements definition phase for the project in order to clearly establish the scope of the project. This will help arrive at more precise cost estimates.

Another critical role estimation plays here is in the form of accurate sizing of the software—typically Function Points or Lines of Code (LOC). The business functionality that the application needs to deliver is detailed to the extent that the level of ambiguity is kept the minimum. All the vendors have the same understanding. Also defined clearly is the technology platform requirements and other performance and related quality needs of the application. Accurate budgets cannot be provided until the scope of the work is thoroughly understood and the Work Breakdown Structure has been completed by the project managers to identify the activities needed to develop the product.

Project Execution Phase

The project execution responsibility now moves to the project manager of the team who has been entrusted with the project. Estimation plays a very major and critical role in several ways throughout the project execution lifecycles.

Project Planning: This is the foundation of the entire project itself. Each activity involved in the project execution is carefully evaluated for its impact in terms of effort, criticality, and the position with respect to other activities. Estimation of the effort for individual activity is essential for arriving at the timeframe by which various milestones are reached. The total elapsed time required to deliver the project (schedule) is thus derived from the plan. Quite often the programmer is not the decision maker as far as the project delivery schedule is concerned. Whereas the business demands its preference of delivery schedule, the IT organization and the project team negotiate the realistic delivery dates with the business based on its technical estimates. As such, once again estimation plays another important role in re-defining efforts for modified activities, their sequence as well as overall delivery schedules.

Resource Allocations: Finding the right number of resources with the right skills required to execute a software project on time and within budget is a tough job that requires a managed resource planning process deployed across all projects in the IT organization. Do not forget the very basic fact that the effort estimation for individual activities has been done assuming that the project team will have a certain minimum level of competency. In software parlance, this is known as productivity of resources. During actual resource allocation you face the reality that expecting the right skilled resources to be available is only wishful thinking. Another situation could arise when you decide to outsource the project either fully or in part. The productivity of the outsourced team could be quite different from that of your own internal IT team. Whatever the reasons may be, the result is a mismatch between the effort that was estimated and the actual capability of the assembled team. Very often this calls for re-estimation.

Project Milestones: Execution of a project without intermediate milestones is akin to driving a car on a highway without any dashboard meters and signs along the road. In both cases, it would be similar to a blind drive with no clue as to when you will reach the end of journey. The software engineering methods have simplified the task of identifying standard milestones in a software project. Requirements, Design, Build, and Test are some of the very common, basic milestones that can occur in a software project. The definition of a milestone will vary if other software project execution lifecycle methods like iterative or agile development methods are deployed. But the challenge here is to estimate effort and schedule for each of the milestones. The estimation technique adopted here is different. The metrics collection process in the organization includes details of effort spent during individual milestones. This information is refined over a number of projects and an average estimated effort as a percentage of total effort and schedule is calculated. By breaking down the effort and delivery schedule estimates at milestone levels based on historic data, the project progress can be tracked more accurately.

Project Monitoring: As discussed in the previous section, estimation plays a key role in tracking the project progress. At the completion of every milestone, the estimation method helps in the following ways:

- Assessing the variance between original estimate and actual effort spent during the milestone; also helps in arriving at the actual productivity of the project team based on actual effort spent

- Re-planning the rest of the project execution milestones by re-estimating the balance activities based on the actual productivity of the project team

- Trapping any scope creep (change in scope) that might have gone unnoticed due to improper project tracking

Trapping scope creep is discussed in detail in Chapter 10, "Tips, Tricks, and Traps."

Project Metrics: Successful implementations of good quality processes require an extensive collection of all project activities metrics. Some of the key attributes for which metrics are collected include

- Productivity
- Defect density
- Effort variance
- Schedule variance
- Cost variance
- Cost of quality

The projects for which the metrics are collected could reflect a wide range of technology, project size, functionality, and complexity. As such, identifying a yardstick by which heterogeneous projects can be compared becomes a necessity. Defining a single yardstick that can measure all varieties of software execution is quite difficult. IT organizations usually identify a couple of the most commonly used measuring units that can encompass most metrics collection processes. A comparison table is also developed for the identified measuring units to facilitate budgeting and other management level decisions. The function point estimation method provides for developing such a yardstick. In fact, some of the attributes mentioned previously, such as productivity and defect density, can be measured with Function Point as a measuring unit.

Estimation and Measurement

Estimation and *measurement* (Figure 2.2) are two faces of the same attribute of a software application: *Size*. This explanation can be extended to other similar attributes of software projects that include effort, schedule, and quality parameters.

"You cannot manage what you cannot measure!" is a very popular statement quoted by measurement gurus. But remember, you can measure something only after it has been created. And if you intend to arrive at an approximate value that defines the size of the software that has yet to be developed, it is then called *estimation*. Whatever the intention, at different lifecycle stages of a project execution, estimation, measurement, or both are employed. To illustrate a few situations, consider the following:

- *Estimation:* During the contract process there is a need to estimate the size, effort, and cost of a software product that is yet to be developed. At every milestone in the project execution stages, the balance of effort required to deliver the project needs to be estimated. Estimation is definitely not done at the end of the project.

- *Measurement:* With the exception of the contract phase and the time preceding the first milestone (for fresh development projects only), measurement activity takes place in all other situations. At the

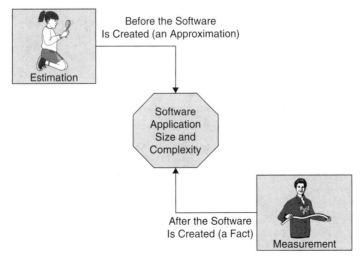

Figure 2.2 *Estimation and measurement.*

completion of every milestone, both measurement of the completed activities and estimation of the balance milestones based on the analysis of the data collated, are done. This helps in tracking as well as making corrections to a project schedule that might be going off track and helps the project deliver on time, and within budget. This topic is discussed in more detail in Chapter 10.

Estimation and Measurement Complexities

The process of estimation and measurement is usually complex due to the very basic fact that every software project and its attributes are unique. As described in Figure 2.3, several variable factors need to be measured.

A good estimation or measurement method must satisfy a wide variety of software application complexities. It is also true that we are yet to develop one method that does it all. A few alternatives address some of the estimations needs, in part. Function Point Analysis method, COCOMO II [1] method, and Lines-Of-Code method are a few examples.

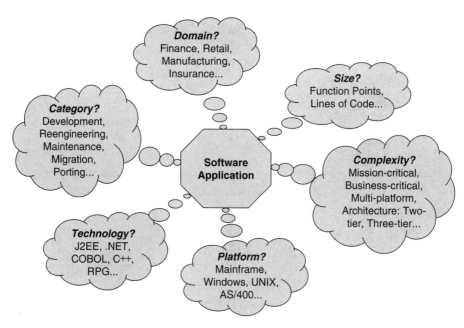

Figure 2.3 *Estimation and measurement complexities.*

The following list introduces some of the key components of a software system and the impact of their variations on estimation methods:

- *Domain:* The business functionality that has to be delivered through the software is the foundation of the rest of the software components. Estimations can vary drastically, based purely on variety of business functions being delivered. The effort to develop an inventory management system might be quite different from the effort to develop a human resources management system.

- *Technology:* The platform, language, database, and other technology components, including the tools that are deployed in the software system, all contribute greatly to the variation in estimations. Coding complexities, skills available (productivity) and the performance parameters that need to be met determine the quantum of total effort to develop the software.

- *Project Category:* A wide variety of software execution processes are adopted, based on business needs. Fresh development, maintenance of existing software systems, and migrating software applications from old to new technology are a few examples of execution processes. In each case, the execution process is quite different, and the related effort varies substantially as well. The estimation method for these needs to be mapped accordingly.

- *Software System Complexity:* Over and above the variants discussed thus far, there are a few other complexities that apply to the software system as a whole. The application could be mission-critical (for example, launching a rocket to the moon or designing a critical healthcare system), business-critical (such as a fund management system or share transaction system), complex architecture-based (such as three-tier or multi-tier architecture or involving integration with many other systems). There could even be strict service-level agreements that need to be met by the software system. Once again, each one of these considerations impacts the estimated effort to develop and deploy.

Each of the above parameters significantly impacts the final estimation. A comprehensive estimation method that can encompass all the complexities and variations, as discussed previously, does not exist today. But does someone really need that kind of estimation method? Independent software programmers working on one-off software projects may not need an elaborate estimation method. Large IT groups handling a wide variety of software project execution, day-in day-out, eagerly look forward to deploying an organization-wide measurement process that could facilitate estimates of various projects on equal terms, whatever their technology or category may be. By far the most popular sizing method used by many IT groups is the Source Lines-Of-Code approach (SLOC). And if you intend to compare and contrast estimates for a variety of software projects across the IT organization, SLOC unit of measurement perhaps should be the last option. This is so because the accuracy of SLOC based estimations cannot be predicted.

Modularized Estimation

A complete estimation process involves evaluating the size (volume) of the software project, evaluating the effort required to deliver the project, and finally, arriving at the costs involved. Although sizing the project can be done by using one of the popular estimation methods, converting the size into effort and costs is somewhat complex. The complexity arises due to the variations in effort and costs that could occur based on factors that include the project development and deployment platform; project execution category (new development, reengineering, maintenance, and migration); skills of the project execution team; and few other environmental factors. Dissecting various components of estimation that facilitate evaluating alternatives is a modularized way of estimating the project. The modularization is simply a process of identifying the individual attributes of the estimation steps and the relation between them. You should be able to plug in the most appropriate component that fits your needs in the chain of events that leads to overall effort and cost estimates.

A careful study of a typical software application will reveal the various components that exist within its boundary. These components can be broadly classified as follows:

- The base *size* of the application
- The *platform* on which the application is developed
- The project execution *type*
- The *skills/competency* of the project team
- Other components such as quality processes and tools, etc.

Estimation of the overall effort to deliver the software application will greatly depend on the complexities related to these components, necessarily in the given order.

Size: This attribute is core to all other attributes and greatly influences the overall effort during the estimation process. Size is directly linked to the business functionality that the target application is expected to deliver. There are a few alternatives for measuring size. Function Points (IFPUG [2]) is the most popular method, giving you the number of Function Points (FP) count based on the functionalities being delivered by the application. FP count is independent of the technology on which the application is/was developed. Lines of Code (LOC) is another method of defining the size of the application. LOC is normally counted for applications that have been completed. The LOC is always available for count in a particular language like COBOL, JAVA, C#, etc. Another popular method to assess application size is based on the number of Use Cases (UC) prepared during scope definition. There are specific uncertainties in the method. Selecting and writing Use Cases at the right level of granularity—and also consistently—is quite complicated.

Technology/Platform: The vehicle to convert business functions into a software application that is capable of input, output, reports, and data storage facilities is the technology. Technology includes several parameters like these:

- Language (COBOL, C#, JAVA, C++...)
- Platform (UNIX, MVS, Windows...)
- Files/Database (VSAM, IMS, IDMS, RDBMS, DB2...)
- Architecture (2 tiers, 3 tiers...)
- Middleware (IBM MQ, MSMQ...)

Choosing the right technology while developing an application is a complex process and depends on several business, technology, and management requirements. There is a direct relation between the size of the software and the effort required to deliver on the technology on which the software is developed (see Figure 2.4). The larger the size of the application, the higher the effort to develop it on a given technology.

Process Type: Depending upon the business need, a software project could be executed in several varieties of processes. These types of projects include development, reengineering, maintenance, enhancement, migration, and porting. Each of these types may adopt different project execution processes. The estimation parameters for these types of projects also vary due to the fact that project effort is mainly driven by the process of execution. For example, development is the fresh creation of a software application as compared to maintenance, which involves activities like corrective, adaptive, and preventive maintenance of

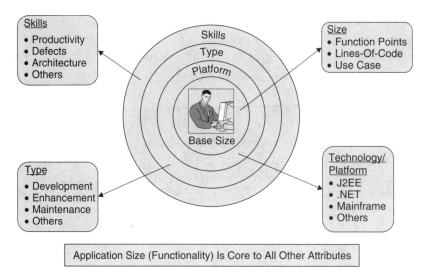

Figure 2.4 *Application components.*

existing software applications. The effort to develop a fresh software system is quite large as compared to executing even a major enhancement to an existing application under the maintenance process.

Skills/Competency: Otherwise termed as "productivity," the unit rate at which software can be delivered depends heavily on the skills of the project team. Within the IT group of an organization, it is not unusual to find different levels of productivity on different technologies, as well as different types of project execution processes. For example, the productivity of the project team working on a J2EE development project will differ with the productivity of another project team working on a COBOL/CICS/DB2 mainframe maintenance project. Beyond the variance in estimated effort due to project size, technology, and type, the productivity factor plays a significant role in finally defining the overall effort estimations.

Others: A number of other indirect factors act as project execution overheads. These include project management, quality assurance, and other related activities. In most situations, the effort for these activities is a percentage of the overall project effort estimations.

The advantages of making the estimation process into a modular form are many. Applying variations to each of the modules will impact the overall estimates. Some key benefits include these:

- If you are able to develop evaluation processes for each of the modules separately, you can mix and match different modules with different degrees of variation depending on project requirements.

- It is possible to do a what-if analysis based on project needs as well as alternatives that you may want to assess on individual modules.

- You can assess the strengths and weaknesses of your team in each of the module areas and organize focused improvement activities.

- Collating historic data of previously executed projects by module will help you analyze organization capabilities.

Case Study—Modularized Estimation

This section provides an example of a Raw Material Issue Module in a Materials Management System. The module facilitates receipt and storage of raw materials sent received from external suppliers in the stores. The module also records all issues to the shop floor from the stores. Overall balance stock in each of the storage bins in the store is tracked, and when the level falls below a predefined threshold level, a message to initiate procurement activities is sent automatically to the purchasing department. This example uses the modularized estimation method to illustrate the steps for calculating the application size, the effort required to deliver the project, as well as the possible cost.

NOTE All data used in this example is for illustrative purposes only and should not be taken as standard data for similar estimates in your organization.

Step 1: Estimate Size

This example does not go into details of identifying various inputs, outputs, interfaces, reports, and tables for the Raw Material Issue Module but simply assumes those factors are known. Assuming that the function point estimation method was applied, a final, adjusted function point count = 380 FP is determined.

Step 2: Evaluate Technology Alternatives

There are a large number of parameters based on which the rating can be calculated for a given technology. This rating can be used as a multiplying factor in overall effort and cost estimates. Table 2.1 shows just a couple of these parameters for a select few technologies. You can develop a larger table suitable to your organization.

Table 2.1 *Productivity Factors Variance Due to Technology*

Technology	Relative User Interface	Build and Test Ease	Tools Availability	Other Overheads	Productivity Factor (T-1)
Mainframe	Low	Medium	High	High	**1.20 ×**
J2EE	High	High	Medium	Low	**0.90 ×**
Microsoft .NET	High	High	Medium	Low	**0.80 ×**
UNIX/C	Medium	Medium	Medium	Medium	**1.35 ×**

Note: Productivity factors provided in all tables in this chapter are purely illustrative figures and are compared against an organization's average productivity across platforms.

You can add other parameters such as database, middleware, and architecture to further evaluate and fine-tune the productivity factor applicable from a technology perspective.

This example is constrained by two factors that determine the technology:

- There is a business need to provide a very high level of user experience to the large customer base. Good GUI (graphic user interface) and ease of navigation is of primary importance.

- At the top IT management level there has been a decision to slowly move all applications to two of the latest technologies, J2EE and .NET.

In view of the above considerations, it has been decided to develop the project on .NET technology. The Technology Productivity Factor for .NET is (T-1) = 0.80.

Step 3: Assess Impact Due to Project Execution Type

The various types of project execution that typically take place in an IT organizations are considered in Table 2.2. Impact on the productivity factor as applicable to various lifecycle stages of each of the project execution types is evaluated. You may want to add others as applicable in your organization.

The existing raw material issue module was originally developed more than two decades ago on a mainframe using COBOL. It was badly designed, unstructured, and had many performance and user interface issues. The module is being totally re-designed and re-built on the .NET platform. As such, this project will be categorized under reengineering

Table 2.2 *Productivity Factors Variance Due to Project Execution Type*

Project Execution Type	Requirements	Design	Build and Test	Other Overheads	Productivity Factor (P-1)
New Development	Medium	Medium	High	Low	0.90 ×
Reengineering	Very High	Medium	High	Medium	1.20 ×
Maintenance	Low	Low	High	Low	0.70 ×
Migration	Medium	Low	Medium	High	0.75 ×

project execution type. The productivity factor for the reengineering project type (P-1) = 1.20.

Step 4: Evaluate Skills/Capability Available

IT organizations typically adopt the metrics collection processes that obtain information about the skills competency of project teams that execute a variety of software projects. A common practice is to collate and average metrics on a given set of technology platforms across different project execution environments. If we intend to make our estimates precise, it would be a good practice to refine the average productivity figures through the skills-based productivity factors as shown in Table 2.3.

Because this example project is 380 FP in size, the productivity factor (S-1) = 1.00 is used.

Table 2.3 *Productivity Factors Variance Due to Project Size*

Project Size	Requirements	Design	Build and Test	Other Overheads	Productivity Factor (S-1)
< 350 FP	Low	Low	Low	Low	0.70 ×
351–750 FP	Medium	Medium	Medium	Medium	1.00 ×
751–1500 FP	Medium	High	Medium	High	1.25 ×
> 1500 FP	High	Very High	High	Very High	1.50 ×

Step 5: Calculate Total Effort

Now all the productivity factors are identified. You can now complete the last few activities to arrive at the overall effort:

- Application Size = 380 Function Points (FP)
- Productivity for the IT Organization (Average Assumed) = 15 Function Points/Person Month
- Other Productivity Factors (as identified previously) = (T-1=0.80, P-1=1.20, S-1=1.00)
- Total Project Effort = (380/15) * 0.80 * 1.20 * 1.00 = ~ 25 Person Months

---

NOTE The above case study is an illustration showing how you can put together a matrix of tables to componentize and modularize various aspects of project execution, technology, and other parameters. Using these parameters and components, you can arrive at a more precise effort and cost estimates. This example has not provided a factor for cost variations; you may want to include your own.

Large Application Systems

Large business organizations that have been in business for several decades have gradually become dependent on their software systems to provide the impetus toward increased business revenues year after year. Although business strategy plays a significant role in shaping the future of the organization, without the active participation of the IT-enabled internal software systems, it becomes extremely difficult for the organization to achieve the growth targets. As a result, more and more organizations become dependent on their internal IT units to continuously improve their cycle time to complete a work-flow process and at the same time show reduction in the total cost of ownership (TCO) of their systems.

So what is the critical issue here? It is very simple. As the business organization grew over several decades, so did the software applications and the IT infrastructure on which this software worked. The IT environment was transformed from a large, monolithic, slow processing, low memory system with a limited number of users to a super fast, gigabyte memory system with a large number of users. The software applications that were working in the old, dinosaurian era had to be transformed gradually to work on the now prevalent jet-age era infrastructure. But the problems did not end there. As the software industry grew, along with growing demands, out came a wide variety of programming languages, platforms, databases, and so on. To further add to the woes of the managers of the software development teams in organizations, every innovation of new programming brought its own breed of developer who had expertise on the state-of-art programming platform of that era.

For every fresh software application development or enhancement, programmers in each era developed their own style of new programs on the latest platform that could deliver state-of-the-art features. At the same time the application could talk with old legacy systems as well. And when the next generation of programming platforms and developers came along, they developed more applications in the newer platform, which connected with the then legacy systems. Thus, life went on …

Heterogeneous Portfolio of Application Systems

In a typical organization, as the business grows, the applications developed to meet the business demands begin mushrooming. Initially these small and medium applications tend to be stand-alone in nature and rarely are there direct interactions between two applications. With ever growing pressure to reduce business process time (turnaround or time-to-market), the need to integrate these individual applications becomes stronger. The integration process addresses two key issues: first, the stand-alone applications talk to each other through an appropriate middleware software, and second, the workflow process provides seamless continuity and presents an end-to-end solution to the user.

NOTE To understand the complexity of a large portfolio of application systems, refer to Figure 2.5.

Does this kind of heterogeneous application portfolio, developed on a wide range of technology platforms and then integrated through middleware, pose a complex situation for estimation processes? Yes, they do. Imagine that you, as part of a development team, are given the project assignment to develop the customer support system on the .NET platform (refer to Figure. 2.5). In a stand-alone application system, you would simply go ahead and size the application and estimate the effort, schedule, and costs. But in a real-life situation, most applications are

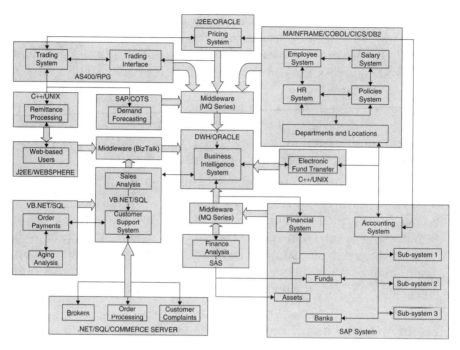

Figure 2.5 *Multi-platform application portfolio.*

integrated as shown in Figure 2.5; thus the effort to develop or introduce a new application must include additional effort to integrate with other existing systems both technically as well as functionally.

Conclusion

The estimation process in any software project is not only integral, but also a very critical component. The success or failure of projects depends heavily on the accuracy of effort and schedule estimations, among other things. Although the final estimated effort seems to be one single entity, in reality this is an aggregation of a number of individual components that has its own complexity and variation based on project situation and functional needs.

Project managers tend to focus more on delivering the project to the agreed specifications, but pay less attention to careful estimation of various activities and various phases of the project execution lifecycle. This has led to serious issues, sometimes resulting in scrapping projects completely. It is very important to understand that almost all the lifecycle stages of a project, from cradle to grave, need a careful dose of accurate estimation of effort, schedule, and costs. The role of estimation in software projects can thus be summarized as follows:

- *Incubation:* Provides a broad guideline in assessing the feasibility and the probability of successful completion of the project itself.

- *Software Contract:* Estimation plays a critical role in defining major contractual agreements, including costs. In situations where the project sponsor needs a tool to determine which technology to use for implementation, good estimation methods prove useful.

- *Execution:* Helps the project team in setting clear targets for effort, schedule, and costs. Also helps the team monitor and mentor the project progress.

- *Complex Projects:* In situations where execution of your project happens in an existing complex IT environment, you should provide for application design complexities due to integration with existing applications. The will result in additional impact on effort, schedule, and costs.

References

1. Boehm, Barry W. *Software Engineering Economics,* Prentice Hall, 1981. http://sunset.usc.edu/research/COCOMOII/index.html

2. International Function Point Users Group (IFPUG). *Function Point Counting Practices Manual (CPM) Release 4.2.*

Other Interesting Reading Material

McConnell, Steve. "The Software-Estimation Story," in *Rapid Development.* Microsoft Press, 1996. Pp. 165–173.

Dreger, Brian J. "Introduction, Function Point Identification and Classification," in *Function Point Analysis,* Prentice Hall, 1989. Pp. 1–4.

CHAPTER 3

A Study of
Function Point Analysis

Why Estimation?

*To err is human. But it is also human
nature to learn through errors.*

To be able to deliver a software project on time and within budget would be a dream come true for most software professionals. From the time a project is conceived until the project is successfully delivered, the project team goes through a number of project lifecycle phases. As discussed in the previous chapter, the project could involve a number of complexities that need to be addressed during the entire lifecycle of the project. They include:

- Understanding each and every activity that takes place in each of the lifecycle phases of the project. You also need to be aware of the sequence and dependency between these activities.

- Knowing approximately how much time each activity may take.

- Identifying the external dependencies for which the team should provide.

- Understanding the known ambiguities in the project, both functional as well as technological.

- Knowing the expected scope of additions and/or changes that may take place during project execution.

- Recognizing how to assess the skills of the project team.

- Identifying the buffers and contingencies the project manager needs to provide for, in order to be able to mitigate known and unknown risks
- Understanding the kind of effort that goes into stringent quality review and tests

Software projects are conceived with the intention of meeting specific business needs of the client organization. In order to meet the business needs, which are time specific, it is essential that the project be completed within a specified timeframe and within budget. The project manager is almost always under tremendous pressure to deliver the project according to the schedule prescribed by the business. This pressure is even greater due to the fact that the estimated time of delivery by the project manager is never acceptable to the business because their expectations are directly mapped to business opportunities, which appear much earlier than the need for the software is articulated. The project manager thus needs tools and techniques that can help in negotiating the best project delivery schedules. These tools and techniques include

- A method to convert activities at the most granular level into measurable effort
- A process to help aggregate these efforts into an overall project effort
- The best practice to convert overall effort into a realistic schedule
- The best practice of allocating the right resources to the right job
- A method to track progress during the project execution
- An important technique: The capability to negotiate a reasonably plausible project schedule with the management and business people

What Is an Estimation Method?

An **estimation method** is a set of processes, supported by appropriate empirical formulae and backed with historical reference data, that help derive predictable results within a decent level of accuracy. There are a number of software project estimation methods available to project managers that help arrive at estimated size, effort, schedule, resource loading, and other similar parameters. A brief discussion on some of the other estimation methods is provided in Chapter 14, "Other Estimation Methods." For an estimation method to become easily acceptable by software developers as well as business and IT groups, the key ingredients of the method should

- Be a method that can be easily understood and deployable
- Allow modularization of the software application components

- Provide predictable results with an accuracy within reasonable limits
- Be comparable across a variety of software projects
- Be backed by extensive regression analysis data
- Facilitate conversion/transformation of the output to other project execution parameters such as schedule, cost, progress, etc.
- Include well-documented instruction manuals, continually updated by recognized bodies

Very few estimation methods truly provide answers to the maximum needs of a software project estimator as described here. Among these is the Function Point Analysis method. The rest of this chapter discusses the Function Point Analysis method in detail, including its applicability to software project estimations as well as the ease with which the method is understood by estimators. Chapters 4, 5, and 6 discuss data functions, transactional functions, and general system characteristics, respectively, while continuing to focus on the core Function Point Analysis method.

Function Points

Almost all engineering disciplines depend on the basic premise of being able to measure the various parameters with which that specific branch of engineering deals. For example, civil engineers can measure various civil structures using the metric system of measurement; electrical engineers can measure through units like watts, volts, amperes, etc.; and mechanical engineers measure outputs through joules, horse power, and other measuring scales. But software engineering is relatively young and we are yet to arrive at a well-defined and universally acceptable unit of measurement for all software systems. Perhaps function points is the nearest to becoming a universal unit of measuring software systems, based on the business functions delivered by the application. Lines-Of-Code is a very poor alternative.

What Is a Function Point?

First, what is this unit of measurement called function point (FP) and how does it help measure the size of a software application?

A **function point** is a unit of measure for arriving at software application size. The software size thus measured (in FP count) is proportional to the functionality delivered by the application. There are many explanations on how the Function Point Analysis (FPA) process helps measure the overall software size. Before considering those details, consider what "functionality" is being measured through the FP count. Most software applications service one of two major categories of user needs: the business need or the functional need of the organization. An order processing application meets the business need, whereas an attendance system meets an internal functional need of the organization. There are exceptions when special software systems are developed to meet technical needs of the IT group of an organization. For example, a middleware system that connects two applications deployed in disparate platforms is an exception to that rule. Whatever the need may be, the FPA method does not differentiate the delivered functional value of the application to the user. The FPA method treats the order processing and attendance system similarly.

Understanding the means through which the functionality is delivered by a typical software application is essential. The ultimate aim is to help the user experience the functionality provided by the application. Consider, for a moment, the software application as though it is a black box to the user. The user experiences all functionalities delivered by the application through the user interface. All the processes, information store, and other extraction of external information are transparent to the user.

Functionality is the process by which information (data) about an entity is fetched, stored, or exported. Figure 3.1 shows the components and the interactions between various processes in a software application. Entities could be of any size and could represent any aspect of a busi-

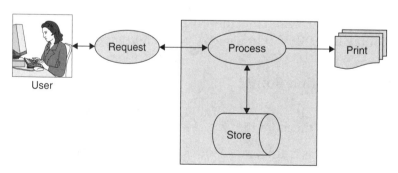

Figure 3.1 *Functional measurement.*

ness, person, product, or other similar concept. A few sample entities include

- An employee
- A customer
- An invoice
- A product or a component
- Payment info
- Salary info

An employee application provides you with the functionality to store, fetch, update, and export (print) information about employees. The functionalities provided by the Customer, Invoicing, Salary, and Inventory applications are similar.

Function Point as a Measuring Yardstick

This section uses an example of an Employee application to illustrate how functionalities are delivered through the software and how the application is sized. This example involves 24 actual attributes that need to be processed for an employee. The attributes include

- Employee Name, Address, Contact #, SSN #, DOB (a total of five attributes)
- Role, Designation, Grade, Department, DOJ (a total of five attributes)
- Educational Qualification(s) (five attributes)
- Previous Work Experience(s) (five attributes)
- Dependents' Information (four attributes)

The basic functionalities that are expected to be provided in the application are the facility to store, fetch, process, and print employee information. These are achieved through various instances of interactions known as **transactions.** The total functionalities received by the user from the employee application can be measured as "x" function points. This number is the collective effort that may be needed to develop the software to process the 24 attributes that define an employee. The activities may include

- Creating data entry screens
- Creating database files
- Generating reports
- Displaying the menu and other cosmetic needs

A single unit of function point may be too small to assign to a single transaction; for example, to measure the size of a data entry screen. Also, in order to keep the effort of working on various components of a software application—such as screens, reports, tables, etc.—comparable to each other through a single measuring yardstick, the function point counting has been appropriately balanced. Consider a few such (illustrative) comparisons:

- Size of a simple data entry screen with 12 data attributes = 3 function points
- Size of a simple report with 15 data attributes = 4 function points
- Size of a simple table (database) with 15 data attributes = 7 function points

Even though the actual process involved to develop each of the components are quite different, the common measuring yardstick for all of them is the function point (FP) unit. In fact it is this unique feature of FP unit, that of being comparable as a unit of work across variety of software development activities, that greatly helps in extending the measuring activity to a larger range of IT-related project executions. Although FP is a unit of work that can measure the functionality or the size of the application under consideration, FP does not give the rate of delivery of a unit of work. The following section discusses some of the uses and benefits of utilizing FP as a standard yardstick to measure a unit of work.

Uses and Benefits of Function Points

The following list introduces some of the direct uses and benefits that can be derived out of the Function Point Analysis method:

- Because the FP count is technology independent, it can be effectively used and reused for sizing a wide variety of software applications.
- Many other metric collection processes are well enabled by measures that are referenced to FP as a base. For example, productivity is measured as FP per person month, defect density per 1000 FP, and cost per FP.
- Project schedules are better evaluated based on the number of FP that can be best delivered in a given timeframe.
- Some of the software project contracts (RFP) are based on expected FP to be delivered. The dollars per FP is a measuring scale in these contracts.

- Scope creep (increase in scope) during project execution is better measured and trapped using FP as a sizing tool.

- Converting the FP count of a software project into total effort is simple, based on the productivity of the project team on the technology platform.

Additional uses of FP are discussed in later chapters. See Chapter 7, "Size, Effort, and Scheduling of Projects," to understand how the function point count can be converted to project estimates.

Function Point Analysis

Although the computer industry existed from way back in the 1940s, there were hardly any well-defined, process-oriented software estimation methods in use. Unlike the hardware industry, where the product capacity was measurable and comparable to proportional costing methods, the software industry was woefully lacking a dependable estimation method. Because software is "soft," fixing its value is a tricky process. At best, designing, developing, and deploying a software application that meets the user's needs can be equated to delivering a service. Until the late '70s, this service was measurable in several ways that include

- *Time and Material:* Perhaps the easiest way to define a contract involves charging for the services delivered. The effort consumed per month by the project team is billed on a monthly basis. This continues until the project is completed and delivered to the user's satisfaction. Overhead costs such as traveling, logistics, etc., are billed on actual expenses. The customer is normally at the mercy of the vendor to complete the project in a reasonable time.

- *Output—LOC:* One of the most popular estimation methods even now is the measure of the software application delivered in Lines-Of-Code. Most software applications are coded using popular languages like COBOL, Visual Basic, C++, and C#, and the connected database system is coded using the SQL language. The final output of almost all these languages is measurable in Lines-Of-Code. The contract for the services delivered is typically agreed based on cost per LOC and delivered after acceptance is complete. The cost may vary based on language, database, and other related parameters specific to the software application.

- *Fixed Price Contract:* The vendor does an internal estimation of the size of application being developed. The estimation could be based on LOC or person months as effort. Based on the accuracy of the estimation and other risks involved, buffer effort, margins, and other overhead costs are added to make this a fixed price contract. The vendor takes the risk of delivering the project within the contract price, whatever the variance between the original estimate and the final effort may be.

There have been many fallacies in these methods. The measure of the service in person months was directly dependent, among other variables, on the capabilities and skills of the project team that was assembled. A time and material project, without a cap on time or cost, would become open-ended, and the customer would have very little control over the project team. Measuring a project size by Lines-Of-Code is even more ambiguous. A few glaring discrepancies are

- The Source Lines-Of-Code (SLOC) count developed to deliver certain business functionality can differ widely when developed using different software languages. This is true because each software language has its own features and functionalities that can address certain aspects of business logic. As such, costing the project based on LOC delivered would be quite risky. The developer team may decide to choose a language that generates maximum LOC.

- Structured and compact coding as compared to free-for-all coding makes a huge difference in the final LOC delivered. Writing compact code is dependent on the skills of the project team members on that language.

- Code generator tools are available that generate the program automatically, based on business logic and other related attributes. The tools often generate code that is much higher than the LOC generated by a good programmer. It would be unwise to cost such projects based on LOC.

Allan Albrecht came up with an innovative way of measuring software size when he was asked by his employer, IBM, to evaluate project productivity. He equated it to the functionality delivered by the software application. He strongly felt the need to arrive at an alternative to LOC as a measure of software size. "He [Allan Albrecht] took the position that the economic output unit of software projects should be valid for all languages and should represent topics of concern to the users of software. In short, he wished to measure the functionality of the software" [1].

After considerable research, Albrecht established the new thought process that all software applications could be measured uniformly based on five key attributes:

- Inputs to the application
- Outputs from the application
- Provision to query
- Internal data store
- External interfaces

These five attributes were easily identifiable for a majority of software applications and they were truly platform independent. Albrecht presented a paper on his research findings at an IBM conference in 1979. Thus was born a remarkable software estimation method that viewed software from a totally new perspective; that of the attributes that were visible and could be experienced by the user of the application. Albrecht introduced the Function Point Analysis (FPA) method in 1979. Universal acceptance of this method of sizing software applications directly led to measuring a few other related parameters, such as productivity, defect density, and effort.

FPA—Objectives

Two views of the business value of software applications existed during this time. The business user viewed the application from the business value perspective and measured its capability by the business functionalities provided by the application. On the other hand, the programmer viewed the software from the technology perspective and valued or sized the application from the perspective of the technology complexity, volume of code written, and other related features like files and reports. The two views were almost completely opposite, but they both were right in their own perspectives (see Figure 3.2).

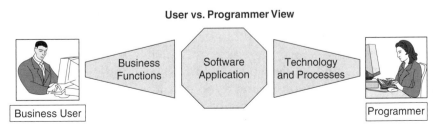

Figure 3.2 *Different views of software.*

Between the two, obviously the business user rates the higher priority because the business need opens the opportunity for IT to develop the new software. Another argument that is heavily in favor of the business user points to the fact that irrespective of technology or processes adopted to develop a software application, the functionality delivered by the application is the same. For example, if an order processing application is to be developed with a defined scope of functionalities, it is almost certain that the end goal would be to meet the scope, irrespective of the technology chosen. Above all, any software project first needs to be budgeted and approved by the sponsor. Typically, management at this level understands the business functionality more easily than the technology and process complexities. It would be far easier to convince the management as well as the business user to approve the project budget based on the functionality being delivered.

Albrecht perhaps had a good measure of the pulse of management, which has the critical role of approving software projects. Management determined the future of IT within the organization. The FPA method developed by Albrecht was thus focusing mainly on sizing an application from the business user's perspective only. The method was completely independent of the technology platform on which the software was being developed.

The FPA method of measuring software size is a significant milestone in the evolution of software estimation methodologies. With one stroke, software size became core to all metrics on software development processes. In fact this measure could address estimation needs through the entire lifecycle of the software application itself, from cradle to grave. Key metrics that are derived out of software size as a base include

- Project effort, schedule, and cost
- Productivity of the developer team
- Defect density
- Quality metrics
- Maintenance costs
- Migration costs

Each of these metrics is discussed in detail in later chapters. The FPA method provided a single yardstick by which many measurement-related metrics could be derived with a fairly decent level of consistency. Much more than providing a tool to measure size, the method also facilitated comparison of totally disparate software systems by using the same common yardstick known as function points.

Other objectives of developing the FPA method were to

- Design an estimation method that was fairly easy to understand, both by the business users of the software as well as the developers.

- Keep learning time to a minimum; ensure that repeated usage quickly builds expertise.

- Make sure the estimated outputs generated through the FPA method are reliable and consistent. It was expected that sizing of existing applications would be within ±10% of actual size and for fresh development projects it would be within ±20% of the final product size.

- Enable the estimated output (size) to be utilized to derive project effort in any technology because the method is independent of technology platform. The productivity on the selected technology would drive the overall effort figures.

- Assure that verification of the output function points could be done by an independent, experienced assessor.

The FPA Model

The FPA model facilitates the measurement of software application size. The output of this method is a count (number) called function points. A *function point* is defined as a unit of business functionality delivered through the software being measured. If application X has a measured count of 500 *function points* (FP), the count signifies that the functionality delivered by the application to the end users is equivalent to 500 business functions.

The FPA model is based on the premise that any software application can be sized based on five key parameters: inputs, outputs, inquiries, internal files, and external interfaces. Clearly all five parameters chosen by Albrecht are those visible to the user and hence are tangible attributes. The most significant part of the software, from the developer's perspective, is the code, which is not visible to the end user and is like a black box. The FPA method does not touch the code part of the software at all.

Figure 3.3 highlights the five key attributes of FPA model as applicable to a typical software application. These attributes collectively and holistically encompass all the parameters of any software application. By measuring complexity and hence the size of these attributes it is possible to measure the overall size of any application. The number of items under each category of attribute can vary in individual applications

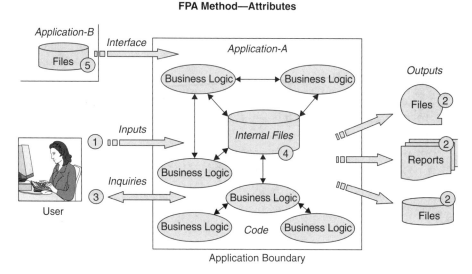

Figure 3.3 *Components of an application.*

based on the business functionality being addressed by these applications. The following list discusses each of the five attributes in detail.

1. *Inputs:* In order for a software application to exist, it is essential that programmers provide the means through which data (business information) can be stored in the files that belong to the application. Moving data from an external source into the application files and updating and maintaining the data are all included under the input attribute. All the CRUD (Create, Read, Update, and Delete) operations are classified under the input attribute. The actual mode of input can vary depending on business needs. Input could be in batch mode, manual, or other modes.

2. *Outputs:* Business information processed through the software application could be output in various forms, modes, and media. A pay-slip, a financial statement, a part item in a store, and a complete inventory report are examples of outputs. The outputs could be printed on company stationery, stored on other media like disk files or tapes, or even displayed on the monitor itself.

3. *Inquiries:* Quite often the user has the need to query a variety of information from the data stored in the application. The output of an inquiry is quite similar to that of outputs discussed previously but the outputs generated here are in their original form. Business

information is not processed; rather it is just sorted or rearranged based on user request and presented in a readable form.

4. *Internal Files*: Every software application basically works on processing data stored within the application and presents the output in the form of business information. As such, all the data that are owned and maintained within the application are stored in files known as **internal files.** These files belong to the application and any modification to the data contents is the responsibility of the application owner.

5. *Interfaces*: A software application that enables users to make business transactions with the software normally interacts with other applications, either within or external to the organization. Having an application that is totally independent and does not feed into or get inputs from another application would be very unusual. Interfacing with other applications is a key attribute that contributes to the size of the application being measured. Typical interfaces are accomplished through intermediate data files, although there could be other modes as well. In the FPA model, interface attributes are defined as files that belong to external applications and are maintained by those external applications. The files do not belong to the application being sized.

The FPA model mandates certain other processes by which the project sizing activity can be made more precise. These include

- Defining a clear boundary of the application being sized. In Figure 3.3, the core part of the application where the internal files and all the code are enclosed is in a boundary. All five attributes of the FPA model that interact with the core are outside the boundary.

- The General System Characteristics (GSC) is another set of 14 attributes that define the overall complexity of the software application being sized. These 14 GSC help the estimator define certain performance and operational aspects of the application. The final application size gets impacted based on the parameters chosen. For more information, refer to Chapter 6, "General System Characteristics."

The FPA Process

The previous section discussed the various attributes of the FPA model—inputs, outputs, inquiries, internal files, and external interfaces—which form the core of the sizing process. And once these are obtained, applying the 14 GSCs to this core data obtained through the five attributes would fine-tune the overall application size. In order to obtain the best results from the FPA model, it is essential that you follow certain well-defined sizing processes and workflows as prescribed in the user manual CPM (*Counting Practices Manual*), version 4.2 by IFPUG [2]. The steps to be followed include

- Identify a good estimator
- Obtain all the relevant artifacts of the application being counted
- Understand the user view
- Identify the type of function point (FP) count
- Determine the scope and boundary of the application
- Count the (unadjusted) data functions
- Count the (unadjusted) transaction functions
- Using the 14 GSC, calculate the value adjustment factor
- Arrive at the adjusted function point (FP) count

A closer look at each of these steps will help you understand the significance as well as the right approach for determining a fairly accurate function point (FP) count of a software application. Figure 3.4 illustrates the sequence of the steps to be followed during the counting process. Although the counting method is fairly simple and easy to follow, it is

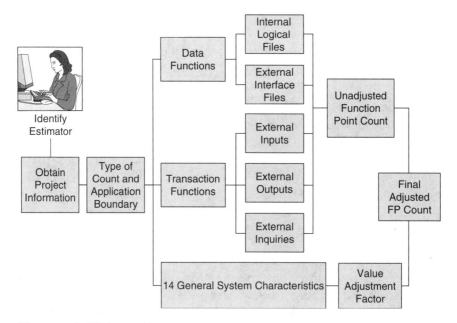

Figure 3.4 *FPA counting process.*

appropriate to be cautious and ensure none of the relevant information is left out or ignored.

Identify Estimator

Your project may not necessarily require a CFPS (IFPUG Certified Function Point Specialist) certified analyst but it is essential to identify an estimator who has the right level of skills to undertake the estimation process. An inexperienced estimator might make all the difference between a good and a bad estimate. Some of the desired skills include

- Fairly good knowledge of the business domain for which the application is being developed
- An understanding of the various components, attributes, and the process of executing an FPA estimation project
- Awareness of the environment under which the application will be deployed
- Analysis of the information received from users to distinguish their task needs from functional requirements, business rules, non-functional requirements, quality attributes, suggested solutions, and extraneous information
- Understanding the software performance expectations from business users in terms of usability, scalability, availability, and reliability
- Experience participating in software development projects in the past

Obtain Project Information

As much as the project scope is a critical input to a successful project execution, it is even more critical to accurate project size and effort estimation. The process of collating project requirements involves activities that include

- Interviewing the key stakeholders and documenting the discussions
- Reviewing any documentation available on the proposed project
- For old software systems, obtaining and reviewing system flowcharts
- Obtaining any other relevant information

Gathering every possible source of information that could enhance understanding of the business functions the software application will address is essential. Having obtained all the information about the requirements of the project, the next step is to separate the functional and non-functional needs. As discussed earlier, functional needs map directly to the business functions that will be delivered through the software application. Ensure that the functional needs are complete in all respects and adhere to a certain minimum level of compliance, such as

- *Non-ambiguous:* The information can be interpreted only in one way.
- *Consistent*: Throughout the document, definitions are repeated consistently.
- *Testable:* Information is clear enough to be testable.
- *Complete:* All relevant information surrounding a function has been fully enumerated.

Estimations performed based on information that follows the rules mentioned here are more accurate. Understand and be aware that you will never get the complete and final set of information that defines the scope of the application being developed. You are expected to dig deeper, ask more questions, and gather information about activities and work-flow processes that have been incompletely explained. Accuracy of the estimation will increase with every additional bit of information thus obtained.

Understand the User View

There is a reason the adage, "The user is king," has been coined. The estimator should be absolutely clear that ultimately the scope has to be understood and defined as it is viewed and perceived by the user. (Refer to Figure 3.2 to see how user and developer perspectives may differ.) The following paragraphs explain several key aspects of user view and explore how it impacts the end FP count due to differences between the ways the estimator and the user see the application.

A Business Function: The user expects certain business process steps to be achieved through the software. Again, the user expects the process to follow certain sequences and related exceptions to occur. The application should address these scenarios. Quite often the user does not convey all the alternatives and exceptions that could occur in such a scenario. Another problem sometimes occurs when the estimator assumes the scenario is based on his own experience and defines the business function without considering the business user's perspective. It is essential that such situations be handled with utmost care. The user view counts. The user is paying for the project and, as a result, the application should meet user needs only.

The ATM Transaction

MyBank wanted a software application to handle ATM transactions. The requirement was quite simple and straightforward; the application should facilitate the following business functions:

- Authenticate user
- Accept request for money
- Deliver required money
- Update account balance
- Close transaction

The project team and the estimator reviewed the requirements and came up with the following steps that were to be addressed in the software application in order to meet the business function:

1. User swipes the ATM card.
2. The software records user information and validates authenticity of the ATM card. If found valid, the process advances to the next step. If not, the transaction is terminated.
3. Requests and accepts the four-digit PIN code from the user and validates this from the user account information available with MyBank.
4. Upon successful authentication of user code, the user is allowed to enter the amount required.
5. The money is dispensed.
6. The transaction is formally declared closed.

The FP count was done accordingly and the project team went ahead with coding. During early acceptance tests, however, certain glaring deficiencies in the functional aspect of the software came up. Some of the key exceptions in the ATM transaction scenario were omitted, such as:

1. While entering the four-digit PIN code, what happens if the user enters the wrong code? This was not addressed.
2. Upon entering the amount to be withdrawn, what happens if it is found that the balance amount in the user account with MyBank is insufficient to service the request?

3. Most important, what happens if the transaction itself does not close properly due to operational problems like network failure or power failures? How does the software reconcile incomplete transactions?

A review and modification of these exceptions resulted in additional coding and, of course, the FP count increased proportionally.

User Approval: Although most user requirements are reviewed and approved by the user, there is a dangerous gap between how the user reads and understands the documented business functions and how the project team has assumed certain functional processes while documenting them. This can lead to lots of rework if this gap not resolved through discussion. At times it is necessary to develop a dummy prototype of the application and get it approved by the user. Using terminology understood uniformly both by the user and the project team is recommended.

Change Management: As the project progresses through various lifecycle phases, the user's view of the scope often changes also. The changes in scope could happen due to various reasons like better understanding of business function, changes in business or technology environment, and others. The project team should be prepared to accept these changes and modify the estimates accordingly.

Determine Type of Count

The FPA process supports three kinds of count that can occur. These depend on the purpose and circumstances under which the count is being done. They are

- Development
- Enhancement
- Application

Development: Software applications that are freshly developed and installed for the first time are considered for development FP counts. The counting is done after the project has been successfully completed, and should essentially meet all user requirements.

Enhancement: Functionality enhancements typically are made to existing applications and done during the maintenance process. Any change in existing functionality in the form of adding, deleting or updating functions are considered part of enhancement process. Each of these change functions (add, delete, and update) are counted separately, and the overall sum total is the enhancement FP count. Bug fixes are also taken as part of enhancement count if the project team that maintains the application is different from the team that developed the application.

Application: During the application maintenance process, re-counting the entire application should be standard practice. Do an FP count after every enhancement process takes place. The revised FP count of the application may not be equal to the sum of the pre-revised FP count and enhancement FP count. A complete, fresh FP count will determine this. Usually the application count is treated as a baseline FP count because this is initialized after every enhancement process.

Table 3.1 provides a quick reference to various types of count as related to software execution processes.

Table 3.1 *Category of Application Count*

Software Execution Process	*Type of Count*	*Comments*
Fresh development	Development	Count after successful installation
Reengineer legacy application to new technology	Development	
Enhance functionality to existing application	Enhancement	Counts only the enhancements (add, update, and delete)
Revise the application count after enhancements are incorporated	Application	Similar to development count
Migrate application to new technology	Development	Separately calculate data migration count (conversion FP)
Bug fixing in existing applications	Enhancement	Only affected functions are counted

Scope and Boundary of Application

The scope of the project encompasses the complete set of functionality being delivered by the application, as expected by the user. If the application is a subset of a large set of applications, then consider only the subset, as defined by the user, with appropriate interfaces to other subsets of applications surrounding the application. Scope defines the functions that need to be included during the count. Sometimes the functions may span two applications. In this situation, the estimator should identify them as two separate applications for counting purposes.

The boundary of an application is well within the overall scope of the application. Boundary is very useful for defining the border between the functions available to the user and the software application being measured.

Defining the application boundary is a critical task that should be done with care. Boundary is defined based on the user's view of which business functions should be available to the user. Figure 3.5 provides an

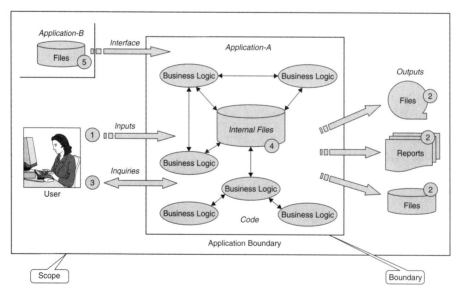

Figure 3.5 *Scope and boundary of an application.*

illustration of boundary, which helps in identifying almost all the attributes of an FPA process. These include identifying the following:

- The user transaction that processes the internal data that belongs to the application.
- Data that is internal to the application. All data that is owned and maintained by the application is treated as internal data. Internal data is always inside the boundary of the application in the form of internal files.
- Which data moves in and out of the boundary of the application. Also identifies which data remains within the boundary.
- Which data is not maintained by the application and hence is termed external to the application.

Sometimes a master system flowchart of existing applications is useful in defining the boundary of the application being counted.

Once the process of defining the boundary is completed, the findings and related assumptions should be reviewed and validated with the user. All the FPA processes that happen next—that is, calculating the data and transaction functions—are heavily dependent on the correct definition of the application boundary.

Count Data Functions

Data function is one of the two most critical components of the entire FPA process. The functionality requirements of the application are met through data functions and are facilitated by means of internal and external files. The focus here is on logical storage of data in the form of files and not the physical implementation. (Refer to Figure 3.3 for a review of the components of the application if necessary. The internal logical files and the external interface files are the data functions shown in this figure.) This section introduces the key standard terms and notations, as described by the IFPUG CPM 4.2 user manual [2].

Data functions typically facilitate the following interactions for the user:

- Add, update, and delete data from internal files (only)
- Refer data from external files (read)
- Index, sort, or arrange data for the purpose of queries and reports

There are two categories of data functions:

- ILF—Internal Logical Files
- EIF—External Interface Files

As mentioned earlier, ILF are owned and maintained by the application under consideration. EIF primarily are files that are referred by the application programs as inputs and they do not belong to the application. Typically EIFs are expected to be ILFs of another external application. Returning again to Figure 3.3, notice that the illustration displays the internal and external files with reference to the application under consideration (Application-A) and the external application (Application-B). ILFs reside necessarily inside the application boundary and EIFs, outside the boundary. In Figure 3.3, refer to circled item numbers 4 and 5.

Each file, whether an ILF or an EIF, contains data. Each element of the data, sometimes referred to as a *field* or a *column*, contains information about an entity. This element is known as a **data element** and this type is called a Data Element Type, or DET. For example, an employee name is a DET. Combining a set of data elements and storing them in a single file is a common procedure. Application design considerations sometimes necessitate these situations. A set of data elements that can be considered as a subgroup within the file is called as a Record Element Type, or RET. What is this subgroup? Consider the example of an employee file that contains complete data about a typical employee. The employee data can be broadly classified into

- Personal information—Name, SSN#, Address, DOB, Gender
- Education information—Qualification, Year of passing, Grade, Institution
- Previous experience—Company, Role, Responsibilities, Period
- Dependent information—Dependent name, DOB, Gender, Relation

You can clearly see here that each of the above classifications of information about the employee contains a set of DETs. The set of DETs together form a subgroup of information about a subclassification of information. The subgroup of information is typically homogeneous in nature and depicts information about a particular behavior of the entity, the employee. In the above example, each of the classifications is an RET and the ILF employee file has four RETs.

It is not enough to know about DETs and RETs that constitute an ILF. A variety of combinations is possible using the DETs and RETs in different real-life situations. In order to address these variations, the FPA process has provided for defining the ILF and EIF into three category of complexity: Low, Average, and High. Based on the combination of the number of DETs and RETs identified in an ILF or EIF, the complexity is identified from a standard, prescribed table by IFPUG CPM 4.2.

Each of the complexity categories—low, average, and high—directly maps to a function point count, which is a constant number. For ILFs, the FP counts are Low –7, Average –10, and High –15. For EIFs the FP counts are Low –5, Average –7, and High –10. These FP counts are defined as **unadjusted function points**. Later, when the other complexity factor known as Value Adjustment Factor (VAF) is imposed on the FP count, you obtain the adjusted FP count. VAF is derived from the 14 GSCS discussed earlier. These are discussed later in this chapter.

For more detail and extensive examples on data functions, see Chapter 4, "Data Functions."

Count Transaction Functions

Transaction function is the second critical component of the FPA process. It is only through transactions that a user can interact with the data that resides in the internal and external files. All transaction functions are outside the boundary of the application and they typically transact with the data functions that reside in the ILFs and EIFs (refer to Figure 3.3). The three basic types of transactions are *inputs*, *outputs*, and *inquiries*. These are the features that are visible to the user, and the execution of the application is done using these functions. The transaction functions provide the following features to the user:

- Provision to add, update, or delete data in the internal files
- Genertation of predefined standard reports
- Provision to query on data from internal and external files

There are three categories of transaction functions:

- EI—External Inputs
- EO—External Outputs
- EQ—External Inquiries

All the transaction functions are termed "external" because they all reside outside the boundary of the application. (See circled item numbers 1, 2, and 3 in Figure 3.3.) All three functions facilitate interactions between the user and the application. Through EIs, the user can input data into the application and maintain them as desired. An EI does not need to be an online data entry system. Inputs through EIs could be offline, batch mode, or other trigger-based inputs. Most applications need to generate reports or other forms of output. These are facilitated through External Outputs (EOs). Reports are normally predefined, repeatable outputs, and as such they are selectable through menu options in the application. The click of a report option in the Report menu generates the desired report (EO). Not all EOs are directed to printers; they can be sent to any other media like tapes, disks, or even monitors. Query features are provided in most applications to facilitate quick validation of certain business functions the user wants. Sometimes queries also provide answers to what-if analysis requirements. External Inquiries (EQ)s are the functions through which queries can be identified and counted during the FPA process. Similar to EOs, outputs from EQs can be directed to any media. Although reports (EO) necessarily contain derived (calculated) data as part of the output, this is not so in case of queries. EQ contains only raw data extracted from the files (ILF or EIF) and are rearranged or sorted according to user needs.

Consider the employee example discussed earlier in relation to data functions. In order to input employee information into the ILF, you need a data entry facility (EI). You can query the list of employees within a certain age group through EQ. If you need a report that provides information on the number of employees in different age groups and the number of dependents associated, you would use an EO to produce it.

The transactions EI/EO/EQ consist of two types of attributes: DET and FTR. You learned about DETs earlier in this chapter. FTR is the File Type Referenced by the transaction. FTR could be in an ILF or EIF. Every file referenced by the transaction is counted as one FTR.

Each EI/EO/EQ transaction type is again categorized into three levels of complexity based on the number of DET and FTR that they service. In order to address these levels, the FPA process has divided EI/EO/EQ into three categories: Low, Average, and High. Based on the combination of the number of DETs and FTRs identified in an EI/EO/EQ, the complexity is identified from a standard, prescribed table by IFPUG CPM 4.2.

Very similar to the FP counting discussed earlier with regards to EIF/ILF, each of the complexity categories—Low, Average, and High— for each type of transaction, EI/EO/EQ, directly map to a function point count that is a constant number. For EIs, the FP counts are Low –3, Average –4, and High –6. For EOs, the FP counts are Low –4, Average –5, and High –7. For EQs, the FP counts are Low –3, Average –4, and High –6. These FP count are defined as *Unadjusted* function points. Later, when the other complexity factor known as *General System Characteristics* based *Value Adjustment Factor* is imposed on the FP count, we then obtain the *Adjusted* FP count. These are discussed later in this chapter.

For more detail and extensive examples on transaction functions, see Chapter 5, "Transactional Functions."

Calculate the Value Adjustment Factor

Figure 3.3 shows the visible five functions available to the user; namely, ILF, EIF, EI, EO, and EQ. These functions capture the operational attributes of the application. Over and above these attributes are another set of attributes known as **technical attributes** of a software application. These technical attributes, although they are not visible to the user, define various technical parameters of the application through which the performance of the application can be controlled.

Based on a number of complexities that could occur in typical software applications, Albrecht came up with a set of technical parameters, which he called *general system characteristics*. There were 14 such GSCs identified. Each of the GSCs could be defined in terms of degree of influence on a scale of 0 to 5, where "0" means no impact and "5" means maximum impact. Table 3.2 describes the 14 general system characteristics that contribute toward arriving at the right value adjustment factor (VAF). The table shows two extreme variations of the total degree of influence (TDI) values. If all 14 GSCs have no impact (lowest values), the VAF works out at 0.65. On the other hand, if all the TDI have maximum impact (highest values), the VAF is 1.35. Between the two extreme ranges exists a variation of 0.70. This means that if the mid-range of values is assumed as 1.0, the 14 GSCs together could have an impact ranging from –35% (0.65) to +35% (1.35).

The VAF was devised to recalibrate the total unadjusted FP count that was arrived at through individual FP counts made by data and transaction functions—ILF, EIF, EI, EO, and EQ. The 14 GSCs were to be applied at the overall application level and not at individual data or transaction functions. The simple formula used here is

Adjusted FP Count = Unadjusted FP Count × VAF

Table 3.2 *Calculate Value Adjustment Factor*

#	GSC Description	Value Range	Lowest Values	Highest Values
1	Data Communications	0–5	0	5
2	Distributed Data Processing	0–5	0	5
3	Performance	0–5	0	5
4	Heavily Used Configuration	0–5	0	5
5	Transaction Rate	0–5	0	5
6	Online Data Entry	0–5	0	5
7	End-User Efficiency	0–5	0	5
8	Online Update	0–5	0	5
9	Complex Processing	0–5	0	5
10	Reusability	0–5	0	5
11	Installation Ease	0–5	0	5
12	Operation Ease	0–5	0	5
13	Multiple Sites	0–5	0	5
14	Facilitate Change	0–5	0	5
	Total Degree of Influence—TDI		0	70
	VAF = (TDI * 0.01) + 0.65		**0.65**	**1.35**

Conclusion

The Function Point Analysis process has been perhaps the most popular estimation method among software professionals. There are quite a number of reasons for the method's popularity:

- FPA maps clearly to the functional needs of the application being counted. This feature makes it easier for the user to validate the mapping of requirements to the components of the actual estimation method itself.

- FPA carefully avoids complexities that could be introduced if variations due to the technology being used are included in the calculation method. The technology component can be separately introduced in the form of productivity of the developer.

- The method provides for varying complexity within each of the attributes being measured. For example each internal file (ILF) can be of simple, average, or complex category. This feature helps finer tuning of the final FP count by the estimator.

- Key characteristics of the application being counted that do not fit into the definition of inputs, outputs, queries, internal, and external files are separately introduced in the form of general system characteristics (GSCs). Several performance and application-quality related parameters that impact the final FP count of the application are provided for fine-tuning FP count.

An estimator attempting to learn and practice the FPA estimation method might not get accurate estimates in the first few attempts. In fact, to check the accuracy of estimates, the estimator will have to wait until the project is completed, and all the data is collated and analyzed. But don't worry; wine gets tastier as it matures over years. With experience, the judgment of using the right parameters to arrive at the right complexity as well as identifying the correct number of attributes to arrive at the unadjusted FP count will make estimates more accurate. Arriving at the GSC-based VAF is most critical to arriving at the final adjusted FP count. An experienced software professional, who understands the larger aspects of application development and deployment, would be able to provide near accurate GSC-VAF. The estimator should obtain help from an expert software professional.

This chapter discussed estimation basics and explored various components of the IFPUG Function Point Analysis method in detail. The three chapters that follow are dedicated to deeper discussions on the three major aspects of the Function Point Analysis method:

- Chapter 4, "Data Functions," delves into all the data-related aspects of the FPA estimation process. Important aspects of data functions, including DET, RET, and other related terms are explained in detail along with examples.

- Chapter 5, "Transactional Functions," covers all the transaction-related complexities, including deep discussions on DET, FTR, and other related items. Examples have been used at appropriate places to help you understand the complexities.

- Chapter 6, "General System Characteristics," (GSC) has been specially provided to address some of the complex FPA attributes. A special section dedicated to mapping GSCs to quality parameters of the application is included.

References

1. Jones, T. Capers. "Foreword," in *Function Point Analysis* (by Brian J. Dreger). Prentice Hall, 1989.

2. International Function Point Users Group (IFPUG). *Function Point Counting Practices Manual (CPM), Release 4.2.*

CHAPTER 4

Data Functions

Introduction

In God we trust, in Data we rest!

Businesses around the world are dependent on IT systems to provide the right data at the right time. Critical and major decisions are made, based on the variety of processed information that these systems produce. Obviously all the information processed is totally dependent on the raw data maintained by the different systems running within the organization. Identifying and structuring the right set of data files for the system being designed is critical both for successful implementation as well as accurate estimation.

The previous chapter focused on the overall FPA estimation method, but only briefly touched on the topics of data and transaction functions. Because professional FPA estimators need a deeper discussion on data and transaction functions, this chapter discusses data functions, as applied and as described by the IFPUG Function Point Analysis method, and provides a number of examples and diagrams.

Creating, maintaining, and processing data into meaningful information are core needs of any software system. Stated broadly, from an estimation perspective, data can be classified into two varieties: data owned by the system and data referred by the system (application). The International Function Point Users Group (IFPUG) [1] has a clear method of differentiating between data owned by the system and the data referred by it. But first consider how a file is defined.

Definition of Files

Estimators are often faced with the dilemma of clearly defining what a "file" is in the context of function point (FP) counts as explained by IFPUG. There are two main areas of conflict:

- Differentiating between logical and physical implementation of data files
- Understanding various technological implementations of data files like flat files, VSAM files, RDBMS system, IMS, IDMS, DB2, and similar databases

The Counting Practices Manual 4.2 (CPM) [1] prepared by IFPUG clearly reiterates that all the attributes involved in FP count should always be seen from the user point of view. Thus identifying files becomes easier if the estimator views files the way the user sees them. In other words, "user view" maps to the concept of logical file.

You can understand a **data file** by considering that

- A set of characters (or numbers) form a data element.
- A set of data elements constitute a record.
- A set of records form a file.

As more and more complex software systems were designed, the structure of data files also became equally complex, moving from the simple files defined here to files having variable records, with each record having variable subrecords and the size of data elements themselves becoming variable.

A user needs neither to be aware of the complexities of defining files nor be worried about implementation issues. The designer is the one to bring the expertise on structuring the right data model for the system that can extract the highest performance, both from data consistency as well as transactions response time perspectives.

A Data File Example

Let's take the example of data files (only) for an Order Processing system. The application has a need to store various pieces of information from every transaction:

- Order details
- Item details

- Item costs
- Sales tax
- Total order cost

Looking at just one Order Details data file from the user point of view, you see a single data file. From the designer's point of view, however, it gets broken down to Order Header file and the Order Details File, which is linked through Order Number as the key. Other files are necessary for sales tax information and more. Which assumption is then correct? Should this be a single file or multiple files? The following sections address these questions.

Data Functions Defined by IFPUG

Before going further, take a few minutes to understand data functions and their attributes as defined by IFPUG. Later in this chapter you will learn more about the key attributes that define a data function.

IFPUG's Counting Practice Manual (CPM) broadly classifies the data function types into two categories: Internal Logical Files (ILFs) and External Interface Files (EIFs). As described in Chapter 3, the boundary of the application being counted decides what is internal and what is external to the system (see Figure 4.1). All files owned and maintained

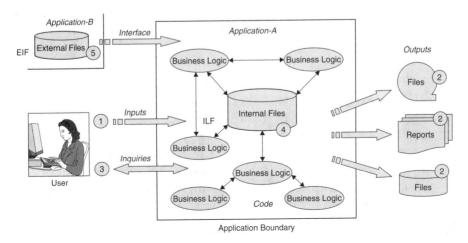

Figure 4.1 *Components of an application.*

by the application being counted are ILFs and all files referenced by the application but outside the boundary of the scope of count, are EIFs. In other words, if the CRUD (Create, Read, Update, and Delete) factor applies to a file in the system, it is likely to be an ILF, and if it is read only, the file is an EIF.

Another critical definition of files by IFPUG reiterates that any consideration of attributes of a file should be based on the fact that it is seen from the user perspective. If we now consider the Order details example, it would be appropriate to consider the Order details as one file (an ILF or EIF as the case may be) and not multiple files as viewed by the data modeler. One may challenge this definition because this rule will lead to fewer function points in the final numbers. Because the IFPUG method is designed to meet the user requirement, it is then seen as counting various attributes accordingly. This approach also increases the comfort of the user because the user is now able to map his or her needs to the function points counting process.

Figure 4.1 describes the various attributes of an application that are needed for function point counting purposes. The ILFs are within the boundary of the application being counted and as such, all ILFs are maintained by the programs belonging to the application. Similarly, the EIFs are external to the boundary of the application being counted and these files are being used for reference purposes only.

ILFs and EIFs

The CPM 4.2 (IFPUG) [2] defines ILF and EIF as follows:

- **ILF:** "An internal logical file (ILF) is a user identifiable group of logically related data or control information maintained within the boundary of the application. The primary intent of an ILF is to hold data maintained through one or more elementary processes of the application being counted."
- **EIF:** "An external interface file (EIF) is a user identifiable group of logically related data or control information referenced by the application, but maintained within the boundary of another application. The primary intent of an EIF is to hold data referenced through one or more elementary processes within the boundary of the application counted. This means an EIF counted for an application must be in an ILF in another application."

The basic difference between an ILF and EIF is that although the ILF is owned and maintained by the application being counted, the EIF is used for reference by the application being considered for FP counting purposes. The EIF referenced by the application being counted must be an ILF to another application.

Embedded Terms

The various embedded terms used in the previous definitions of ILF and EIF—control information, user identifiable, elementary process, and maintained—are explained in detail in the sections that follow.

Control Information

Control information is the data that influences an elementary process of the application being counted. It specifies what, when, or how data is to be processed. In other words, the behavior of an application, when being executed, can be controlled by means of control information. Instead of executing a set of workflow processes manually, you can record them in the required order and in a format that can be understood by the system on which the application is being executed. On a given trigger, the system automatically executes the workflow-related subsystems (applications), which then process and generate the required outputs. The control information itself can be stored in a data file format and can be an ILF to the application being counted.

Example 1

At the end of every work day, all sales data entered in the application has to be processed, analyzed, and used in reports that are generated in a given format. The control information data file will have all the workflow process-based instructions, such as "collate sales data for the day from given sales data files, arrange in certain order, process and analyze the data, and finally generate reports." For each of these processes, predefined applications are identified. In a typical mainframe platform, a JCL (Job Control Language) file can be treated as an ILF under the control information category.

Example 2

A large plant that manufactures circuit boards depends heavily on continuous power supply availability. Upon failure of electricity, the backup power supply needs to kick start without a break in power supply.

The control information file maintains the trigger and subsequent workflow processes by which the backup power needs to come up. The application that reads the control information has a set of other support sensors and connected equipment, which takes care of starting and stopping the backup power supply.

User Identifiable

The term **User Identifiable** refers to defined requirements for processes and/or groups of data that are agreed upon, and understood by, both the user(s) and software developer(s). The intent here is to ensure that all inputs that are taken in order to design a data file are identified from the user point of view. It is essential that the inputs thus agreed are documented and signed off on by the user as well as the software developer.

Example 1

A large shoe store requires an order processing application to process and generate orders to the suppliers of a variety of shoes. Practical requirements of the order processing system are discussed in detail with the user and then mutually agreed on and recorded. Care is taken while defining the various data items that need to be stored and processed by the order processing application. The name and the attribute of each data element are identified in a manner that is easily understood by the user. For example, shoe type, size, material, color, price, and gender (male/female) could be some of the information about the order that is identified and approved by the user. The data item for the application thus becomes the user identifiable inputs.

Example 2

The finance department needs a new salary processing application to be designed and developed. Here the user is the finance department and the requirements described by them are recorded. Various data items are required to process employee salary: basic salary, allowances, deductions, and tax, are provided and approved by the user. Thus the data processing requirements are user identifiable and are the basic inputs for the design of the salary processing application.

Elementary Process

An **elementary process** is the smallest unit of activity that is meaningful to the user. The elementary process must be self-contained and leave the business of the application being counted in a consistent state. The process of getting user inputs, validating, and updating the inputs to a data file is termed an **elementary process.** The elementary process is said to be complete when the data updating to a file is complete in all respects and there is a consistency in the updated information.

Example 1

Take the very simple situation of an application that maintains company employee information. The information stored includes employee generic information, dependent information, educational background, work experience history, etc. The elementary process here encompasses full and complete information update of all employee information in a single transaction. In other words, if the program that is written to record employee information does not provide for updating the full set of information mentioned here, it is not considered as conforming to an elementary process.

Example 2

In an invoicing system, the information to be recorded includes the generic information of the invoice (invoice #, date, customer, total amount, excise/tax id, etc.), details of the items invoiced, taxes, and other overheads. In order for the data recorded to be consistent, the elementary process here requires all information about the invoice to be processed in a single transaction.

Maintained

The term **maintained** is the ability to modify data through an elementary process. Examples include, but are not limited to, adding, changing, deleting, populating, revising, updating, assigning, and creating data.

You also must understand that each of these terms (adding, changing, and so forth), requires a different set of elementary processes. This is enumerated in detail as follows:

- The **add** elementary process first creates a blank record for the user to input, validates identified data items, and then populates all the contents in each of the data elements and finally creates a new record in the file when saved.
- The **update** elementary process fetches an existing record from the file, allows the user to change required data items, and then facilitates updating the revised data into the file upon saving.

- The **delete** elementary process first fetches the requested record, allows the user to identify the information and approve delete process, and then removes the record from the file. It could be a physical or logical deletion.

Rules for Identification of ILFs and EIFs

In order to ensure that the various files being included in the FP counting process for an application are rightly identified, it is critical that the definitions of embedded terms mentioned in the earlier sections of this chapter are strictly followed. It will help identifying the right ILFs and EIFs that are involved with the application being counted. There are several benefits:

- The true user view is captured to identify ILFs and EIFs.
- Clear differentiation between ILFs and EIFs happens based on correct demarcation of application boundary, again based on user view.
- The various workflow processes decide the maintenance activities that are associated with each data file.
- The core of any application is the information it stores and processes. This information storage happens in the form of data files. As such, correct identification of data files also facilitates identifying other related attributes of FP counting, such as transactions, reports, interfaces, etc.

The following sections define identification rules as given in CPM 4.2 (IFPUG). The identification rules are limited to classifying a file as an ILF or EIF. Once identified, to further determine the complexity of each of the files, a separate set of rules is provided.

ILF Identification Rules

To identify ILFs, look for groups of data or control information that satisfy the following definition of an ILF. All the following counting rules must apply for the information to be counted as an ILF:

- The group of data or control information is logical and user identifiable.
- The group of data is maintained through an elementary process within the application boundary being counted.

Figure 4.1 shows the ILF inside the boundary of the application. Basically ILF are owned by the application. As far as the function point counting process is concerned, it does not matter in what form the ILF is maintained within the technology platform on which the application is being developed. Each ILF could be stored in various alternative forms; for example, as RDBMS table, simple text file, VSAM file, and other generic file types.

All the data that is core to the application is stored in the ILFs. The ILFs facilitate modification of data in each file. Other operations, like queries and reports, can be done using the ILF.

EIF Identification Rules

To identify EIFs, look for groups of data or control information that satisfy the definition of an EIF. The following counting rules must apply for the information to be counted as an EIF:

- The group of data or control information is logical and user identifiable.
- The group of data is referenced by, and external to, the application being counted.
- The group of data is not maintained by the application being counted.
- The group of data is maintained in an ILF of another application.

In Figure 4.1, the EIF is outside the boundary of the application. Unlike the ILF, which belongs to the application, the EIF is treated as an external reference data file only. If the application simply refers to a file that belongs to another external application, the file is identified as an EIF. As mentioned in the preceding rules, an EIF does not allow any updates or maintenance process to be executed by the application. Typically, the EIF concept is used to provide data interface between two applications. Similar to the usage of ILF, the EIF can also be used in various processing situations that include data entry operations through EI, queries through EQ, reports through EO, and other interfaces through EIFs themselves.

Determining Complexity of ILFs and EIFs

As described earlier in this chapter, a data file contains a set of records consisting of a set of data elements. Because this definition is the basic and common component of any data file, ILF or EIF, you can now proceed further to categorize ILF and EIF into three large groups of complexities: Low, Average, and High.

IFPUG has defined a clear process of identifying an ILF or EIF as Low, Average, or High and also has a fixed number of unadjusted function points assigned to each of these categories. Only two major components of any data file decide its complexity: data elements (DET) and record elements (RET). The sections that follow explain the attributes of DET and RET and provide examples to support the definition.

DET

A data element type (DET) is a unique, user-recognizable, non-repeated field. In simple terms, it is a field within a record of a file or a column in a database table (file), but the mapping of a field or column in the file should be with respect to the data element recognized from the user point of view. This definition makes understanding a data element a bit complex. This section discusses the rules for identifying a DET, followed by a number of examples that illustrate various situations and mapping to user view. Please read them carefully and try to understand the implications as applicable to practical situations. Improper interpretation of data elements (and later, RETs) might lead to improper counting of unadjusted function points. Here are the rules (from IFPUG CPM 4.2) [3]:

Rule 1: "Count a DET for each unique *user recognizable,* non-repeated field *maintained* in or retrieved from the ILF or EIF through the execution of an elementary process." Under normal circumstances, if you consider an employee file with employee information and other relevant information, such as dependent information, academic information, experience, etc., the DETs that might generally be required are

- Employee name, SSN#, Date-of-Birth, Permanent Address, Date-of-Joining
- Dependent's name, Date-of-Birth, Gender
- Academic qualification, University/Institution, Year, Grade
- Work Type, Grade, Duration, Employer, Salary

The preceding set of DETs can be mapped to data elements from the user view. But if you explore a bit deeper you will find that "Employee name" is actually split into first name, middle name, and last name. The basic doubt an estimator gets here is whether they are three different DETs or a single DET. Figure. 4.2 has the two different views of the same DET—Employee Name. A similar dilemma arises when we explore the "address" part of the DET. The address is normally split into house #, street, city, ZIP Code, and country. Are they five separate DETs or a single DET?

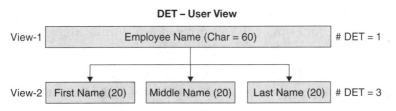

Figure 4.2 *Two views of DET.*

The answer to all such concerns is the philosophy of estimation explained by IFPUG: follow the user view. Typically "Employee name" is a single entity from the user view and it is the application designer (programmer) who splits this to make data processing easier and more presentable. As such, if this is a design-related split, you should count Employee name as one single DET. But there are situations wherein the user asks for the Employee name to be split in order to facilitate certain business-related requirements. In such situations, you should count this as three DETs as mentioned earlier (and as shown in View-2, Figure 4.2). In the same manner, you can visualize the address as one or more DETs based on user view only. There are situations when the user has asked for ZIP Code to be separated in order to process information data based on ZIP Code. In such cases, the ZIP Code is counted as a separate DET.

Rule 2: "When two applications maintain and/or reference the same ILF/EIF, but each maintains/references separate DETs, count only the DETs being used by each application to size the ILF/EIF" [4].

Example 1

Application A may use an Employee Name, SSN #, Address, City, State, and Zip Code. Application B may use the same ILF but also use employee salary information DETs like Basic Salary, Allowances, Deductions, Tax, and Net Salary. Application A would count six DETs; Application B would count five DETs. This is a situation of different data elements in the same file being referenced by different applications and hence different counts of DETs.

Example 2

Application X maintains and/or references an ILF that contains Employee Name, SSN#, and Address. Application Y maintains and/or references the Dependent's Name, Date-of-Birth, and Gender. Application X would count three DETs; Application Y would count three DETs, both from the same ILF.

Rule 3: "Count a DET for each piece of data required by the user to establish a relationship with another ILF or EIF" [5]. Note that under normal circumstances, the relationship between two files is established per the design requirements specified by the designer and hence cannot be counted as additional DETs. But there could be specific situations wherein the user has a need to establish a relationship between two files (ILF or EIF), and in this situation the linking data element is counted as a DET.

Example

A specific user requirement intends to track payments made against all the invoices received. The ILF, which maintains invoice information DETs, has an additional reference DET (foreign key) called payment voucher #, which is also a DET in the payment voucher ILF. Here the payment voucher # is counted as an additional DET in the invoice ILF. This is a user requirement.

RET

A *record element type* (RET) is a user-recognizable subgroup of data elements within an ILF or EIF. There are two types of subgroups:

- Optional
- Mandatory

Optional subgroups are those that the user has the option of using. The user may choose to use one or none of the subgroups during an elementary process that adds or creates an instance of the data.

Mandatory subgroups are subgroups where the user must use at least one subgroup.

Defining, designing, or identifying the right set of RETs for a given ILF or EIF has significant importance in the whole process of data modeling for an application. Sometimes the entire FP count may get distorted if the assumptions made while identifying the right set of DETs and RETs are incorrect. And in these situations, classification of mandatory and optional subgroups (within an RET) are critical.

Consider the earlier example of a data file with information about employees and their dependents. Here the employee data becomes

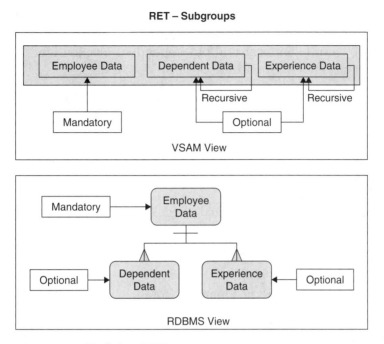

Figure 4.3 *Defining RET.*

mandatory and dependent data becomes optional. In other words, mandatory RET contains data or information that is absolutely essential for a record to exist. Optional RET may or may not have data or information that needs to exist for all or every record of an employee. Every employee record will have generic information about the employee that is mandatory, but every employee record is not required to have the optional dependent data.

Figure 4.3 shows alternate ways of depicting a data model and shows how records are designed based on multiple RETs within a record. The VSAM (a mainframe file handling system) has the ability to store multiple RETs within a record. In the example shown in Figure 4.3, the RETs are employee data, dependent data, and experience data. On the other hand, if the same group of employee information has to be designed in an RDBMS system, the employee data, dependent data, and experience data become three tables connected to the employee data as the base table through a reference key. In both situations (VSAM and RDBMS) the employee data is of mandatory subgroup category because without the mandatory category, other groups of information do not look meaningful.

The dependent and experience data are optional subgroups because they depend on the employee data. A particular instance of an employee record can exist without dependent or experience data (or both) but it cannot exist without the employee data.

RET Rules: One of the following rules applies when counting RETs:

- Count a RET for each optional or mandatory subgroup of the ILF or EIF, or
- If there are no subgroups, count the ILF or EIF as one RET.

Example

An apparel store uses an invoice data file (ILF) that stores the following information:

- Invoice #, Invoice Date, Customer Name, Sales Tax, Total Invoice Amount
- Item #, Item Code, Rate, Quantity, Cost

Two subgroups of information are involved: generic information about the invoice, and the details of the items invoiced. Mapping to the definition of RETs, you will observe that the generic information of the invoice is the mandatory subgroup and the item details is the optional subgroup. This also means there are two RETs in this data file: invoice generic data and items data.

Some of the expert estimators follow a different form of explanation to determine multiple RETs in a data file. They presume that whereas a mandatory RET can have only one set of data in one record, the optional RET can have multiple, recursive sets of data for the same mandatory RET. For example, an employee ILF will have one mandatory RET that stores the generic information about the employee, but the same record can have multiple subgroups containing employee dependent(s) data that is termed optional. Similarly an invoice ILF will have the generic data about the invoice as one subgroup, mandatory RET but multiple subgroups of item details as optional RET.

Complexity and FP Count Contributions

As explained earlier in this chapter, the two key attributes that define and size a data file (ILF and EIF) are DET and RET. IFPUG has a well-defined matrix table between DET and RET variations that derives complexity of an ILF/EIF. As the number of DET or RET increases in a given ILF/EIF, the complexity of the file also varies upward from low to average and then to the high category.

Table 4.1 *ILF/EIF Complexity Factor*

Range	*1 to 19 DET*	*20 to 50 DET*	*51 or More DET*
1 RET	Low	Low	Average
2 to 5 RET	Low	Average	High
6 or more RET	Average	High	High

Table 4.1 gives the reference matrix that can be used to determine the complexity factor of each ILF/EIF.

After you refer to Table 4.1 and determine the complexity of an ILF/EIF, you then have to assign the actual FP contribution (count) to the ILF/EIF, based on the complexity factor. Two separate tables can help you with this, one each for ILF and EIF, providing the exact FP contribution for each of the complexity categories of simple, average, and high.

The contribution FP count table for ILF is given in Table 4.2.

The contribution FP count table for EIF is shown in Table 4.3.

Step-by-Step FP Contribution Calculation Process

The following six sequential steps provide you the guideline to assess and count the FP value for data functions:

1. Determine whether the data file is an ILF or EIF, based on the application boundary defined by user.
2. Determine the number of DETs and RETs that exist in each of ILF/EIF by following the rules explained earlier in this chapter.
3. Determine the complexity factor (Low, Average, or High) from Table 4.1 based on number of DETs and RETs counted for each ILF/EIF.

Table 4.2 *ILF FP Contribution*

Functional Complexity Rating	*Unadjusted Function Points*
Low	7
Average	10
High	15

Table 4.3 *EIF FP Contribution*

Functional Complexity Rating	Unadjusted Function Points
Low	5
Average	7
High	10

4. Using the complexity factor, for each ILF, find the FP contribution (unadjusted FP count) from Table 4.2.

5. Using the complexity factor, for each EIF, find the FP contribution (unadjusted FP count) from Table 4.3.

6. Add FP contribution for all ILFs and EIFs to get the total unadjusted FP count for data transactions.

The following chapters explain how the unadjusted FP count can be converted to an adjusted FP count using the value adjustment factor.

Tips to Remember

Many practical situations could lead to ambiguous identification of various ILF and EIF parameters during actual FP counting. Here are a few tips to remember:

- An ILF or EIF may appear repeatedly in multiple sections of the same application during the counting process. Ensure that once a specific, identified ILF or EIF is defined and recorded, any subsequent appearance of the same ILF or EIF should be ignored. Duplicate counting of the same ILF or EIF will lead to erroneous FP count. For example, an ILF for employee data may appear in the employee data update module as well as in the employee job maintenance module. Count the employee ILF only once. But if in the event of multiple occurrences of the same ILF you find that the data element information varies, take the maximum data element count.

- The basic definition of an ILF or EIF maps them to a logical implementation of a file. Do not confuse this with the physical implementation of an existing data model in an RDBMS system. You should identify an ILF or EIF based on user view and ensure it is a logical implementation only. Do not map an ILF or EIF to a table in an RDBMS system without checking the basic rule.

Case Study: Counting ILF/EIF of an Invoicing Application

The user requires an invoice processing application to be developed. The module needs to meet the following user requirements:

- Maintain, inquire, and print invoices.
- Include customer information in the invoice. The customer data is maintained by another application.
- Maintain, inquire, and print items information.
- Inquire and report invoices summary for various customers.

This data model can be implemented in various types of databases (relational, IMS, IDMS, etc.). But remember that from the user perspective, this is supposed to be platform independent and as such, only the files and the entity relationship between files need to be taken into consideration while processing the FP count for ILFs and EIFs.

You can now prepare the list of possible fields in each of the entities shown in Figure 4.4. The data elements assumed here are illustrative only and might change significantly in different real-life situations.

The Entity-Relation (E-R diagram) in Figure 4.4 shows the following four groups of information:

- Invoice Data
- Customer Data
- Item Data
- Item Details Data

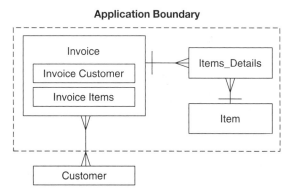

Figure 4.4 *Invoice data model.*

Table 4.4 *Invoice ILF Identification*

ILF Identification Rule	*Does the Rule Apply?*
The group of data or control information is logical and user identifiable.	Yes. The complete data information of the Invoice together with Item details is user identifiable.
The group of data is maintained through an elementary process within the application boundary being counted.	Yes. The elementary process maintains the Invoice and Item Details data.

Follow IFPUG rules and determine whether each of the preceding items is an ILF or EIF.

The analysis of Invoice Data is given in Table 4.4.

Based on the above analysis, the Invoice Data file, maintained within the boundary of the application being counted, is an ILF.

The analysis of Customer Data is given in Table 4.5.

Based on the above analysis, the Customer Data file is not an ILF. Table 4.6 explores whether this file fits the EIF identification rules.

Based on the above analysis, the Customer Data file is an EIF.

The analysis of Item Data is given in Table 4.7.

Based on the preceding analysis, the Item Data file, although maintained within the boundary of the application being counted, is not an ILF.

The analysis of Item Details Data is given in Table 4.8.

Table 4.5 *Customer ILF Identification*

ILF Identification Rule	*Does the Rule Apply?*
The group of data or control information is logical and user identifiable.	Yes. The complete data information of the Customer is user identifiable.
The group of data is maintained through an elementary process within the application boundary being counted.	No. The elementary process does not maintain the Customer data.

Table 4.6 *Customer EIF Identification*

EIF Identification Rule	Does the Rule Apply?
The group of data or control information is logical and user identifiable.	Yes. The complete data information of the Customer is user identifiable.
The group of data is referenced by, and external to, the application being counted.	Yes. The Customer data is referenced by and external to the Invoice application.
The group of data is not maintained by the application being counted.	Yes. The Customer data is not maintained by the Invoice application.
The group of data is maintained in an ILF of another application.	Yes. The data is maintained in the Customer application.

Table 4.7 *Item Data ILF Identification*

ILF Identification Rule	Does the Rule Apply?
The group of data or control information is logical and user identifiable.	No. The data information of the Item is partial because it does not contain details of each item as identified by the user.
The group of data is maintained through an elementary process within the application boundary being counted.	Yes. The elementary process maintains the Item data.

Table 4.8 *Item Details ILF Identification*

ILF Identification Rule	Does the Rule Apply?
The group of data or control information is logical and user identifiable.	No. The data information of the Item Details is partial as it does not contain details of each item as identified by the user.
The group of data is maintained through an elementary process within the application boundary being counted.	Yes. The elementary process maintains the Item data.

Table 4.9 *Item Information ILF Identification*

ILF Identification Rule	Does the Rule Apply?
The group of data or control information is logical and user identifiable.	Yes. The data information of the Item Information is complete and is user identifiable.
The group of data is maintained through an elementary process within the application boundary being counted.	Yes. The elementary process maintains the Item information data.

Based on the above analysis, the Item Details Data file, although maintained within the boundary of the application being counted, is not an ILF.

Based on the user perspective, Item data alone and Item Details alone are not ILFs, but when combined, the Item Information is user identifiable. You must combine the two data files to form a single group of data items as identified by the user.

Apply the analysis to Item information Data as given in the Table 4.9.

Based on the above analysis, the Item Information, maintained within the boundary of the application being counted, is one ILF.

Table 4.10 counts the DETs and RETs in each of the ILF/EIFs, which can then be used to define the complexity that will further determine the FP contributions.

Table 4.10 *DET and RET Identification*

File Fields	Counting Process
Invoice Entity	**RET 1 (mandatory)**
Invoice #	DET 1
Invoice Date	DET 2
Sales Tax #	DET 3
Discount Amount	DET 4
Gross Amount	DET 5

Table 4.10 *DET and RET Identification (Continued)*

1a. Invoice Customer Entity—Subgroup	RET 2 under Invoice Entity (mandatory)
Customer Id	DET 6
Customer Name	DET 7
Customer Address	DET 8
Shipping Address	DET 9
1b. Invoice Items Entity—Subgroup	**RET 3 under Invoice Entity**
Item #	DET 10
Item Description	DET 11
Rate	DET 12
Quantity	DET 13
Cost	DET 14
Items Entity	**RET 1 (mandatory)**
Item #	DET 1
Item Description	DET 2
2a. Items Details Entity—Subgroup	**RET 2**
Item # (foreign key)	Previously counted as DET 1
Item Category	DET 3
Item Rate	DET 4
Customer Entity	**RET 1 (mandatory)**
Customer Id	DET 1
Customer Name	DET 2
Address	DET 3
Shipping Address	**DET 4**

Table 4.11 *DET/RET Identification*

Rule	Rule Applies?	1-Invoice Entity	2-Items Entity	3-Customer Entity
Count a DET for each unique user-recognizable, non-repeated field maintained in or retrieved from the ILF or EIF through the execution of an elementary process.	Yes	14	4	4
When two applications maintain and/or reference the same ILF/EIF, but each maintains/references separate DETs, count only the DETs being used by each application to size the ILF/EIF.	No	NA	NA	NA
Count a DET for each piece of data required by the user to establish a relationship with another ILF or EIF.	No	NA	NA	NA
Count a RET for each optional or mandatory subgroup of the ILF or EIF.	Yes	3	1	1
Or, if there are no subgroups, count the ILF or EIF as one RET.	Yes	NA	1	1

Table 4.11 applies the DET and RET counting rules and so that you can check whether it matches the numbers identified previously.

The exact FP contribution can now be evaluated (see Table 4.12) using the contribution figures provided by IFPUG.

Table 4.12 *FP Count*

Entity	File	DET	RET	Complexity	Unadjusted FP Count
Invoice	ILF	14	3	Low	7
Items	ILF	4	1	Low	7
Customer	EIF	4	1	Low	5

Conclusion

The data functions constitute the core part of an application and all transactions are designed to manipulate data functions. Counting the FP value of data functions is critical though the counting process is not very complex. Key points to note while counting data functions include

- Identify all data files that are within the scope of the application that is being evaluated for FP count
- Segregate data files that are maintained by the application being counted and those data files that are only referred but not maintained by the application
- Data files particularly are user identifiable because the FP method follows the logical implementation of files

Identifying ILF/EIF: User View versus Programmer View

During the process of defining and identifying the right number of ILF/EIF, programmers often tend to go a bit overboard in including files that are needed from an application design perspective, but actually not seen from the user view. All files that are not included in the user view have to be discounted in the FP counting process. Determining correctly whether an ILF/EIF belongs to an application can involve quite a bit of ambiguity. Here are a few examples of ILF/EIF that can be included and also those that can be generally excluded from an application FP count.

ILFs that are generally included:

- Any application data that is maintained by an external transaction like employee, invoice, inventory, payroll, banking, accounts, etc.
- Online help data maintained within the application
- Control information maintained within the application
- Error logs and audit data maintained within the application
- All files that are identified and approved by the user

ILFs that are generally excluded:

- Sort files, temporary files, work files, indexes, and similar files that are purely envisioned by the programmer from the design perspective. They are intended to enhance the performance of the application.
- View or join files introduced due to design/build requirements.

- Files not maintained by the application being counted and those being used for reference only.
- Files that are set up to track and monitor transactions from beginning to end.

References

1. International Function Point Users Group (IFPUG). *Function Point Counting Practices Manual (CPM), Release 4.2.*

2. Ibid.

3. Ibid.

4. Ibid.

5. Ibid.

Other Interesting Reading Material

Garmus, David, and David Herron. "Sizing Data Functions" in *Function Point Analysis: Measurement Practices for Successful Software Projects.* Addison-Wesley, 2004. Pp. 93–109.

CHAPTER 5

Transactional Functions

Introduction

Transactions are the means through which data is transformed into meaningful information. Static data is of very little use to the business. A good transaction processing system provides continuous data updates, collating and compiling it into useful information and then presenting it in a readable form.

Transactions are also the vehicle through which the user accesses the raw as well as processed data. Three categories of transactions are available to the user:

- The transaction to input data into the system
- The transaction to query information from the system
- The transaction to generate reports

Chapter 3, "A Study of Function Point Analysis," focused on the overall FPA estimation method, but that chapter simply introducd data and transaction functions. Because professional FPA estimators need a full understanding of data and transaction functions, Chapter 4 focused on data functions, and this chapter discusses transaction functions in more detail, supported by a number of examples and diagrams.

The International Function Point Users Group (IFPUG) has specified a clear method to differentiate between various types of transactions. But first you need to understand how a transaction is defined.

Definition of Transactions

The FPA estimation method prescribes three basic types of transaction functions: inputs, inquiries, and outputs. (These functions have been discussed previously in this book: Refer to Figure 3.3 in Chapter 3 for more information.) Through these transaction functions, the user is able to interact with the application. Most transaction functions are predefined, and the look and feel as well as the processing logic of the functions are frozen during the software design and development process. Data entry screens, online queries and report generation are some of the practical examples of transaction functions.

While attempting to estimate the size and effort required to design, develop, and test these input/output transaction functions, estimators normally encounter a conflict situation about which items to include and which ones to exclude. Understanding the basic concept of how external entities interact with internal intelligent software is helpful at this point.

Mapping a human system to a software application shows similarities in its execution processes. The various attributes specified by the IFPUG method to define an application system—input (EI), output (EO), inquiry (EQ), internal file (ILF), and external interface file (EIF)—can all be equated to important parts of a human system:

- The main memory or storage area, part of the human brain (gray cells), is the ILF.

- Inputs to the brain come through the eyes, ears, and nose. They are the EI/EQ.

- Outputs from the brain can be made through the mouth (voice), hands, etc. They are EO.

The information stored in the brain is not of much use unless there are means to extract it to the outer world and take advantage of the quality of the content. The various input/output mechanisms facilitate information from the brain so that it can be transacted and made available to the external user. The information extracted could be raw data or processed data. The transaction vehicle provides for this flexibility.

Case Study

Take the example of a mobile phone. Very similar to the brain and the human system, you can map various components that include input, output, interface, and data storage in a mobile phone.

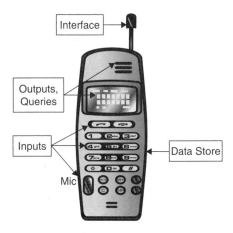

Figure 5.1 *Input and output components of a mobile phone.*

Figure 5.1 identifies the various modes of transactions that are similar to the transaction screens or windows provided for a typical software application.

Similar to a human brain or a mobile unit, a software application requires multiple modes of input as well as output through which a user can transact with the application to record or obtain desired information. In a way, the user is seldom able to actually see and feel the design and code that comprises a software application—that is what makes it similar to a black box. By providing access facilities to this black box, the user is allowed to view, access, and manipulate the information stored there. These access features are the transaction screens in the application.

In translating the various features of the mobile phone to FPA transaction functions, you will be able to do the following mapping:

• The keypad, including the navigation buttons, are input facilities and each of the keys has a built-in function to perform a specific action under different situations. You can map these keys to External Inputs (EI).

• The display screen as well as the speaker facilitates output that can be seen or heard. These elements can be mapped to External Outputs/Inquiries (EO/EQ).

- The antenna of the mobile phone is the basic means of connecting with an external wireless network. This can be mapped to External Interface File (EIF).

- The mobile phone has its own data storage facility that is mapped to Internal Logical File (ILF).

Albrecht's Definition of Transactions

Perhaps after careful evaluation of the various modes and alternatives of input and output that can exist for a software application, Albrecht identified three major forms of transactions: External Inputs (EI), External Outputs (EO), and External Inquiries (EQ). The term *external* is being used here to indicate that the transactions occur from outside the application boundary and interact with data stored inside the boundary. This remarkable evaluation by Albrecht has resulted in significant consolidation of several forms of input/output transactions into just three varieties. Key achievements that resulted include

- A learner of IFPUG FPA estimation method feels comfortable in quickly understanding and adapting to a small number of simple input/output categories.

- An expert estimator can map a large variety of input/output mechanisms to these three categories of transactions. (These are discussed later in this chapter.)

- With a few exceptions, almost all user interaction requirements are provided for through only three modes of transaction with the application.

- By separating input, output, and queries into three categories and assigning appropriate weights to the FP counts, Albrecht gave the estimators a method to measure the FP count more accurately.

Ingredients of a Transaction

This section explores what constitutes a transaction, its relation to application development, and how it helps in sizing and defining the effort to develop a transaction. Figure 5.2 explains the architecture of a transaction that typically begins as input from an external user; then passes through the user interface layer, the application, and the database; and finally exits in the form of output on a printer or other external devices.

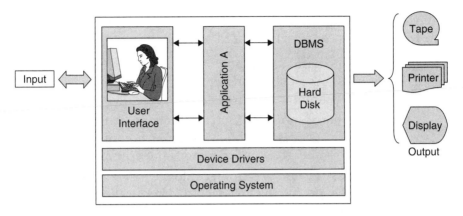

Figure 5.2 *Definition of a transaction.*

The transaction architecture shown in Figure 5.2 can be split and mapped to the three varieties of transactions defined by IFPUG as follows:

- The interaction between the external user and the database through the application, facilitating data maintenance in the database, is typically an External Input.

- The interaction between the external user that results in accessing data from the database and resulting in an external output on external device is typically an External Output.

- In a situation where the interaction between the external user and the database results in an extraction of raw (unprocessed) data, the transaction is typically termed an External Inquiry.

A transaction that occurs between the user and the software application is facilitated through a user interface. To explain this in software parlance, the **user interface (UI)** is the experience that the user gets while interacting with the application. The UI is backed with appropriate business or workflow logic in appropriate language code. This code facilitates the instructions given by the user to appropriately interact first with the system and then the data at the back end, extracting meaningful information and finally bringing it back to the user through the same UI.

IFPUG's Counting Practices Manual 4.2 (CPM) [1] clearly states that all the components involved in FP count should be seen from the user's point of view. While identifying the components that can be considered a transaction, it is essential that the estimator understand various possible modes of transactions that could occur in the software industry:

- Transactions are assumed to be platform independent during the sizing process. As such, transactions could be character-based screens or GUI (Graphic User Interface) screens.

- The basic mode of input/output transactions could vary over a wide variety of devices. Keyboard, mouse, pointing devices, bar code readers, or other sensors are some of the examples.

- The mode of transaction execution could vary depending upon the design and the processing need of the application. Online and batch execution are two basic variations. In some situations, transactions get triggered based on set parameters. For example, a department store might trigger a stock replenishment transaction when the stock level of a particular product falls below the predefined minimum store level. A second example might be that of a GPS tracking system installed in a car that triggers a transaction and warns the driver of certain traffic congestion ahead on the highway.

All the preceding examples are considered transaction functions and need to be included in the FPA counting method.

As more and more complex software systems were designed, the transaction media became equally complex, moving from simple character-based screens to GUI-based graphic screens, and, more recently, to wireless devices. Some of today's hand-held devices are capable of multiple varieties of transactions including telephone, e-mail, music, and camera functions.

A user does not need to be aware of the complexities of defining the transactions nor be worried about implementation issues. The designer must work hard to design the right transaction mode for the system to extract the highest performance, both from data consistency as well as response time perspectives.

Transactional Functions Defined by IFPUG

Transactional functions provide the means for a user to transact with the application. These functions facilitate the processing of data contained in the system, and convert and present it in a form desired by the user.

Unlike data functions, all the transaction functions belong to the application being counted and are directly related to the data processing requirements of the user.

The IFPUG FPA method sets certain parameters that clearly define the rules for identifying a transaction. These definitions include the following:

- The transaction is visible or accessible to the user.
- All transactions are identified to be outside the boundary but within the scope of the application being counted.
- The various data elements that constitute the transaction necessarily move from outside to inside the application boundary and vice versa.
- The transaction could be invoked through various means of input (batch or online) or through a variety of hardware devices, sensors, and more.

The FPA method also clearly differentiates between various types of transactional functions. These differences are identified by assessing the intent of each of the transactions. A few rules are enumerated as follows:

- The External Input (EI) transaction is primarily designed to maintain one or more Internal Logical Files (ILF). The term *maintain* includes processes like add, update, delete, and populate.
- Two other transactions, External Output (EO) and External Inquiry (EQ), are quite similar in many respects. But the key differentiator is in their intent. Whereas EQ fetches and produces data that is raw and in its original form, the EO fetches as well as processes the data and delivers in an analyzed form.
- Another differentiator between EO and EQ is that the facility of updating an ILF is allowed only in an EO transaction process.

Figure 5.3 describes the various attributes of an application that are needed for function point counting purposes. The EI/EO/EQ are all outside the boundary of application being counted. The next section describes the three transactional functions as explained by IFPUG and then further explains various parameters and terms used to define them. Examples for each of the parameters will help illustrate the definition in different contexts.

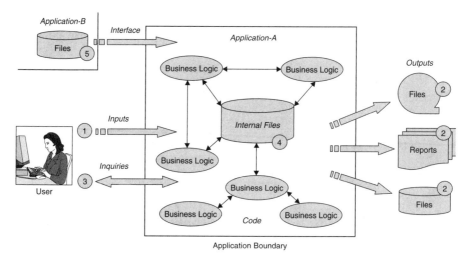

Figure 5.3 *Components of an application.*

EI, EO, and EQ

The CPM 4.2 (IFPUG) defines EI, EO, and EQ as follows:

External Input

"An external input (EI) is an elementary process that processes data or control information that comes from outside the application's boundary. The primary intent of an EI is to maintain one or more ILFs and/or to alter the behavior of the system."

External Output

"An external output (EO) is an elementary process that sends data or control information outside the application's boundary. The primary intent of an external output is to present information to a user through processing logic other than or in addition to the retrieval of data or control information. The processing logic must contain at least one mathematical formula or calculation, or create derived data. An external output may also maintain one or more ILFs and/or alter the behavior of the system."

External Inquiry

"An external inquiry (EQ) is an elementary process that sends data or control information outside the application boundary. The primary intent of an external inquiry is to present information to a user through the retrieval of data or control information. The processing logic contains no mathematical formula or calculation, and creates no derived data. No ILF is maintained during the processing, nor is the behavior of the system altered."

Chapter 4, "Data Functions," explains that one single physical transaction like EI (or EO/EQ), as seen by the user, may not translate into one logical transaction. A designer may combine more than one logical transaction into one physical transaction to facilitate usage convenience. Identify these design-related differences and count the occurrence of true logical transactions.

Embedded Terms

This section explains in detail the various embedded terms used in the preceding definitions of EI, EO, and EQ.

Elementary Process

An **elementary process** is a defined unit of activity that is understood by the user. When a transaction is executed, the process facilitates transmission of information between the user and the application across the boundary of the application. The elementary process helps define how and when the information that is being processed can be termed as complete in all respects. The key definition to remember is this: The elementary process that processes a set of data and then either updates, inquires, or reports an output should leave the final business information of the system in a consistent state.

Example 1

An HR application is required to maintain all information about every employee of the organization. Additional information, such as dependent data, employee experience, and employee academic records is also maintained for every employee. The design of an EI that facilitates recording of this information conforms to the definition of elementary process of this EI. When an employee record is updated, the process should facilitate update of all the attributes of the employee, including his or her dependent, experience, and academic data. If the EI process does only a partial data update, it is conforming to the elementary process requirement of an EI. As such, the process may not be counted as a valid EI.

Example 2

A typical invoicing application for an apparel store must process and record three types of information:

- The invoice details, such as invoice number, date, and customer details

- Item details for every item procured, like item number, quantity, and rate

- Invoice payment details, including total cost, tax, and other reference data

An elementary process is considered to be completed if the EI design facilitates processing and recording of all the above sets of information.

Control Information

Control information is the data that influences an elementary process of the application being counted. It specifies what, when, or how data is to be processed. This has been discussed in detail (with examples) in Chapter 4.

User Identifiable

The term **user identifiable** refers to defined requirements for processes and/or groups of data that are agreed upon, and understood by, both the user(s) and software developer(s). This has also been discussed in detail (with examples) in Chapter 4.

Processing Logic

The behavior of a transaction is often controlled by the **processing logic** that goes behind its intent. Just as a transaction itself is designed based on user requirements, the processing logic that is built into the transaction is based on user requirements. A few popular examples of processing logic include the following:

- Validating input data. The data could be raw data or an output of a mathematical equation, etc.

- Determining whether the process meets a defined business rule.

- Establishing whether the transaction meets its minimum conditions to be accepted as a standard transaction like EI/EO/EQ.

Maintained

The term **maintained** is the ability to modify data through an elementary process. Examples include, but are not limited to, adding, changing, deleting, populating, revising, updating, assigning, and creating. This has been discussed in detail (with examples) in Chapter 4.

Rules for Identification of EI, EO, and EQ

In order to ensure that the various transactions included in the FP counting process are rightly identified, it is critical that the definitions of embedded terms mentioned in the earlier sections of this chapter are strictly followed. This will help you identify the right EI, EO, and EQ involved with the application being counted. There are several benefits:

- The true user's view is captured to identify EI, EO, and EQ.
- Clear differentiation between EI, EO, and EQ happens based on the correct processing logic involved—again, based on the user's view.
- The various workflow processes decide the maintenance activities that are associated with each transaction.

The following sections define identification rules as given in CPM 4.2 (IFPUG). The identification rules are limited to classifying a transaction as an EI, EO, or EQ. Additionally, a separate set of rules is further provided to help you further determine the complexity of each of the transaction.

EI Identification Rules

To identify EI, look for transactions that satisfy the following criteria of an EI. All the following counting rules must apply for the information to be counted as an EI:

- The data elements being transacted are input from outside the application boundary.
- One or more Internal Logical Files (ILF) are maintained through the transaction.
- The processing logic applied for a transaction is unique and has not been used in another transaction of the same application.

EO/EQ Identification Rules

To identify EO, look for transactions that satisfy the following criteria of an EO. All the following counting rules must apply for the information to be counted as an EO:

- The information residing in data elements being transacted is sent outside the application boundary.
- One or more files (ILF/EIF) are referenced through the transaction.
- The processing logic applied for a transaction is unique and has not been already used in another transaction of the same application.
- The one unique rule that differentiates EO and EQ is the usage of a mathematical formula or calculation (derived data) in the processing logic. If the output contains derived data, the transaction is an EO; and if it does not contain any derived data, the transaction is an EQ.

Table 5.1 provides a summary of elementary process identification rules for the three types of transaction functions (EI/EO/EQ).

Table 5.1 *Elementary Process Identification Rules*

Identification Rule	EI	EO	EQ
The process is the smallest unit of activity that is meaningful to the user.	Y	Y	Y
The process is self-contained and leaves the business of the application in a consistent state.	Y	Y	Y
The primary intent of an elementary process is to maintain an ILF or alter the behavior of the system.	Y	N	N
The processing logic of the elementary process contains at least one mathematical formula or calculation.	NA*	Y	N
The processing logic of the elementary process alters the behavior of the system.	Y	Y/N	N
The primary intent of the elementary process is to present information to a user.	N	Y	Y
The data moves from outside to inside the application boundary (or vice versa).	Y	Y	Y
An ILF is maintained by the elementary process.	Y	Y/N	N

*NA = Not Applicable.

Table 5.2 *DET and FTR Identification Rules*

Identification Rule	EI	EO	EQ
Count an FTR for each ILF maintained.	Y	Y	NA*
Count an FTR for each EIF referenced.	Y	Y	Y
Count one DET for each user-recognizable, non-repeated field that enters or exits the application boundary and is required to complete the input/output/query process.	Y	Y	Y
Count one DET for each message sent (for example, an error/confirmation message).	Y	Y	Y
Count one DET for each action button.	Y	Y	Y

*NA = Not Applicable.

Table 5.2 provides guidelines on how to apply the DET and FTR counting rules for the three types of transaction functions: (EI/EO/EQ).

Determining Complexity of EI, EO, and EQ

IFPUG has defined a clear process of identifying an EI, EO or EQ as simple, average, or complex and also has assigned a fixed number of unadjusted function points to each of these categories. Only two major components of any transaction decide its complexity; that is, Data Elements (DET) and File Type Referenced (FTR).

- *DET:* A **data element type** is a unique user-recognizable, non-repeated field. In simple terms, it is a field in a file or a column in a database table (file), but the mapping of a field or column in the file should be with respect to the data element recognized from the user's point of view. For more details and examples, refer to Chapter 4.

- *FTR:* A **file type referenced** (FTR) is a file, internal or external, that has been accessed by the transaction.

FTR rules: The following rules apply when counting FTRs:

- Count an FTR for each file referenced by the transaction.
- Count an FTR for each file maintained.

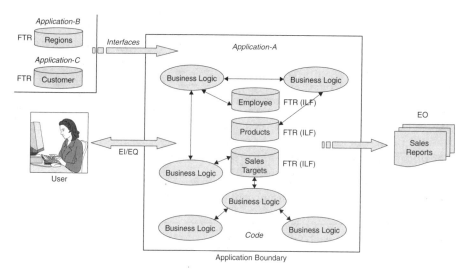

Figure 5.4 *Identifying FTR in transactions.*

Example

The marketing department of a cosmetics sales and distribution company requires the sales reporting application to maintain as well as generate periodic sales reports. Various reports are produced; for example, reports by salesperson, region, and product are all generated.

Figure 5.4 has captured the gist of the way an FTR is identified in most transaction functions. The following list explains the assumptions made in the figure:

- *Employee* is the salesperson file that stores personal details of all salespeople.

- *Products* is the file that contains all information of the various varieties of cosmetic products sold and distributed by the company.

- *Sales Targets* is the file that maintains the quarterly and annual sales targets set for each salesperson. The targets are regional as well as product-specific.

- *Regions* is the file that stores data of all regions on which the salespeople operate. This file is maintained by Application B; hence this file in an external file.

- *Customer* is the file that is maintained by Application C and is also an external file.

The transactions that can be identified for normal sales activities processing are

- The data entry modules (EI) required to maintain the employee and products need one FTR each. But to maintain the sales target data, you need to reference two external FTRs (the region and customer data files). Counting one FTR for each file, you get a total of three FTRs to maintain sales target data. But only the sales target file (an ILF) is updated. The regions and customer (EIF) are only referenced.

- For generating the regional, customer-specific sales reports we need all the files—employee, products, sales targets, and region—as well as customer files. Count each one as one FTR. For this sales report example, you need a total of five FTRs.

Complexity and FP Count Contributions

As explained earlier in this chapter, the two key attributes that define and size a transaction (EI, EO, and EQ) are the DET and FTR. IFPUG has a well-defined matrix table between DET and FTR variations that derives complexity of an EI/EO/EQ. As the number of DET or FTR increases in a given EI/EO/EQ, the complexity of the transaction also varies upward, from simple to average and then to the high category.

External Inputs

Table 5.3 gives the reference matrix that can be used to determine the complexity factor of each EI.

Table 5.3 *EI Complexity Factor*

Range	1 to 4 DETs	5 to 15 DETs	16 or More DETs
0 to 1 FTR	Low	Low	Average
2 FTRs	Low	Average	High
3 or more FTRs	Average	High	High

Table 5.4 *EO/EQ Complexity Factor*

Range	1 to 5 DETs	6 to 19 DETs	19 or More DETs
0 to 1 FTR	Low	Low	Average
2 to 3 FTRs	Low	Average	High
4 or more FTRs	Average	High	High

External Outputs/External Inquiries

Table 5.4 gives the reference matrix that can be used to determine the complexity factor of each EO/EQ.

After you decide the complexity of an EI/EO/EQ, you then have to assign the actual FP contribution (count) to the EI/EO/EQ based on the complexity factor. There are two separate tables, one for EI/EQ and another for EO, that provide the exact FP contribution for each of the categories of complexity (simple, average, and high).

The contribution FP count table for EI/EQ is given in Table 5.5.

The contribution FP count table for EO is given in Table 5.6.

Step-by-Step FP Contribution Calculation Process

In order to ensure that the estimator is able to clearly identify all the transactions that are applicable and are also those identified by the user, it is essential that the following steps are executed in the given sequence:

1. Determine whether the transaction is an EI, EO, or EQ, based on the processing logic required by the user.
2. Determine the number of DETs and FTRs that exist in each of EI/EO/EQ by following the rules explained earlier in this chapter.

Table 5.5 *EI/EQ FP Contribution*

Functional Complexity Rating	Unadjusted Function Points
Low	3
Average	4
High	6

Table 5.6 *EO FP Contribution*

Functional Complexity Rating	Unadjusted Function Points
Low	4
Average	5
High	7

3. Determine the complexity factor (simple, average, or high) from Tables 5.1 and 5.2 based on number of DETs and FTRs counted for each EI/EO/EQ.
4. Using the complexity factor for each EI/EQ, find the FP contribution (unadjusted FP count) from Table 5.3.
5. Using the complexity factor for each EO, find the FP contribution (unadjusted FP count) from Table 5.4.
6. Add FP contribution for all EI/EO/EQ to get the total unadjusted FP count for transactional functions.

The following chapters explain how the unadjusted FP count can be converted to adjusted FP count using the value adjustment factor.

Case Study: Counting EI/EO/EQ of an Invoicing Application

This case study was first introduced in Chapter 4 to explain the identification of data files. This chapter revisits the case study to identify the transactional functions required to facilitate easy user interactions. As you may recall, in this example, the user needs an invoice processing application. The module needs to meet the following user requirements:

- Maintain, inquire and print invoices.
- Include customer information in the invoice.
- The customer data is maintained by another application.
- Maintain, inquire and print items information.
- Facility to inquire and report invoices summary for various customers.

The transactional functions EI/EO/EQ can obviously be developed in any technology like J2EE, .NET, or mainframe/COBOL, but it does not really make a difference while identifying each of the transactions because they are basically technology independent.

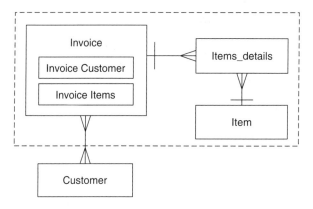

Figure 5.5 *Invoice data model.*

The Entity-Relation (E-R Diagram) in Figure 5.5 shows the following four groups of information:

- Invoice Data
- Customer Data
- Item Data
- Item Details Data

Follow IFPUG rules and determine whether each of these groups requires EI, EO, or EQ. Start with individual data handling transactions and then move on to the consolidated invoice transactions.

The analysis of Item transactional functions is given in Table 5.7.

Based on this analysis, the Item transaction function maintained within the boundary of the application is not being counted as an EI.

Table 5.7 *EI Identification—Item Data*

EI Identification Rule	Does the Rule Apply?
The process is the smallest unit of activity that is meaningful to the user.	No. The Item Data by itself does not conform to complete and meaningful information.
The process is self-contained and leaves the business of the application in a consistent state.	Yes. The process is self-contained and leaves the business in a consistent state.

Table 5.8 *EI Identification—Item Data and Item Details*

EI Identification Rule	Does the Rule Apply?
The process is the smallest unit of activity that is meaningful to the user.	Yes. The Item Data and Item Details together conform to complete and meaningful information.
The process is self-contained and leaves the business of the application in a consistent state.	Yes. The process is self-contained and leaves the business in a consistent state.

Now consider the analysis of Item and Item Details transactional functions together as given in Table 5.8.

Based on this analysis, the Item and Item Details transaction function, maintained within the boundary of the application is being counted as an EI. This EI can be utilized by the user to maintain data about all the items being transacted through the invoice.

CRUD Transactions

Special discussion is necessary at this stage to analyze the differences in the basic elementary processes for each of the CRUD (Create, Read, Update, and Delete) categories of functional transactions associated with a typical EI. The following list explains the basic variations in the way each of the transactions happen:

- **Create** transactions involve creating a blank record in the data file, obtaining all relevant data element contents from the user, and then populating the data elements in the blank record with the content obtained from the user.

- **Read** transactions normally require scanning the data file and obtaining the data element contents of an identified record. Normally this transaction is combined with other transactions like Update and Delete.

- **Update** transactions involve fetching an existing record from the data file, displaying it to the user, obtaining any changes, and finally writing it back to the data file with necessary updates.

- **Delete** transactions require fetching an identified record from an existing data file, displaying and obtaining confirmation from the user to remove it, and then logically (and sometimes physically) removing the record.

Table 5.9 *EI Identification—Invoice, Item Data, and Item Details*

EI Identification Rule	*Does the Rule Apply?*
The process is the smallest unit of activity that is meaningful to the user.	Yes. The Invoice, Item Data, and Item Details together conform to complete and meaningful information.
The process is self-contained and leaves the business of the application in a consistent state.	Yes. The process is self-contained and leaves the business in a consistent state.

If you evaluate the elementary process involved in each of the preceding CRUD transactions, you will find that except in the case of a Read transaction, all others are unique. As such, while counting EI for a data maintenance transaction, you will be counting them as three EIs, one each for Create, Update, and Delete. The complexity of these three EIs might vary depending on the number of data elements (DETs) involved in each of the transactions. Typically the Delete transaction does not require all the DETs to be displayed before accepting confirmation to delete.

The customer data information does not require transactions to be counted because it has been stated that this information belongs to an external application. The customer data has been used in the invoice application for reference purposes only.

Now consider the analysis of Invoice, including the Item and Item Details transactional functions, as given in Table 5.9.

Based on the above analysis, the Invoice that includes Item and Item Details transaction functions maintained within the boundary of the application is being counted as an EI. This EI can be utilized by the user to maintain data about all invoices being transacted through the Invoice application.

Invoice System—FP Counting Process

You can now count the DETs and FTRs in each of the EI/EO/EQ (for the entire invoice application) and then use the count to define the complexity that will further determine the FP contributions (see Table 5.10).

You can now apply the DET and FTR counting rules and check whether the count matches the numbers identified previously (see Table 5.11).

Table 5.10 *DET and FTR Identification for the Invoice Application*

EI Contents	Counting Process
Items Entity	FTR 1
Item #	DET 1
Item Description	DET 2
1a. Items Details Entity—Subgroup	FTR not counted
Item # (foreign key)	Previously counted as DET 1
Item Category	DET 3
Item Rate	DET 4
Invoice Entity	FTR 1 (RET 1)
Invoice #	DET 1
Invoice Date	DET 2
Sales Tax #	DET 3
Discount Amount	DET 4
Gross Amount	DET 5
2a. Invoice Customer Entity—Subgroup	FTR 2 (EIF from external application)
Customer Id	DET 6
Customer Name	DET 7
Customer Address	DET 8
Shipping Address	DET 9
2b. Invoice Items Entity—Subgroup	RET 2 under Invoice Entity (optional)
Item #	DET 10
Item Description	DET 11
Rate	DET 12
Quantity	DET 13
Cost	DET 14

Table 5.11 *DET and FTR Counting Rules for Invoice*

Rule	Rule Applies?	Items	Invoice
Is the data moving in from outside the application boundary?	Yes	Yes	Yes
An ILF is maintained by the EI.	Yes	Yes	Yes
Count an FTR for each ILF maintained.	Yes	1	2
Count an FTR for each EIF reference.	Yes	0	1
Count one DET for each user-recognizable, non-repeated field that enters or exits the application boundary and is required to complete the external input.	Yes	4	14
Count one DET for each message sent.	Yes	1	1
Count one DET for each action button.	Yes	2	2

Table 5.12 *FP Contribution for Invoice*

Entity	Trans.	DET	FTR	Complexity	Unadjusted FP Count
Items	EI	4	1	Low	7
Invoice	EI	14	3	Low	7

The exact FP contribution can now be evaluated using the contribution figures provided by IFPUG (see Table 5.12).

NOTE This case study describing FP counting does not cover the complete FP counting requirements of an invoice system. The counting stops at unadjusted FP count. The next chapter discusses the value adjustment factor used to convert the unadjusted FP to adjusted FP count.

Conclusion

The ability to clearly identify the complete and correct number of transactional functions for an application does not happen in the first attempt—it is best done through a couple of iterations. Reviewing all the transactions through iterations will help resolve certain overlapping and multiple usage processes, including

- Helping to identify repetition of processing logic across multiple transactions
- Rationalizing common data elements, such as files referenced that are spanning across multiple transactions

Identifying EI/EO/EQ—User View versus Developer View

During the process of defining and identifying the right number of EI/EO/EQ, it is not uncommon for developers to go a bit overboard in including transactions that are needed from an application design perspective but actually not seen from the user view. All such files that are not included in the user view have to be discounted from the FP counting process. Determining whether an EI/EO/EQ belongs in an application is sometimes a difficult task. Here are a few examples that illustrate the EI/EO/EQ that can be included and also those that can be generally excluded:

EI/EO/EQ that are generally included:

- Any application data file that is maintained by an external transaction, such as employee, invoice, inventory, payroll, banking, accounts, etc., has a mandatory requirement to provision CRUD operations on each of the data files.

EI/EO/EQ that are generally excluded:

- Transactions for online help data not maintained within the application
- Transactions for error logs and audit data that are maintained within the application but not defined as a user requirement

References

1. International Function Point Users Group (IFPUG). *Function Point Counting Practices Manual (CPM) Release 4.2.*

Other Interesting Reading Material

Garmus, David, and David Herron. "Sizing Transaction Functions," in *Function Point Analysis: Measurement Practices for Successful Software Projects.* Addison-Wesley, 2004. Pp. 111–143.

CHAPTER 6

General System Characteristics

Introduction

Programmers will always dream about capturing the complete, total, and true requirements of a software application. Most likely, that will never happen unless the user is the actual programmer! From time immemorial, experts have tried their best to dissect a software application into various components, architectural layers, work-flow processes, technology aspects, and more. No doubt these efforts have improved understanding and enhanced the design of many software development processes. There is a limit to the requirements that are captured; the rest is assumed.

The Function Point Analysis method defined by IFPUG does its best to facilitate capturing of scope of the software application to the maximum extent possible. Broadly, the scope (requirements) is classified into two distinct areas:

- Business functionality as desired and visible to the user. These are classified as files (internal and external), input, output (reports), and inquiries.

- Application characteristics (behaviors) that explain various attributes during actual execution, such as performance, security, usability, and more.

Whereas the business functionality is visible to the user, the application characteristics are visible to the programmer (designer) and experienced by the user. Obviously, the business functionality, the application behavior-related information, and scope are provided by the user. But in real-life situations, emphasis is placed on capturing maximum information on the business functions of the application. The performance, security, and other behavioral requirements are vaguely enumerated. It is left to the application designer to define these. And unless the designer is truly immersed in the IT environment of the organization where the application is being deployed, true justification in capturing these behavioral attributes becomes difficult.

Before going into more detail on the general system characteristics in the context of a typical software application, including how to measure them and incorporate the impact on the final function point count of an application, briefly consider two very basic but critical definitions of software application from a software professional's perspective: functional and non-functional requirements. Later, this chapter will link the non-functional requirements to the general system characteristics (GSCs).

Functional and Non-Functional Requirements

Chapters 3, 4, and 5 discussed the FPA method, including data and transactional functions and how to implement them in actual counting situations. This chapter is specifically dedicated to explaining the concept of general system characteristics (GSCs) that are applicable to the application being counted as a whole system. Before going into detail on the 14 GSCs, their attributes, and their impact on the final function point (FP) count, consider the two broad subsections of a software application, popularly known as the **functional** and **non-functional** requirements.

Functional Requirements

Functional requirements (FR) refer to the business functionality that the application is expected to address. In simple terms, FR define what the product (application) should do. FR are the core of any software application and define the critical business services that are expected to be facilitated when the user works with the application. Functional requirements are visible to the user and can be validated through well-defined test procedures. Some of the common FR include:

- Collecting input on predefined business functions, process them, and then provide appropriate output

- Enabling predefined business rules to be embedded in various transactions initiated by the user
- Facilitating storage of a large amount of business critical data in a specified format
- Facilitating a wide variety of processed output in the form of reports in a predefined format
- Providing a good user interaction interface that forms the means of communication between the user and the application
- Ensuring that the behavior of the application is predictable and is consistent

Non-Functional Requirements

Non-functional requirements (NFR) define the system properties and specify the behavioral pattern under various operating conditions. They are also called *constraints* that are imposed on the application. The NFR are not directly visible to the user and it is quite difficult to validate them in a simulated environment. As the name suggests, NFR do not address any of the direct business functions expected from the application. Some key NFR properties that could be attributed to an application include

- Reliability
- Response time
- Performance
- Security
- Availability
- Scalability
- Capacity

Often the NFR turn out to be more critical than the FR. For example, the lack of certain functionality in a system can be managed through manual or alternate means, but improper design leading to a system crash because of an increase in user base can lead to the application being totally unusable. This is discussed in more detail later in the chapter.

Introduction to General System Characteristics

The data and transactional functions discussed in earlier chapters together represent the total business functions that are delivered through the application being counted. Truly this is the logical representation of the functionality and does not address the physical implementation of the functions in an IT environment. In other words, data and transactional functions are the *what* of the application features, and the physical implementation of these functions is the *how* of the features being deployed in a given hardware/infrastructure environment.

The Function Point Analysis (FPA) method by IFPUG has captured the critical implementation features of typical applications through 14 general system characteristics (GSCs). These 14 GSCs encompass almost all the major implementation complexities that can exist, and through careful evaluation of each of the GSCs, the estimator can arrive at a final function point (FP) count that includes logical as well as physical implementation properties of the application being counted. Chapter 3 briefly discussed this.

Although the data and transactional functions (unadjusted FP) remain the same regardless of their implementation, including technology and infrastructure, the GSCs play a significant role in defining the final (adjusted) FP count that is dependent on the implementation environment. The 14 GSCs are

 1. Data Communications
 2. Distributed Data Processing
 3. Performance
 4. Heavily Used Configuration
 5. Transaction Rate
 6. Online Data Entry
 7. End-User Efficiency
 8. Online Update
 9. Complex Processing
10. Reusability
11. Installation Ease
12. Operational Ease
13. Multiple Sites
14. Facilitate Change

Every application being counted needs a mandatory evaluation on all 14 GSC parameters in order to arrive at the final, adjusted FP count. It is important to know that as much as the user's view is important to agree and count data and transactional functions, it is equally critical and essential that the 14 GSCs are evaluated based on the user's view. While gathering information from the user about the business functions that need to be delivered, it would be advisable to educate the user about the importance of the 14 GSCs that define the properties of the application and agree on the attributes that the user expects.

Degree of Influence (DI)

While evaluating the 14 GSCs, provision has been made by the FPA method to assess the impact of each of the GSCs based on a range of increasing complexity factor. This range varies in value between 0 and 5, with 0 as the lowest complexity and 5 as the highest. Based on user input, the estimator must evaluate the complexity number (0 to 5) for each of the 14 GSCs. The sum of the degree of influence for all of the 14 GSCs is known as **total degree of influence** (TDI).

You can easily calculate the two extreme ranges of values for TDI by assuming the lowest and the highest degree of influence values for each of the 14 GSCs:

- The TDI value is = 0 when all the 14 GSCs have the lowest degree of influence
- The TDI value is = 70 when all the 14 GSCs have the highest degree of influence

If you take the mid-range of TDI value as average (between 0 and 70), it is obvious the TDI has a variation range of ±35%.

The FPA method offers a well-defined explanation for each of the 14 GSCs in order to arrive exactly at the degree of influence. This next section goes through each of these explanations and provides appropriate support definitions. From a practitioner's perspective, it has been observed frequently that estimators tend to make mistakes in arriving at the right degree of influence for each of the GSCs. Thus the final FP count does get impacted to a great extent. Sometimes this leads to lack of credibility of the FPA estimation method itself.

Guidelines for General System Characteristics

After considerable research and deliberations, IFPUG has come up with explanations on how to evaluate and assess the level of degree of influence for each of the 14 GSC parameters. This section provides the details as defined by IFPUG.

GSC-1: Data Communications

Every application should have at least two layers architecturally: the client layer and the server layer. Depending upon the complexity, environment, and other factors, these layers could extend to more layers or the other networking hardware and communication protocols may be introduced within the two layers. The overall complexity of the application will vary with the complexity of these layers. The Data Communications GSC defines the level of complexity based on the communication environment that is envisaged for the application being counted. Table 6.1 describes the degree of influence attributed to each level of complexity.

GSC-2: Distributed Data Processing

Data movement is critical to business applications. The Distributed Data Processing GSC helps measure the complexity that arises due to the intensity and complexity involved in data handling processes in the application (see Table 6.2). All data processing measured is within the application boundary. In most situations, this GSC impacts typically with the GSC-1 Data Communications.

Table 6.1 *Data Communications*

DI	Guidelines
0	Application is pure batch processing or a stand-alone PC.
1	Application is batch but has remote data entry or remote printing.
2	Application is batch but has remote data entry and remote printing.
3	Application includes online data collection or TP (teleprocessing) front-end to a batch process or query system.
4	Application is more than a front-end, but supports only one type of TP communications protocol.
5	Application is more than a front-end, and supports more than one type of TP communications protocol.

DI = Degree of Influence.

Table 6.2 *Distributed Data Processing*

DI	Guidelines
0	Application does not aid the transfer of data or processing functions between components of the system.
1	Application prepares data for user processing on another component of the system such as PC spreadsheets and PC DBMS.
2	Data is prepared for transfer; then it is transferred and processed on another component of the system (not for end-user processing).
3	Distributed processing and data transfer are online and in one direction only.
4	Distributed processing and data transfer are online and in both directions.
5	Processing functions are dynamically performed on the most appropriate component of the system.

DI = Degree of Influence.

GSC-3: Performance

Applications that serve a large user base, are mission-critical, or business-critical typically have stringent performance requirements. The parameters are provided by the user. Faster response time, performing at the same level at peak user logins, higher throughput, etc., are some of the performance requirements set by the user. The performance requirements are addressed during the design phase (see Table 6.3). Depending on the platform, technology, and tools used for developing the application, the effort can vary over a large range.

GSC-4: Heavily Used Configuration

Quite often the software architect comes across the situation where the hardware on which the application is to be deployed has serious processing limitations. The limitation could be due to various reasons, including CPU availability, storage capacity, and other interfacing components (see Table 6.4). Sometimes the hardware is already overloaded with other important applications. In these situations, innovative design and programming techniques are required.

Table 6.3 *Performance*

DI	Guidelines
0	No special performance requirements were stated by the user.
1	Performance and design requirements were stated and reviewed but no special actions were required.
2	Response time or throughput is critical during peak hours. No special design for CPU utilization was required. Processing deadline is for the next business day.
3	Response time or throughput is critical during all business hours. No special design for CPU utilization was required. Processing deadline requirements with interfacing systems are constraining.
4	Stated user performance requirements are stringent enough to require performance analysis tasks in the design phase.
5	Performance analysis tools were used in the design, development, and/or implementation phases to meet the stated user performance requirements.

DI = Degree of Influence.

Table 6.4 *Heavily Used Configuration*

DI	Guidelines
0	No explicit or implicit operational restrictions are included.
1	Operational restrictions do exist, but are less restrictive than a typical application. No special effort is needed to meet the restrictions.
2	Some security or timing considerations are included.
3	Specific processor requirements for a specific piece of the application are included.
4	Stated operation restrictions require special constraints on the application in the central processor or a dedicated processor.
5	There are special constraints on the application in the distributed components of the system.

DI = Degree of Influence.

GSC-5: Transaction Rate

With increase in the user base, an application that is business-critical to the user demands that each user is serviced at the same rate of response on the transactions. In complex, algorithm-based applications, the architecture must be multi-layered in order to be able to scale up to peak transaction rates (see Table 6.5).

GSC-6: Online Data Entry

Interactive and real-time data entry features are common among user interface intensive data entry screens of software applications. The GSC for Online Data Entry defines the complexity of an application based on the percentage of application that has online, interactive data entry features (see Table 6.6). Some of the complexities seen in online data-entry screens are real-time data validations as well as reference information for faster data entry operations.

Table 6.5 *Transaction Rate*

DI	Guidelines
0	No peak transaction period is anticipated.
1	Peak transaction period (for example, monthly, quarterly, seasonally, annually) is anticipated.
2	Weekly peak transaction period is anticipated.
3	Daily peak transaction period is anticipated.
4	High transaction rate(s) stated by the user in the application requirements or service level agreements are high enough to require performance analysis tasks in the design phase.
5	High transaction rate(s) stated by the user in the application requirements or service level agreements are high enough to require performance analysis tasks and, in addition, require the use of performance analysis tools in the design, development, and/or installation phases.

DI = Degree of Influence.

Table 6.6 *Online Data Entry*

DI	Guidelines
0	All transactions are processed in batch mode.
1	1% to 7% of transactions are interactive data entry.
2	8% to 15% of transactions are interactive data entry.
3	16% to 23% of transactions are interactive data entry.
4	24% to 30% of transactions are interactive data entry.
5	More than 30% of transactions are interactive data entry.

DI = Degree of Influence.

GSC-7: End-User Efficiency

As more and more organizations are IT enabled, the variety of users with varying levels of IT experience grows. Basically the GSC for End-User Efficiency measures the capability of the end user and defines the complexity value, which is inversely proportional to the awareness level of the user. Most software product vendors have now been moving toward providing a high level of user experience that is oriented toward making applications easier to use.

Table 6.7 *End-User Efficiency*

DI	Guidelines
0	None of the 16 activities
1	One to three of the 16 activities
2	Four to five of the 16 activities
3	Six or more of the 16 activities, but there are no specific user requirements related to efficiency
4	Six or more of the 16 activities, and stated requirements for end-user efficiency are strong enough to require design tasks for human factors to be included (for example, minimize key strokes, maximize defaults, use of templates)
5	Six or more of the 16 activities, and stated requirements for end-user efficiency are strong enough to require use of special tools and processes to demonstrate that the objectives have been achieved

DI = Degree of Influence.

The IFPUG FPA method defines the following set of 16 activities that can capture the need for varying level of End-User Efficiency (see Table 6.7):

- Navigational aids (for example, function keys, jumps, and dynamically generated menus)
- Menus
- Online help and documents
- Automated cursor movement
- Scrolling
- Remote printing via online transactions
- Pre-assigned function keys
- Batch jobs submitted from online transactions
- Cursor selection of screen data
- Heavy use of reverse video, highlighting, colors underlining, and other indicators
- Hard copy user documentation of online transactions
- Mouse interface
- Pop-up windows
- As few screens as possible to accomplish a business function
- Bilingual support (supports two languages; count as four items)
- Multilingual support (supports more than two languages; count as six items)

GSC-8: Online Update

Many business-critical applications have a mandatory need to keep the data up-to-date to the last transaction level. This could also mean that all resources attached to the application are more frequently busy. Every transaction is complete and closed online. Typically online data entry goes together with online update. Sometimes stringent audit needs and backup and recovery requirements are tied up with critical online systems. Table 6.8 presents the guidelines for the Online Update GSC.

GSC-9: Complex Processing

In a number of situations, due to the complexity of the business functions, heavy transaction processing or even complex algorithmic needs

Table 6.8 *Online Update*

DI	Guidelines
0	None
1	Online update of one to three control files is included. Volume of updating is low and recovery is easy.
2	Online update of four or more control files is included. Volume of updating is low and recovery is easy.
3	Online update of major internal logical files is included
4	Protection against data lost is essential and has been specially designed and programmed in the system
5	High volumes bring cost considerations into the recovery process. Highly automated recovery procedures with minimum operator intervention are included.

DI = Degree of Influence.

are necessary. The Complex Processing GSC captures the complexity based on presence (or absence) of the following five components (see Table 6.9):

- Sensitive control (for example, special audit processing) and/or application specific security processing
- Extensive logical processing
- Extensive mathematical processing
- Much exception processing resulting in incomplete transactions that must be processed again (for example, incomplete ATM transactions caused by TP interruption, missing data values, or failed validations)
- Complex processing to handle multiple input/output possibilities (for example, multimedia or device independence)

GSC-10: Reusability

Reuse of code can happen in two situations: software development with reusable codes or software development for reuse purposes. For example, if you have a predesigned set of software codes (sometimes known as *objects*) and the project team uses these predeveloped objects, this process is then known as *software development with reusable codes*.

Table 6.9 *Complex Processing*

DI	Guidelines
0	None of the five components
1	Any one of the five components
2	Any two of the five components
3	Any three of the five components
4	Any four of the five components
5	All five of the 5 components

DI = Degree of Influence.

When the project team develops fresh code with the intention of using this code again in future development projects, the process is known as *software development for reuse*. The Reusability GSC refers to the second category. While developing an application, portions of the code are earmarked for reuse and componentized to facilitate reuse either within the same application or in other applications. The degree of componentization is captured through this GSC (see Table 6.10).

Table 6.10 *Reusability*

DI	Guidelines
0	No reusable code.
1	Reusable code is used within the application.
2	Less than 10% of the application considered more than one user's needs.
3	Ten percent (10%) or more of the application considered more than one user's needs.
4	The application was specifically packaged and/or documented to ease reuse, and the application is customized by the user at source code level.
5	The application was specifically packaged and/or documented to ease reuse and the application is customized for use by means of user parameter maintenance.

DI = Degree of Influence.

GSC-11: Installation Ease

Often estimators come across specific needs from the user that stipulate that the software be installable on different hardware configurations. Combined with these complexities, frequent upgrades to the next versions of the OS or technology platform also require the software design and coding to be more structured in order to facilitate smooth conversions (see Table 6.11).

GSC-12: Operational Ease

Once installed and configured on a given platform, the application or the software system should not need any manual intervention, except during serious breakdown situations. To attain this status, maximum design and coding effort is needed and hence the Operational Ease GSC will have maximum degree of influence value. Although some of the parameters given in Table 6.12 are oriented more toward mainframe and legacy systems, the estimator can map these to newer platforms appropriately.

Table 6.11 *Installation Ease*

DI	Guidelines
0	No special considerations were stated by the user, and no special setup is required for installation.
1	No special considerations were stated by the user but special setup is required for installation.
2	Conversion and installation requirements were stated by the user, and conversion and installation guides were provided and tested. The impact of conversion on the project is not considered to be important.
3	Conversion and installation requirements were stated by the user, and conversion and installation guides were provided and tested. The impact of conversion on the project is considered to be important.
4	In addition to item 2, automated conversion and installation tools were provided and tested.
5	In addition to item 3, automated conversion and installation tools were provided and tested.

DI = Degree of Influence.

Table 6.12 *Operational Ease*

DI	Guidelines
0	No special operational considerations other than the normal backup procedures were stated by the user.
1–4	One, some, or all of the following items apply to the application. Select all that apply. Each item has a point value of one, except as noted otherwise. • Effective startup, backup, and recovery processes were provided, but operator intervention is required. • Effective startup, backup, and recovery processes were provided, but no operator intervention is required (count as two items). • The application minimizes the need for tape mounts. • The application minimizes the need for paper handling.
5	The application is designed for unattended operation. Unattended operation means no operator intervention is required to operate the system other than to start up or shut down the application. Automatic error recovery is a feature of the application.

DI = Degree of Influence.

GSC-13: Multiple Sites

If the user base is spread across several country locations, customizations that are specific to a country are additional installation specifications that need to be addressed. Additional effort is consumed due to additional testing at different locations if the customizations are different. The Multiple Sites GSC sometimes goes together with GSC 11, Installation Ease. Table 6.13 presents the range of influence for the Multiple Sites GSC.

GSC-14: Facilitate Change

The Facilitate Change GSC addresses the capability of the design and code structure to facilitate easy maintenance. Although the parameters in Table 6.14 are focused more on query and report, there are a number of other situations that could be attributed to facilitating easy modifications and maintenance of usage. Examples include hard coding data into the code (remember the great Y2K problems), business logic, and

Table 6.13 *Multiple Sites*

DI	Guidelines
0	User requirements do not require considering the needs of more than one user/installation site.
1	Needs of multiple sites were considered in the design, and the application is designed to operate only under identical hardware and software environments.
2	Needs of multiple sites were considered in the design, and the application is designed to operate only under similar hardware and/or software environments.
3	Needs of multiple sites were considered in the design, and the application is designed to operate under different hardware and/or software environments.
4	Documentation and support plan are provided and tested to support the application at multiple sites, and the application is as described by item 1 or item 2.
5	Documentation and support plan are provided and tested to support the application at multiple sites and the application is as described by 3.

DI = Degree of Influence.

Table 6.14 *Facilitate Change*

DI	Guidelines
0	None of the five characteristics
1	A total of one item from the five characteristics
2	A total of two items from the five characteristics
3	A total of three items from the five characteristics
4	A total of four items from the five characteristics
5	A total of five items from the five characteristics

reports being inflexible. The following five characteristics can apply for the application:

1. Flexible query and report facility is provided that can handle simple requests; for example, and/or logic applied to only one internal logical file (count as one item).

2. Flexible query and report facility is provided that can handle requests of average complexity; for example, and/or logic applied to more than one internal logical file (count as two items).

3. Flexible query and report facility is provided that can handle complex requests; for example, and/or logic combinations on one or more internal logical files (count as three items).

4. Business control data is kept in tables that are maintained by the user with online interactive processes, but changes take effect only on the next business day (count as one item).

5. Business control data is kept in tables that are maintained by the user with online interactive processes, and the changes take effect immediately (count as two items).

All the tables describing the degree of influence for each of the 14 GSC have been directly adopted from the IFPUG CPM 4.2 manual [1].

AUTHOR'S NOTE I did a fairly detailed search across various books, technical papers, etc., on the function point method, looking for an explanation of how the 14 GSCs map to various lifecycle stages of the software development activity. The findings were very insignificant and disappointing. Most authors simply explained the 14 GSCs, their degree of influence, the calculated value adjustment factor, and moved on. I am making an attempt to provide an explanation of the 14 GSCs as actually mapped to the non-functional requirements of a software application. This is in an early stage of research. The next section, "GSC and NFR," has been dedicated to this explanation

---

GSC and NFR

There is no shortcut to success! If you are looking for a quick and dirty way to arrive at estimates that are nearly accurate, you will end up with only dirty estimates. A survey among software professionals once revealed that, on average, professionals spend approximately 4 to 16 hours on project effort and cost estimates. The projects could be as small as a $100,000 or as large as $2,000,000. I fail to understand why the software professionals neglect the most critical aspect of a software project—proper estimation. The success of the project itself depends on accurate estimations. Whatever tools, techniques, or expertise one may have, it would be quite risky to do the effort and other estimates of a $2 million project in just two days! If one has to justify the estimates, it is critical that the estimator understands and spends quality time in understanding the high-level architecture of the application. These and other observations are discussed more fully in Chapter 10, "Tips, Tricks, and Traps." The desired behavior of a software application depends to a great extent on the internal engine of the system. In a civil engineer's language, a good metaphor for the internal engine would be the architecture of a building; for a car designer it is the engine, carburetor, and perhaps the transmission system. Software applications also rely heavily on the architecture that holds together various layers, components, and interfaces. Various properties of the application that decide the behavior of the system during actual execution from no load to full load are also dependent on the way the engine is designed. Knowing the environment in which the engine is expected to perform is also important for architects. The heart of the system should be built with a strong base, and architecture is the heart of a software project.

Understanding the deeper implications of various dimensions of IT architecture is essential. Figure 6.1 outlines the layers, tiers, and levels

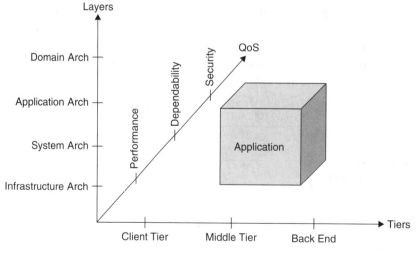

Figure 6.1 *IT architecture.*

of service. IT architecture addresses the enterprise level environment that exists in an organization. A detailed understanding of this will help you map the attributes of the IT architecture to the GSCs. The various components of the IT architecture can be broadly classified into three dimensions [2]:

1. Layers
2. Tiers
3. Quality of service

Layers

Typically, there are three layers that define the logical organization of IT architecture:

1. *Technical architecture* consists of two subarchitectures (layers):
   - *System architecture*—defines the technology, standards, and system software products for development and deployment of applications and components
   - *Infrastructure architecture*—deals with the underlying network and communications environment, and the system management architecture required to operate/manage all components of the architecture
2. *Application architecture*—involves architectural decisions, patterns, guidelines and standards required to design and deploy application/business components on the given technical architecture. It extends the technical architecture to provide for application developers to deploy business/application components
3. *Domain architecture*—is derived from business requirements and is concerned with design of applications and components that enact business processes. Domain architecture delivers functional/business services to end-users

Tiers

The tier is the other dimension of IT architecture. In a distributed computing environment, separating out the processing needs as well as data handling needs is achieved by providing appropriate tiers like the front tier, middle tier, and the back-end tier.

- Front tier typically addresses all the client (user) facing processes like that on a desktop, a mobile device, or other similar user interface devices.

- Middle tier typically addresses the server side processes, business logic, etc. The middle tier shares the processing load between the client and the back end tiers through *application servers.*

- Back-end tier is the real RDBMS system that handles the data storage, retrieval, and archival processes. Other file handling systems on legacy systems are also considered among back-end tier.

Quality of Service (QoS)

The third dimension and a key factor that heavily controls the architecture of a software application is the Quality of Service. Critical attributes like scalability, availability, and reliability, which define the performance of an application under different load conditions, are defined and measured under this service. Quality of Service generally covers system performance, as opposed to system functionality. QoS requirements specify not what the system does, but how the system satisfies its clients while doing what it does.

ISO/IEC 14143-1: Definition of User Requirements

ISO/IEC 14143-1 defines Functional Size as "a size of software derived by quantifying the Functional User Requirements." ISO/IEC 14143-1 defines the fundamental concepts of Functional Size Measurement (FSM) and describes the general principles for applying an FSM method by distinguishing between three categories of user requirements:

- Functional User Requirements
- Quality Requirements
- Technical Requirements

The IFPUG FPA method captures the Functional User Requirements.

The Quality Requirements as defined in ISO/IEC 9126:1991 describe the degree to which the functional or technical requirements are met. ISO/IEC 9126:1991 defines the following types of characteristics as part of the quality model:

- Functionality
- Reliability
- Usability
- Efficiency
- Maintainability
- Portability

The ISO 9126 QoS framework provides for a very specific description of various performance-related attributes, as shown in Table 6.15.

A careful review of the quality model described reveals the fact that most of these parameters map to some of the 14 GSC attributes defined by the IFPUG FPA method. The only component of the ISO/IEC 14143-1 that is not covered by the IFPUG FPA method is Technical Requirements. It is clear from the basic definition of the IFPUG FPA method that the Function Point sizing method is independent of the technology on which the software is deployed. As such, the Technical Requirements are not included in the IFPUG FPA method.

Table 6.16 maps the 14 GSC attributes to the QoS attributes (NFR).

The non-functional requirements thus can be mapped to a great extent to the 14 GSCs. (*Author's note:* This is still under research.) While you are capturing the functional requirements of the application, prepare a questionnaire that captures the non-functional requirements as well. The NFR information would be useful in identifying the right degree of influence for each of the 14 GSCs.

From the Dinosaur Era to the Jet Age

Earlier chapters introduced this idea, but it is worth pausing for a moment here to do a quick recap on how hardware platforms, software languages, databases, and other middleware have evolved over the last 40+ years. Along with mainframes, there exist even now, systems that have serious memory, storage, and processing limitations. State-of-art systems also exist that are becoming smaller in size but much faster and cheaper than their predecessors. In this context, if you review the various degree of influence (DI) parameters defined for each of the 14 GSCs, you will see that many of the definitions are no longer valid in today's high-performing technology platforms, languages, databases, and other infrastructure facilities.

Take the example of the Data Communications GSC: DI-5 requires that the system support more than one type of TP communication protocol. The latest platforms have these features built-in and the programmer simply has to invoke them with a minimum of effort. Similarly, the complexities attributed to the Distributed Data Processing GSC can be solved through component load balancing, network load balancing, or clustering techniques. But yes, to set up these techniques, expertise and effort are required. This continues to be an area of ongoing research.

Table 6.15 *ISO 9126 QoS Framework*

Function	Subcategory	Description
Functionality	Interoperability	System should interact with other systems.
	Security	Attributes of software that bear on its ability to prevent unauthorized access, whether accidental or deliberate, to programs and data.
Reliability	Availability	System should be able to maintain a specified level of performance in case of software faults. Percentage time that the system should be accessible to provide the desired service.
	Recoverability	System should be capable of re-establishing its level of performance and recovering the data directly affected in case of a failure and on the time and effort needed for it within the designated time and effort.
Efficiency	Performance	Attributes of software that bear on response and processing times and on throughput rates in performing its function. System should meet the desired performance expectations (response, processing time, throughput rates).
	Resource usage	Attributes of software that bear on the amount of resources used and the duration of such use in performing its function.
Usability	Understandability	Attributes of software that bear on the users' effort for recognizing the logical concept and its applicability.
Maintainability	Manageability	The system should be able to provide mechanism to manage the data and applications.
	Reusability	The degree to which a software module or other work product can be used in more than one computing program or software system.

Table 6.15 *ISO 9126 QoS Framework (Continued)*

Function	Subcategory	Description
Portability	Conformance	System should adhere to the standards/conventions related to porting.
	Installability	Attributes of software that bear on the effort needed to install the software in a specified environment. System should be installable to a given environment with less effort.

The Relationship among GSC, NFR, and Technology Platform

Despite knowing well the different GSCs and non-functional requirements for an application that is being counted, a basic doubt may arise on how you actually assign the right number for the degree of influence (DI) for a given GSC. Different technology platforms provide a wide variety of built-in multi-processing, multi-threading, large-volume data processing and storage facilities. Do you then discount the degree of influence if a selected platform provides that GSC requirement as a built-in feature? Here are some examples to consider:

Example 1

GSC-5 Transaction Rate: Most of the latest hardware as well as the operating systems themselves provide built-in features that facilitate high transaction rates. High-speed storage disks are available with high-speed disk access timings, high bandwidth network, and CPUs with high MHZ processing speed. All these together give you a built-in high transaction facility. The dilemma here is whether to fix a low degree of influence value to this GSC because the technology platform is state-of-the-art.

Solution: If the user requirement is met by hardware as well as the operating system capabilities together, then the DI value would be low (1 or 2).

Example 2

GSC-9 Complex Processing: Old legacy systems had limitations on processing capabilities that were compensated through virtual memory and exploitation of disk space. The software designer had to use ingenuity to architect the system in order to be able to utilize the hardware platform to the maximum. Now with a wide variety of alternatives, like high-speed CPUs, multi-processors, multi-threading, and many other features built

Table 6.16 *GSC and QoS Mapping*

#	GSC Description	QoS Mapping	QoS Description
1	Data Communications	Maintainability: Manageability	
2	Distributed Data Processing	Efficiency: Resource Usage	
3	Performance	Efficiency: Performance	Attributes of software that bear on response and processing times and on throughput rates in performing its function. System should meet the desired performance expectations (response, processing time, throughput rates).
4	Heavily Used Configuration	Efficiency: Resource Usage	Attributes of software that bear on the amount of resource used and the duration of such use in performing its function.
5	Transaction Rate	Scalability	Ability to scale up to peak transaction loads.
6	Online Data Entry	Efficiency: Performance	
7	End-User Efficiency	Usability: Understandability	Attributes of software that bear on the users' effort for recognizing the logical concept and its applicability.
8	Online Update	Efficiency: Performance	
9	Complex Processing	Functional Requirement	
10	Reusability	Maintainability: Reusability	The degree to which a software module or other work product can be used in more than one computing program or software system.

Table 6.16 *GSC and QoS Mapping (Continued)*

#	GSC Description	QoS Mapping	QoS Description
11	Installation Ease	Portability: Installability	Attributes of software that bear on the effort needed to install the software in a specified environment. System should be installable to a given environment with less effort.
12	Operation Ease	Reliability: Recoverability	System should be capable of re-establishing its level of performance and recovering the data directly affected in case of a failure and on the time and effort needed for it.
13	Multiple Sites	Portability: Conformance	System should adhere to the standards/conventions related to porting.
14	Facilitate Change	Maintainability: Manageability	The system should be able to provide mechanisms to manage the data and applications.

into the platform, complex processing needs in applications very rarely test the full capability of the platform. Once again, should the estimator assign a low degree of influence value to the GSC due to platform capabilities?

Solution: If the user requirement is met by hardware as well as the operating system capabilities together, then the DI value would be low (1 or 2).

Case Study

A large, high-tech manufacturing company was developing a Web-based application. The application was intended to provide online technical support to the onsite service engineers who were working on maintenance activities on the company's high-tech machinery. The performance requirements as specified by the user group were as follows:

Efficiency Requirements

- *Down Time:* The application system needs to be up on a 24/7 basis.
- *User Population:* Currently the system has 3,000 users with approximately 300 concurrent users. They are expected to work on the

Table 6.17 *Mapping of NFR to GSC*

NFR Specified	GSC	DI
Down Time	GSC-12 Operational Ease	5
User Population	GSC-5 Transaction Rate	5
Performance Requirements	GSC-3 Performance	4
Growth in Data Volumes	Not Applicable	
Archival	GSC-12 Operational Ease	5
Environmental	GSC-7 End User Efficiency	3–4

system in three shifts: 6 AM to 2 PM, 2 PM to 10 PM, and 10 PM to 6 AM. The peak time range is from 9 AM to 2 PM.

- *Performance Requirements:* The customer would like to see a performance similar to the other existing systems' performance. Currently, the response of existing applications at peak load averages around 2.4 seconds for most transactions.

Data Requirements

- *Growth:* Facilitate easy growth in data volumes.
- *Archival:* Provide automatic backup and recovery facilities.

Environment Requirements

The customer prefers to have the finished product support Internet Explorer 6.5, Netscape, and possibly a Mac browser. Additionally, if the finished product does support multiple browsers, the customer is willing to specify the required version of the browser. Performance tuning should be geared to Microsoft IE 6.5.

This case study provides some input on how the estimator can map the user requirements with respect to performance and other environmental specifications to the GSC (see Table 6.17). The mapping will get more refined with experience.

Conclusion

Understanding the complexity of the 14 GSCs and capturing the actual applicable attributes for a given application is somewhat complex. Estimators tend to shy away from this part of the IFPUG FPA estimation process and sometimes simply assume the VAF as 1.0 by default. There have also been situations when organizations have simply done away with the GSC and VAF calculations. They stop at counting the unadjusted function points and transform this count into effort, schedule, costs, etc. This is not a good practice. The estimator may choose to skip the VAF calculations, but the programmer cannot escape the resultant increase in development effort for complex applications.

The estimator should obtain help from a good architect if he or she is not confident in arriving at the right attributes for the GSCs. The GSCs can be mapped to the non-functional requirements, which in turn define the architecture of the application being designed. Based on the architecture and QoS parameters, the GSC attributes can be defined.

References

1. International Function Point Users Group (IFPUG). *Function Point Counting Practices Manual (CPM) Release 4.2.*

2. Kolathur, Somakumar, and Kingshuk Dasgupta. *Architecture Reference Model (ARM)—Defining IT Architecture.* Infosys Technologies, Ltd., 2001.

Other Interesting Reading Material

Dreger, Brian J. "FPA General Application Characteristics: Rules and On-line Parts System Example," in *Function Point Analysis.* Prentice Hall, 1989. Pp. 62–77.

Garmus, David, and David Herron. "General System Characteristics" in *Function Point Analysis: Measurement Practices for Successful Software Projects.* Addison-Wesley, 2004. Pp. 145–160.

CHAPTER 7

Size, Effort, and Scheduling of Projects

Importance of Size

A person intending to build a house typically estimates the overall size of the house in number of square feet. While buying an office table, you may specify the size as *Length × Breadth × Height*. Almost every object used in daily life can be sized by using one or more parameters. Because software is "soft," it is always quite difficult to size it as accurately as other material products like a house, a car, or a television. Software professionals traditionally have been measuring the size of software applications by using different methods; Lines-Of-Code (LOC) is the oldest and most popular method used.

Whatever the level of approximation, LOC does give some sense of software size. For example, you can differentiate between two applications developed in the same language that have LOC figures of 20,000 and 50,000. Measurement of software size (in LOC or other units) is as important to a software professional as measurement of a building (in square feet) is to a building contractor. All other derived data, including effort to deliver a software project, delivery schedule, and cost of the project, are based on one of its major input elements: software size.

Key Inputs to Software Sizing

In software estimation parlance, scope of work (also expressed in terms of business functionality provided) is one of the key inputs that determine

149

the size of the final product being delivered. Software estimators sometimes confuse *size* and *effort*. **Size,** in a software development context, is the complete set of business functionalities that the end user gets when the product is deployed and in use. And the person months required to produce the software application of a given size is the **effort**. For example, in an invoicing application, the user gets the capability to prepare invoices for products sold to customers. The features provided in the invoicing application are equivalent to the functionality available; hence, the size of the application. The amount of time spent by the programmers to design and build the invoicing application is the effort. IT organizations should practice recording metrics of past sizing activities and use the information and experience to size future projects. In his technical paper, "Size Does Matter: Continuous Size Estimating and Tracking," Mike Ross observes, "The secret to making progress in sizing these new environments (software applications) is to identify the *unit of human thought* in the abstraction being used. Next, the organization must go through a calibration process, starting with projects for which the actual size can be determined in terms of that *unit of human thought*" [1].

Differentiate Functions from Production Effort/Costs

While negotiating the price of a product, both the buyer and the seller normally assume that the final price includes all aspects of the product; that is, features (functions), look and feel (user interface), quality and reliability (performance), and more. When two products of the same type (family) are being compared, very rarely are products 100 percent identical. To illustrate, compare any two products (for example, mobile phones like Nokia and Samsung, laptops like IBM and Toshiba, or software products like Oracle and Microsoft SQL Server); none of these products are the same in all respects. Similarly, each software project has its own unique requirements, and as such, estimating the cost of the project will also be unique if you adopt the process of assessing effort based on software features, such as quality, scalability, and reliability, which are normally unique for each project.

Estimating the effort and cost of software development projects is perhaps much more complex than estimating the production costs of most consumer products as well as other areas of project execution, whether it involves construction, manufacturing, services, or other elements. Table 7.1 provides some insight into the key differences between a typical product development and software development activities.

Table 7.1 *Activity Comparison for Products and Software Development*

#	Activity Description	Typical Product/Service	Software Development
1	Functions/ Features Clarity	Very clear, defined, and definite	Somewhat vague; can and will change during development phase
2	Quality attributes	Accurately measurable	Measurable but cost of quality varies based on team skills
3	Tools availability	Well-established tools available in the market	Tools with somewhat ambiguous claims on productivity gains
4	Skills/ Competency of workers	Defined	Defined
5	Production effort	Can be estimated very well	Quite loosely estimated
6	Effort/Cost Estimation	Definite	Gut feel + Buffer + Contingency; typically overruled by managers
7	Changes during production	Negligible	Very frequent
8	Specification & Design	Well-defined, reviewed, and signed-off before start of production	Loosely defined, keeps changing throughout the lifecycle of product development
9	Rework/ Improvements	Almost impossible to modify once the product is delivered	Always possible to modify even after it goes into production

Over and above the ambiguity and ever-changing scope (functionality and features) in the software development projects shown in Table 7.1, if you add issues related to the target technology platform on which the software is being developed, the cup of woes would be full to the brim. No wonder that the question that bothers a software development project team is, "Can there be an alternative and better-defined method of estimating project execution effort and costs?" On second thought, wouldn't it be wonderful to have a standard yardstick that can measure different products with different sets of functions against the same measuring scale? This yardstick should provide the user with a true comparison facility. For example, a measuring tape can measure a table size, the number of square feet in a house, the height of a tower, the distance between two locations, and more. All the items are different in nature but the measuring unit (yardstick) is same. Further, if you measure two similar items (such as the distance between locations) using the same measuring tape, you can compare the two measurements and even define a relative size ratio between them.

Function Point Analysis Method

The Function Point Analysis (FPA) methodology-based estimation model designed by Allan Albrecht of IBM in 1979, and now owned and continuously upgraded by IFPUG [2] (International Function Point Users Group), is perhaps the nearest to separating the functions delivered by a product from the technology platform on which the product is developed and hence the path to deriving the total effort and cost to deliver the application. The uniqueness of this FPA method enables the estimator to clearly size the software application (product) based purely on the functions that are expected to be delivered by the application. Perhaps it is due to this unique feature in the FPA method that its popularity and usage, as compared to other estimation methods, is the highest in the software developer community.

To understand the uniqueness of the FPA method, consider the example of a mobile phone, as shown in Figure 7.1. From a mobile phone user's perspective, the various functions the user expects to experience are

- To be able to communicate with contacts, friends, and family at will, irrespective of physical location and environment
- Instant, online access to the directory of contact numbers
- Provision to send SMS (text) messages to anyone, any time
- Internet browsing facility
- Storing and playing music

The FPA method is built on the premise that the function point (FP) count finally determined is based totally on the user's perspective of the functions expected to be delivered with the final product.

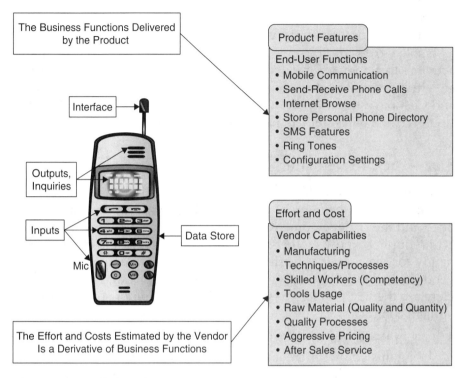

Figure 7.1 *Defining size.*

In Figure 7.1, the Product Features map clearly to the end user functions that are expected to be delivered from the product (mobile phone). The FP counting method provides key inputs and maps to this aspect of Product Size.

Now consider the other half of the effort and cost-calculation activities (other than Product Sizing), which contribute toward arriving at the overall product pricing. Figure 7.1 shows those activities as:

- Manufacturing techniques/processes
- Skills/Competency of the workers
- Effective usage of right tools
- Raw material
- Quality process
- Pricing
- After sales service

A careful review of these parameters exposes the fact that most of these activities and processes are vendor specific and depend on the team assembled to deliver the project. The Effort and Cost text box contains all activities that point to vendor capabilities. Understanding the two different attributes of a production activity in terms of Product Size and Effort and Cost paves the way for further discussion and focus on Size as the single, critical measurement attribute in software development projects.

Size—The Differentiator

In a typical software development project scenario, the end user (or business user) is the owner (customer) of the application being developed and the IT development team or an external (outsourced) vendor is the supplier. Knowing the size of the application would come in very handy for the customer in situations where an evaluation of multiple vendors, including the internal IT development team, is being done. Here are the key pointers to successful negotiation of software development contracts:

- When the application's size is predetermined, the user can avoid being misled by different vendors on various functional complexities of the application. Instead, the vendors could be asked to provide their quotes for the defined size of the application being developed on a given technology platform.

- The user may not have a deep knowledge of the internals of the application development process or even the technology involved (sometimes the technical architecture and coding of a project is compared to a black box). Despite this situation, the user can still manage all project contract execution activities based on the final size of the product that needs to be delivered and accepted.

- "An experienced estimator can produce reasonably good size estimates by analogy if accurate size values are available for the previous project and if the new project is sufficiently similar to the previous one" [3].

- "Basically, function points are the quantified representation—or size—of the functions (or transactions) and data that go together to operate as a computer application. They provide a rough unit of size that is based upon the *software component* of the requirement" [4].

- Because functional features are separated through the size model, this opens the opportunity for the customer to choose the technology platform on which the application needs to be developed.

Development costs on different technology vary based on skills available, and this leads to better control over cost and budget constraints.

- Function points are perhaps one of the best methods to estimate the size of an application. The method is quite ambiguous and therefore flexible enough to be molded into a variety of estimation needs, such as software development, maintenance, reengineering, enhancement, etc. Source Lines of Code (SLOC) or LOC is a poor alternative.

- "...'*Size*' refers in a very general way to the total scope of a program. It includes the breadth and depth of the feature set as well as the program's difficulty and complexity" [5].

The Yardstick

The business value delivered by software systems, in the form of functions provided, is one of the key inputs to the size of the system. This size can be used as an effective yardstick to facilitate many needs of an IT organization. In much the same way a measuring tape can be used to measure height, length, width, and depth of a variety of material objects and places, size can be an effective yardstick for software estimation in projects ranging from simple to complex.

Inputs to Sizing

The size of a software application can be measured in several measuring units. Popular sizing units include Source Lines of Code (SLOC), function points (FP), object points, and feature points. Each measuring unit is unique in the sense that the measuring unit defined by the SLOC method does not have a clear and measurable equivalent ratio with, for example, function points or object points. Each measuring unit also measures the application size from a different perspective. For example,

- SLOC measures the total lines of code that can be counted in the software application. The SLOC are specific to the technology platform on which the application was developed. For a given application, the SLOC count will vary for different technology platforms. The number of SLOC, if written in COBOL, would be far higher when compared to SLOC written in C, although the delivered functionality would be the same in both cases.

- Function points (FP) count measures the business functionality delivered by the application being counted. The size measured through FP method is independent of the technology on which the application is developed. Therein lies the comforting fact that when two different experienced estimators are given an application, the size they measure in function points will be within a comfortable variance range.

- Object points measures the size of an application by counting the number of screens, reports, and interfaces (known as *objects*) required to complete the coding. The objects themselves can be classified into different level of complexity such as simple, average, and complex.

- Feature points [6] is a variant of function points. Developed by Capers Jones, this method adds another measurable attribute, the complexity of algorithms. Here the size is measured in feature points count very similar to function point count.

Source of Inputs

For any type of estimation, it is important to have detailed information about the application/system. This is also the case with function point estimation. For estimating the size of an application using function point analysis, the following information about the application is required:

- Scope (specifications) of the application
- Data being maintained by the application
- Data being referenced (but not being maintained) by the application
- Logical grouping of the data being used by the application
- Input to the application, in terms of data within the defined application scope
- Output from the application like reports, queries, etc., within the scope of application requirements
- The general behavioral characteristics of the system

These inputs can be categorized into two distinct types of requirements, typically called *functional* and *non-functional* requirements. The requirements information can be obtained from the following artifacts:

- Functional requirements:
  - Business process
  - Business work flow

- Conceptual data model
- Functional specifications or use case specifications
- Input on external applications, if any, including details of interface with other applications
- Non-functional requirements:
  - Documents stating the performance requirements and other infrastructure details, like multiple sites, reliability, scalability, availability, usability, etc.

Accuracy of Requirements

The quality and accuracy of the requirements specification is critical to correct sizing. The specifications need to be complete, correct, and up-to-date for the size calculation. The result of wrong size estimation will lead to incorrect effort projections, schedule calculations, and other project planning and project costs because these activities are based heavily on the size information.

Details of all the functionality required by the user at the time of project initiation may not be available, which can lead to scope change later (also known as *scope creep*). The specifications should include the business data and reference data. Following are some of the points that must be specified to ensure the accuracy of the requirements specifications documents:

- Objectives of the proposed system
- Business requirements
- Scope and boundary
- Business events/functions
- Screens and reports
- External interfaces
- Operating environment; hardware, operating system, technology platform, and network protocols
- Specific communication requirements
- Performance requirements
- Special user requirements
- Data migration
- Architectural requirements
- Constraints/issues

Role of Size in the Software Development Lifecycle

The purpose of evaluating and estimating the size of a software application is to move the estimation process forward to arrive at effort, schedule, and costs of executing the project. As such, it is essential for the estimator to understand the relation between the various categories of size units (SLOC, FP, object points, and feature points) to its applicability in the software development lifecycle stages. The typical lifecycle stages of software project execution considered here are (1) the requirement phase, (2) the design phase, (3) the build (construction) phase, and (4) the test phase. Consider the following points:

- The Source Lines-Of-Code (SLOC) is the most ambiguous of all the sizing units and is highly unreliable as far as the estimation process is considered. Obviously, estimations are done when the application is yet to be developed. Predicting the SLOC that the application will generate upon project completion would be quite an uphill task.

- The other concern is to relate the SLOC count to the lifecycle stages of software project execution. Although the total SLOC generated at the end of project completion is measurable, coming up with an estimation formula that would give you the break-up effort for various lifecycle stages of project execution individually would be complex. To better illustrate, consider an application in COBOL that generates 50,000 SLOC. How do you relate this SLOC count to the effort it would take to complete the lifecycles stages (requirements, design, build, and test)? Experts in COBOL may be able to provide an approximate effort that it takes to code and test a given count of SLOC. The estimator will then have to convert the code and test (build) effort to the total project execution effort through extrapolation methods. Every bit of error in calculation of code and test effort will be multiplied during the extrapolation.

- Function points is perhaps the nearest method to providing a measuring unit that spans across all the standard lifecycle phases of software project execution. Function point count of an application under development depicts the total functionality that the user expects to be delivered. If you have the data on the delivery rate of the project team, the total project effort can thus be calculated by dividing the FP count by the delivery rate (productivity). Further, the total project execution effort can be now divided into lifecycle phase efforts based either on historic data from your own organization or industry standard data.

For example, consider a project that has a count of 1,000 FP. Assuming a delivery rate (productivity) of the project team on a selected platform to be 15 FP per person month, you get a total effort of approximately 67 person months (1,000 FP divided by 15 FP per person month). If you assume a lifecycle phase breakup of effort as

- *Requirements:* 15 percent
- *Design:* 20 percent
- *Build:* 40 percent
- *Test:* 25 percent

The total project effort can be divided according to the preceding percentages. The percentage breakup of effort can be fine-tuned by taking feedback from completed projects and applying corrections as applicable through continuous improvement cycles.

- Feature points are quite similar to function points.
- Object points looks at the number of objects (screens, reports, etc.) likely to be generated in the software. The effort estimated for objects is similar to that of SLOC and it is focused on the code and test phase of the project execution lifecycle. The full effort is calculated by extrapolation as is done in the case of SLOC estimation.

Impact of Delivery Rate

Sizing a software project is important, but knowing the delivery capacity of your programmers is even more critical. The foundation of a predictable project execution is the ability to attain repeatable delivery processes. Having a good handle on the IT organization's delivery rate helps IT managers commit to project delivery timelines with higher confidence.

Measuring the actual productivity of the programmers in an organization is a lengthy and iterative process. Depending on the size of the IT organization and the variety of technology platforms in use, the definition of productivity becomes more and more complex. The following sections discuss some of these complexities and variations.

Productivity Drivers

Productivity, sometimes known as *delivery rate*, can be viewed as the ratio of output/input. In a software development parlance, output is typically the software product and input is the effort spent by the programmers. The three major ingredients that define productivity are

- Software product (application)
- Software production process (the software project lifecycle activities)
- Software development environment

The productivity measuring team should be able to define and measure each of these ingredients in order to be able to calculate delivery rate figures.

Software Product

The product that is the final delivered output is also called the **software application**. Other secondary outputs that are delivered during a typical software development project are documentation for requirement specification, design, test plans, test results, and operations manual. In project management, these are called *project deliverables*.

Software Production Process

Various activities that take place during typical software development lifecycle stages need different process definition. Typical lifecycle activities are

- Requirement analysis and specification
- Architecture
- Detailed design
- Build and unit test
- System and integration test

Different activities in each lifecycle stage need varied skills and competencies. Even with a well-defined process for executing each of the lifecycle activities, the competency of the individual resource controls the productivity for the lifecycle activity.

Software Development Environment

The general environment under which the software project team works contributes toward significant variation in productivity. A good development environment supported by tested and productive tools plays a big role in productivity improvements of the project team. A robust quality control mechanism backed further by reusable software components, artifacts, and best practices further enhances productivity rates.

This is perhaps the most difficult part of setting up a well-structured IT organization. It takes considerable length of time to achieve the maturity in defining, deploying, and accepting a wide range of highly productive tools and an equally large number of reusable components that lead to high productivity figures.

Productivity Measurement

Among the three ingredients that impact software development productivity (the product, the development resources and processes, and the environment), the output is the software product and the input is the effort spent during software production stages. The environment, under which the production takes place, controls the variation in input efforts.

Figure 7.2 shows that different lifecycle stage activities require resources with an appropriate level of competency. The most common roles involved in a typical software development project are

- Project manager
- Technical architect
- Business analyst
- Programmers
- Testers

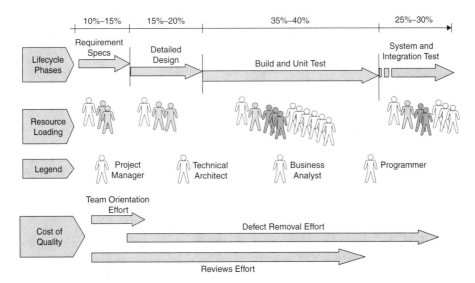

Figure 7.2 *Productivity parameters.*

The number of resources for each category for each lifecycle stage is directly dependent on the project size. Over and above the effort spent by each of the resource categories, a substantial amount of effort goes toward quality and audit-related checks throughout the project execution lifecycle. This quality-related effort is part of the *cost of quality*. **Cost of quality** is the cost an organization spends to attain a certain level of quality output.

Measuring Input

Input is the effort spent by various resources throughout the project execution lifecycle toward various kinds of activities like requirement analysis, high level and detail design (architecture), build and unit test, and system and integration tests. Also included are efforts toward cost of quality activities, as shown in Figure 7.2. The efforts thus can be classified as:

- Requirements/business analysis effort = # business analysts × assigned duration
- Architecture and design effort = # architects/technical leads × assigned duration
- Coding and unit testing effort = # programmers × assigned duration
- System and integration effort = (# testers + # programmers) × assigned duration
- Cost of quality = # reviewers × assigned duration for each + effort spent on defect removal + effort spent on orienting project team

Productivity

Adding all these efforts gives the overall effort for the entire project.

Productivity of the team = application size/total effort

Organization-wide baselines for different technologies are prepared using the preceding methods and are used in future projects. Execution of the future projects is improved through experience. In the absence of specific technology baseline productivity, the technology that is the closest is chosen. For example, if the productivity information for C++ is not available, you can start with the productivity figures of C or Java. If nothing close is found, you can use the weighted average productivity from Capers Jones's table of the languages and databases involved. (Refer to http://www.spr.com for more details on Capers Jones's tables.)

Often IT organizations face a dilemma while defining the list of software project execution activities that are included or excluded while calculating the delivery rate of the project team. There is no defined rule for this. It is best defined by individual organizations, based on the project execution processes they have adopted. Following is an illustrative list of activities that can be included when expressing the productivity for a typical software project:

- Requirement analysis
- High level design
- Detailed design
- Build and unit test
- Integration testing
- System testing
- User testing support
- Product quality checks and reviews

Different organizations adopt different methods of including or excluding certain lifecycle activities. Following is an illustrative list of some of the activities that are typically not considered while calculating productivity:

- Project management effort
- Configuration management effort
- Additional quality assurance efforts towards attaining SEI-CMMI Level 4-5
- User acceptance testing activity
- Developing prototype
- Warranty support
- Holidays and personal leaves

Effort and Schedule

Sizing the project by using function points, SLOC, or other methods is a job only half done. Transforming the size to a deliverable effort within a comfortable schedule makes the project planning a complete success story. Further, the total project effort (for example, in person months) that needs to be consumed in a given schedule provides the guidance to do a proper resource loading.

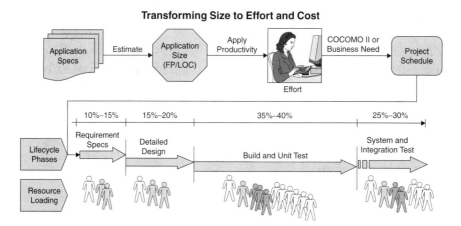

Figure 7.3 *Deriving effort and costs.*

Once the phase-wise resource loading details are available, you can apply the resource rate to each category of resource—such as project manager, architect, analyst, and developer—for the duration of the assignment. Thus the total base cost for the project is calculated. You can then add project management, configuration management, and other overheads as appropriate to get the gross cost. Figure 7.3 shows the broad parameters that are to be taken into account during different lifecycle stages of the project execution.

Deriving Effort

The overall project effort (typically measured in person months) is directly dependent on two critical inputs: application size and project team/programmer productivity. The steps to calculate each of these items are as follows:

- From the given specification for the application, calculate the size of the application. The size can be estimated by using one of the popular estimation methods, such as
  - *Function points method:* Output will be in FP count.
  - *Object points method:* Output will be a list of classes of simple/medium/complex categories.
  - *SLOC method:* Output will be a "gut feel" of lines of code.
- Make sure that you have the productivity (delivery rate) available for the technology platform on which the application is being developed. For every language there are available average productivity figures

that should be adjusted by the historic project productivity data for your own IT organization. Productivity of your project team:

- Is based on competency of programmers
- Is specific to a given technology
- Is dependent on the software development environment

- Convert application size to effort (in person months):

  - Effort = Application size × productivity

- The effort thus derived is the total project effort that would be spent for all the lifecycle stages of the project, from requirements creation through user acceptance. Add project management and configuration management effort as applicable. The effort is also the aggregate of the individual effort spent by each of the resources assigned to the project.

Scheduling

Transforming the overall project effort into a delivery schedule (elapsed time) is somewhat tricky. If the right approach is not applied, the risks of project failure are high. There are three alternatives to calculate the schedule:

- Use popular scheduling methods like COCOMO II.
- "Gut feel" scheduling based on past experience.
- Schedule driven by business user need.

The schedule data that can be obtained by one of these methods is in the form of duration required to deliver the project itself. For example, the schedule could span 10 months from the start date of the project. The schedule thus encompasses all the lifecycle stages of the entire project. From the total duration given to the project team, the project manager must divide the time into lifecycle-based segments. The lifecycle phase percentage is also to be based on historical delivery information of the IT organization. For example, with 10 months of elapsed time, the schedule can be split as follows:

- *Requirements:* 2 months (20 percent)
- *Detailed design:* 1.5 months (15 percent)
- *Build and unit test:* 4 months (40 percent)
- *System and integration test:* 2.5 months (25 percent)

Resource Loading

Resource loading is a complex activity and has to be worked on with extreme care. Improper assignment of resources will have an impact on

Table 7.2 *Resource Loading Chart*

Resource	M1	M2	M3	M4	M5	M6	M7	M8	M9	M10	Total PM
Project manager	1	1	1	1	1	1	1	1	1	1	10
Technical analyst		1	1	1					1	1	5
Business analyst	2	3	3	3	3	3	3	3	2	2	27
Programmer			4	4	6	8	10	8	6	4	50
Configuration controller			1	1	1	1	1	1	1	1	8
Total effort	3	5	10	10	11	13	15	14	11	8	100

[M1 = Month 1] [Total PM = Total Person Months].

project delivery schedules as well as the quality of outputs. Resource loading requires two critical mapping considerations:

- The right resource role for the appropriate lifecycle stage. For example, you need to know when to assign a project manager, an architect, or a programmer.
- The right duration of assignment. This includes when to assign and when to release. The effort spent by each resource is determined by tactful resource allocation method.

For Figure 7.3 shown earlier in this section, the resource loading patterns are displayed illustratively in Table 7.2. For your project, you can prepare a table showing resource role assignments for the appropriate durations. For example, assume a total project effort of 100 person months. This effort includes project management and configuration management effort. Table 7.2 illustrates the typical resource loading based on the percentage breakup of elapsed time, as given in the example in this chapter.

NOTE The elapsed time percentage need not be exactly equivalent to resource person months spent in a given lifecycle stage. For example, the requirements phase could be 2 months (20 percent) elapsed time, but the actual resource efforts spent as shown in the table for months M1 and M2 is only 8 (3+5) person months, which is only 8 percent of the total effort for the project. Typically, maximum effort is spent during the build and unit test phase.

Costing

Once the resource loading chart (as shown in Table 7.2) is complete, it is fairly easy to attach the rate per hour (or rate per week/month) for each of the resource roles, such as project manager, architect, analyst, developer, etc. The steps are

- Arrive at the rate per time unit for each of the resources.
- From the resource loading chart, obtain the duration of assignment for each category of resource (project manager, architect, analyst, developer).
- Multiply the individual resource allocation duration by the rate to obtain individual resource costs.
- Aggregate the individual costs to get the overall project cost for resources.
- Add overheads and buffers as applicable.

Conclusion

Sizing development effort using a well-established estimation method like FPA can be a very powerful yardstick you can use to effectively estimate a number of software project execution processes. Through well-defined sizing and costing methods, IT groups within organizations can derive a variety of benefits in various activities that include software contracts, project management, cost of ownership, IT budgets, outsourcing costs, and more. Here are some key areas of direct benefit:

- Because software is "soft," it has always been a difficult product to measure in real terms. FPA-based sizing can provide a reliable yardstick by which to measure software.
- Size and complexity are key, and the core input, to all software estimations. All the subsequent information about software projects, such as effort and schedule based on the skills of the team and cost based on resource rates, can now be better estimated.
- For a CIO, the comfort of being able to compare and equate two different applications (systems) in their IT organization for purposes of TCO (Total Cost of Ownership), budgets, or other strategizing

purposes has always been another area of serious concern. For example, equating an Order Management System with a Payment Processing System on TCO or number of resources deployed would be quite difficult. Even if the two systems belong to the same organization and have been developed on the same technology platform, equating them on any terms would be a difficult task. Sizing the two applications using a common yardstick (like FP count) would perhaps be the nearest to showing their relation accurately.

• Skills or competency of the software development team (productivity) can be better compared through a common yardstick like FP count even if skills are measured across different technology platforms.

• Measuring and monitoring the quality metrics such as effort and schedule variance and also code defect density, etc., can be done by using the sizing technique.

• For a CIO, there are a number of cost-saving, better budgeting, and project monitoring facilities that can be fine-tuned through application sizing methods.

References

1. Ross, Mike. "Size Does Matter: Continuous Size Estimating and Tracking." Quantitative Software Management, Inc.

2. International Function Point Users Group (IFPUG). *Function Point Counting Practices Manual (CPM) Release 4.2.*

3. Peters, Kathleen. "Software Project Estimation." Software Productivity Centre Inc., kpeters@spc.ca

4. Robyn, Lawrie, and Paul Radford. "Using Function Points in Early Life Cycle Estimation." CHARISMATEK Software Metrics.

5. McConnell, Steve. *Rapid Development.* Microsoft Press, 1996.

6. Feature Points, developed by Capers Jones of Software Productivity, Inc., is a variant of IFPUG Function Point Analysis. www.spr.com/products/feature.shtm

Other Interesting Reading Material

McConnell, Steve. "Effort Estimation; Schedule Estimation," in *Rapid Development*. Microsoft Press, 1996. Pp 182–198.

Jones, Capers. *Applied Software Measurement, Second Edition*. McGraw-Hill, 1996.

———. *Software Quality: Analysis and Guidelines for Success*. International Thomson Computer Press, 1997.

———. *Estimating Software Costs*. McGraw-Hill, 1998.

CHAPTER 8

Estimation Flavors

Change Forever

The only thing that's constant is change!

As a quick recap of the discussion on "Large Application Systems," in Chapter 2, you may recall that, over a period of several decades, as business organizations grew, software applications and their IT infrastructure grew as well. The IT environment was transformed from a large, monolithic, slow-processing, low-memory system with a limited number of user systems to a super fast, gigabyte-memory system with a large number of user systems. The software applications that were working on systems in the old, dinosaurian era had to be transformed gradually to work on the now prevalent jet age infrastructure.

Most business organizations that depend on IT systems to prop up their business and help it grow year after year are under constant pressure to keep their IT systems up-to-date. Part of the maze includes the large number of business applications that run on a variety of software technology platforms, along with an equal number of infrastructure systems. At any given time, the IT folks are grappling with one or more of the following situations:

- There is an urgent need to design and develop new application modules to facilitate newer business opportunities.
- Upon completion and successful commissioning of newly developed applications, there is an immediate need to move these into maintenance mode.

171

- A considerable number of small, medium, and large applications that are in production and serving business functions in the organization are required to be maintained on a continuous and long-term basis.

- With recent upgrades in some of the vendor-supplied operating systems and other infrastructure software, the IT organization has also decided to upgrade their obsolete infrastructure. This makes it necessary to port all the applications running on the old infrastructure to the new infrastructure.

- A number of business critical applications have reached their limit on user scalability and encountered user interface limitations. These are now being migrated to state-of-art technology platforms.

- Quite a number of applications that were developed in earlier years are no longer being used because they have outlived their utility. The business does not need them. These must be retired after ensuring that all relevant data is extracted and interfaces with other applications have been carefully severed.

- Applications that were developed by different user groups were found to have duplicate functionalities. In addition, applications servicing the needs of one business unit have been developed in a different technology platform over the past several years. Now the applications must be reengineered to consolidate them into a single technology platform.

What was a state-of-art technology platform in IT a few years back is obsolete today. In fact, even a system that was recently successfully developed and deployed is already designated as a "legacy" system. At any given time in an IT organization, changes are happening continuously. Some of the changes include these:

- New applications are being developed.
- Applications are under maintenance.
- Enhancements are happening on some systems.
- Upgrades to the latest operating systems and infrastructure are in progress.
- Applications are being migrated to newer technology platforms.
- Applications are being reengineered to facilitate consolidation and being upgraded to newer technology.

Obviously, a wide variety of estimation methods are needed to facilitate the estimation of projects of the different types mentioned here. This chapter explores some of the most commonly needed estimation flavors. The focus here is on function points as a base to these estimation flavors.

Development Projects

In a true sense, development projects in IT organizations should be addressing a totally new business or internal organization need. But quite often the business users raise requests for development projects that are really extensions of existing business opportunities. As such, although the project requires doing fresh development of a business application, interfaces to other existing applications also are often required. IFPUG [1] defines the development project as the function point (FP) count delivered to the user with the first installation of the application. In certain situations, a large enhancement to an existing application may also be called a development project.

Whatever the context may be the fact remains that the business functionality the development project needs to provide was previously nonexistent in another software application. Thus the software project team needs to understand the scope of the new development project in collaboration with the business and user groups. Transforming a new business concept into detailed requirements that can feed estimation methods is quite an uphill task during the early stages of application development. Perhaps only after a couple of iterations of functional upgrades to the existing application can the users expect to get a system that meets most of their business functional needs.

Functional Decomposition of Modules

If an estimator wants to do total justice to the process of estimating the size and effort required to develop a new business application, it is essential that the estimator completely and clearly understands the business functions of the application under development. This will help in two situations:

- If the specifications provided by the user are complete and detailed, the estimator will be able to quickly divide the application into modules and sub-modules and then proceed to estimate effort for individual activities.
- If the specifications are sketchy and incomplete or partial, an estimator with a good background in the business functions being developed will be able to identify the missing functional elements and arrive at a fairly good estimate of effort.

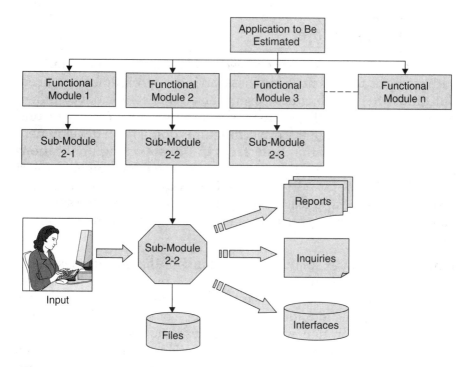

Figure 8.1 *Functional decomposition.*

The first step is to break the application under development into smaller functional modules that meet all the business functions that can be serviced through a homogeneous set of workflow activities. Identifying the right level of modules that encompass all the functions within a homogeneous set of activities may be a bit difficult to achieve in the beginning. But through practice, one starts to observe a pattern of such groups of functions that constitute a module or sub-module (See Figure 8.1).

Case Study—Invoicing Application

An invoicing system provides a simple case study. The application takes care of all invoicing that happens in an apparel manufacturing firm. All the related activities connected to invoicing are also serviced by the application. The key business functions addressed by the invoicing system are

- Creating the invoice at the factory
- Collecting the amount through cash or credit card

- Updating the inventory balance on the shelf
- Generating daily sales reports by product, daily, weekly, and monthly
- Producing sales analysis reports
- Maintaining customer data across locations
- Reconciling sales to pending orders

Having identified a high-level business function need of the invoicing application, you can now try to define the different modules and sub-modules that constitute the invoicing system as a whole. (*Note:* This example is provided as an illustration only and does not in any way claim to mimic a real invoicing system in an apparel manufacturing firm.) The modules are

- Invoicing module with the following sub-modules:
  - Invoice Creation module
  - Apparel Item module
- Sales Reports module with the following sub-modules:
  - Sales Summary module—daily/weekly/monthly/product-wise
  - Sales Analysis module
  - Sales to Pending Order Reconciliation module
- Customer Info module with the following sub-modules:
  - Customer Master module
  - Locations module
  - Banks Master module

As mentioned earlier, this list of modules and sub-modules is not an exhaustive list but just an illustration of how the modules can be identified based on homogeneity of functions.

Having identified all the modules and sub-modules, you can next identify the various input, output, reports, interfaces, etc., for each module and sub-module. These attributes can be fed into any estimation method the estimator is comfortable with and be used to arrive at the estimated effort for the application as a whole. Ensure that appropriate level of additional effort is apportioned based on the type of estimation method used. This is explained in the following sections under different estimation methods.

Other methods identify various components of an entire software application that can be input to any estimation method. But I find that from a software professional's perspective, breaking the application into functional modules is somewhat akin to designing the business function based on business workflow. Another added advantage of this method is that by the time the estimations are done, the estimator has a high-level design of the application already in place.

Development—Function Point Analysis Method

The Function Point Analysis estimation method is perhaps most suited in such situations where the scope and other inputs are somewhat ambiguous. The detailed requirements could be captured through the typical requirements specifications method or through the use case method. In either case, the business functions can be well mapped to the various attributes of the function point estimation method.

Having captured high-level requirements from the functional users, next categorize the application into modules and sub-modules as explained in the previous section. Now segregate the five basic attributes defined by the FP method for each of the sub-modules, namely:

- External Inputs (EI)
- External Outputs (EO)
- External Inquiries (EQ)
- Internal Logical Files (ILF)
- External Interface Files (EIF)

As shown in Figure 8.2, you start identifying specific FP counting attributes for each of the sub-modules and then record them carefully. As you move from sub-module to sub-module, you will observe some emerging patterns of attributes:

- Certain functions seem to repeat in more than one sub-module.
- Interface files identified in one sub-module are actually internal file to another sub-module.
- Internal files are sometimes shared by more than one sub-module.

The data and transaction functions identified for each sub-module in Figure 8.2 are provided as examples only. As discussed earlier, some of the external interfaces identified in some of the sub-modules may happen to be internal files of another sub-module. In this situation, the external interface files are not counted. The General System Characteristics (GSC) are applied to the entire application to arrive at the value adjustment factor (VAF). The aggregate FP count from all the modules and sub-modules is multiplied by the VAF factor to arrive at the final adjusted FP count.

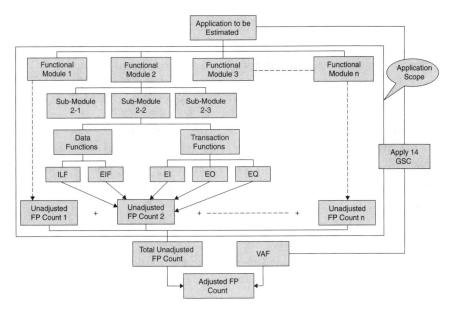

Figure 8.2 *Module level FP counts.*

Reengineering Projects

Software reengineering is the process of redesigning and rewriting existing software applications. There could be several reasons for an application to be reengineered:

- Aging applications are not able to scale up to higher performance requirements.

- Years of maintenance tends to damage the original structure of the application and can lead to frequent breakdown or make the code prone to defects.

- The platform on which the application was originally written is no longer supported by the vendor.

- The user has a compelling need to move the application to the latest GUI-based technology.

- The application no longer facilitates easy maintenance due to bad structure.

This list is not an exhaustive one. There could be several business, technological, or other reasons for a user group to resort to reengineering of an existing application. A detailed discussion on the concept and process of software reengineering is beyond the scope of this book.

The broad objectives of application reengineering include

- Restructuring the existing application without altering the existing functionality
- Making the application modular in order to facilitate easy maintenance and enhancements
- Rewriting the application in a new language on a new technology platform to facilitate improved performance as well as improved usability
- Cleaning up the data that has accumulated defects or errors over years of usage
- Planning for the future and designing a scalable and fault tolerant system

The basic process of reengineering is reverse engineering to understand the business functions being delivered by the application (see Figure 8.3).

Although reengineering is done to lessen the risk for the business impact due to inherent structural, business functions, and technology weaknesses in the existing application, you should also be aware that a newly developed application has to go through its own lifecycle of defects and other hiccups before it is stabilized, even if it is a reengineered application.

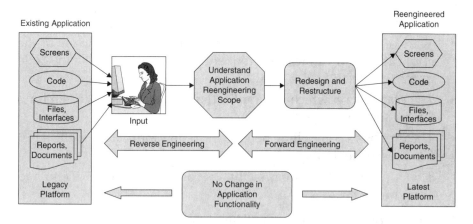

Figure 8.3 *Reengineering applications.*

Whatever the reasons to reengineer and whatever the method or process of reengineering adopted by the project team, the basic fact remains that the overall functionality of the application is not expected to change.

Reengineering—Function Point Analysis Method

Apart from a difference in the process of collating inputs to define the scope of the application, the rest of the process to arrive at an FP count for a reengineering project is similar to a fresh development project. The following steps will help in calculating the FP count and the reengineering effort:

- While working on the reverse engineering process, as you are reviewing the various components of the existing application, begin assessing the FP count of each of the components as it fits into the FP analysis method.
- Each screen identified will be an input (EI), and if the documentation provides information on other batch inputs, count them also as EI. There could be situations wherein the physical appearance of an EI might combine several logical EIs. You will have to identify them logically and then count them as appropriate.
- Count all the query screens or query outputs as EQ.
- Identify the reports that are generated through the application and count them as EO.
- Identify all the logical files that are owned and maintained by the application and count them as ILF.
- Identify interfaces from other applications and count them as EIF.
- Identify the GSC parameters and calculate the VAF.

After the completion of the reverse engineering activities, when you start working on the redesigned process, review all the listed FP attributes, keeping in view the revised structure and design of the target application. Some of the attributes among EI, EO, EQ, ILF, EIF, and GSC might undergo changes. The revised FP count will be the actual size of the application that has to be taken into consideration for all further calculations of effort, schedule, and cost. Choose the target technology platform, select the productivity for the target platform as applicable to your project team, and proceed to calculate the overall effort for the project.

The one major difference between fresh development and reengineered projects is the existence of data from the legacy application in

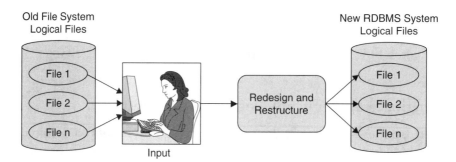

Figure 8.4 *Migrating data.*

the latter case. While migrating to the latest platform through reengineering, it is also necessary that the large volume of data that exists in the old application be transformed into the new database in the target platform (see Figure 8.4).

The IFPUG method does include the method to count data migration FP. This is termed Conversion Function Points (CFP). When data is transformed from the source platform to the destination platform, CFP are counted. Typically, CFP are counted in the reengineering and migration category of software projects.

The conversion of data from source to target format is dependent on several factors that constitute the objective of reengineering or migration activity. These factors include

- Converting source data format to target data format
- Transforming data sometimes to suit changes in business functions in the target applications. For example, when an old legacy application is reengineered to a newer technology platform and in the process a considerable amount of new functionality is added, this situation requires moving old data supported by the legacy application to the new application data format and also providing for storing additional data in the new format. This will mean transforming data using business logic so that the target data is understood and accepted by the reengineered application.
- Splitting or consolidating data from one or more source logical files to one or more target logical files based on target application data requirements.

For software professionals, the conversion process would require writing programs that read data from the source file, transform the data to suit the target file, and populate the transformed data into the target file. The fundamental question that arises here is how to count these programs. Under which category of FP counting attribute will this be accounted for? The IFPUG FPA method identifies the data migration process as an External Input process (EI). The inputs to the EI are the data elements that are read from the source file. The transformed data elements are written to the target database that is the ILF of the application being reengineered.

A very common concern among estimators is this: How many EI do you need to count while transforming a large database containing more than, say, 250 files? Will this be a single EI because all the conversion programs are likely to be consolidated into one batch file and then executed in a batch mode?

The answer lies in the process you adopt while identifying a source or target file. As discussed earlier in this chapter, files are identified as logical files that store and process data about one defined entity. For example, for an entity called *employee*, the data file can contain data about the employee, his or her dependents, work experience information, and maybe academic qualifications. All this information put together can be identified as one logical file with three or four record element types (RET). Also, one EI needs to be considered to transform data from the source employee file to the target employee file. The steps that the estimator needs to follow in order to arrive at the number of EI required to count the FP for data migration include these:

- From the source database, identify each logical file based on the business entity that the file or set of files addresses.
- For each logical file identified, assign one EI and calculate the DET and RET based on actual data elements that cross the boundary of the application and enter the target database logical file.
- Find the complexity of each EI identified and add them together to arrive at the total conversion function points (CFP).
- Normally the target database files would have already been counted as ILF for the target application As such, do not make the mistake of counting them again during data migration FP counting.
- Ensure that the source files are not counted as ILF or EIF because they only provide inputs to the EI.

It would be appropriate to remind the estimators that in reengineering projects, provision should be made for some of the additional activities that are not seen in normal development projects. To enumerate a few:

- Quite often it is found that the documentation of the source application is either in bad condition and not up-to-date or it does not exist at all. The reengineering analysts will have to obtain the information by actually reading the code and interviewing the existing users. This is quite tedious and will require additional effort.

- While testing the final product, over and above system and integration tests, the user will expect parallel tests and regression tests to be done to ensure that the outputs of tests are matching with similar tests done on the source application. Remember that this is a very time-consuming activity and quite often leads to code and even design changes.

Migration Projects

Migration projects are quite similar to reengineering projects. Typically the main objective of a migration project is to transform the current application from a legacy platform to a newer platform. Quite often the transformation is straightforward and may not involve any reengineering or even any change of design or application architecture. Release of a new version of a platform sometimes calls for a migration effort. For example, when Microsoft released the .NET version of Visual Basic, the applications in old VB6 were migrated to VB.NET by users who wanted to access the features of the new platform.

The effort to migrate an application to a target technology platform is typically less than a reengineering project for applications of similar size. The steps to follow while counting FP for migration projects include

- Count the FP for the source application as described in the "Reengineering Projects" section earlier in this chapter. Assuming that the functionality existing in the source application remains the same, the FP count will not change for the target application platform.

- Because migration of technology often involves migration of data as well, count the conversion FP as described in the reengineering CFP process.

- Identify the productivity figures for the target technology platform. Convert the FP count of the project, including CFP, to effort using this productivity.

In situations where the migration effort involves very little change in code structure and also in situations where the technology platform vendor provides a ready-to-use tool that can migrate the code from the older version of the platform to the new version, the estimation process would use a different productivity data as applicable while using conversion tools.

Maintenance Projects

The software application maintenance community is perhaps the largest category among software professionals. Almost without exception, all development projects move to maintenance mode after successful deployment in production. The software maintenance process has been quite elaborately defined by SEI/CMMI processes. Broadly, there are three categories of maintenance; namely, corrective, adaptive, and preventive maintenance. These encompass the majority of software application maintenance activities. It is not within the scope of this book to delve into these maintenance processes. However, the process of estimating various maintenance activities that typically take place in maintenance projects is discussed.

First consider the contractual (or otherwise) obligations that need to be met in typical maintenance projects:

- Depending on the size and complexity of the application being maintained, a certain number of full-time equivalent resources (FTE) are assigned to the maintenance project.

- The maintenance team will be working on the following main categories of activities at any given time:

  - *Production Support:* The level 1 and level 2 kind of activities that involve the first level of interaction and support to users. Other production support activities include executing batch jobs, uploading or downloading data extracts, troubleshooting, and other operational activities.

  - *Bug Fixes:* The corrective category of maintenance activity that involves identifying the problem and fixing it within a specified time.

  - *Enhancements:* Done to upgrade/enhance the application with additional functionality from time to time based on business needs. Enhancements are typically of two categories: minor and major. Minor enhancements take less effort as compared to major enhancements. The actual definitions of efforts that identify minor or major enhancement categories are specific to organizations. For example, in some IT organizations, enhancement effort up to 80 hours per enhancement is classified as minor enhancement and beyond 80 hours but within a certain upper limit of 250 hours, is classified as major enhancement.

Request for Service

In a typical application maintenance project scenario, the maintenance activity is triggered through a request for service (see Figure 8.5). A user issues a request, sometimes also known as a *ticket*, to address a problem during application usage. This user request gets transmitted to the maintenance team responsible for handling maintenance requests. Depending on the type of problem, the request could be a bug fixing type or an enhancement type. Once the request is received, the maintenance team typically follows these steps:

1. Study the request and do an impact analysis of the request. The impact analysis provides information that includes the number of programs, screens, files, and other parts of the application that are impacted.

2. Based on the information obtained through the impact analysis process, an estimation of the effort and elapsed time to fix the request is calculated.

3. A formal sign-off and approval to proceed with the maintenance activity is obtained from the user.

4. The impacted programs, screens, files, and reports are all modified by the maintenance team.

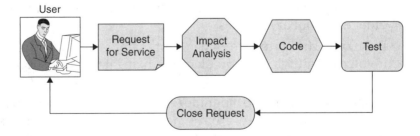

Figure 8.5 *Request for service.*

5. The modified portion of code and all other impacted programs, screens, files, and reports are thoroughly tested as per standard testing processes. Once the testing is complete, the modified application is deployed into production.

6. The request is then formally closed.

Estimating Maintenance Requests—Function Point Analysis

The application maintenance activities are normally covered by the enhancement category of project execution under the IFPUG FPA methodology. Estimating FP count for bug fixes is difficult, but minor and major enhancements can be estimated by applying the application enhancement FPA method. As defined by IFPUG CPM 4.2, the three major processes that could be normally involved during application enhancement are as follows:

- Functions that are freshly added to the existing functions, changed or modified, and deleted.

- Due to the added, changed, or deleted functions, sometimes the data structure also gets impacted. Any change in the structure of logical files that result in conversion of the data to map to the restructured functions is counted as conversion function points (CFP).

- Occasionally the overall changes in functions due to maintenance leads to a change in the values of the general system characteristics (GSC) attributes. As such, the value adjustment factor (VAF) also could change.

The FP counting formula provided by IFPUG for a maintenance activity is

$$EFP = [(ADD + CHGA + CFP) * VAFA] + (DEL * VAFB)$$

The explanations for various variables mentioned in the formula above are

- *EFP (Enhancement FP):* The total function point that is counted for the maintenance activity as a whole. This will be the final, adjusted FP count.

- *ADD (Added FP):* Function points that were added during the maintenance activity. This is unadjusted FP count.

- *CHGA (Changed FP):* The functions that were modified during the maintenance activity are counted here. Ensure that the FP value is counted after the actual change or modification has been done.

For example, suppose that you have been required to modify a screen (EI) that is of medium complexity (4 FP). After you added a number of data elements (DET), you found that the complexity of the screen (EI) had changed from medium to complex. The FP to be taken into consideration would be the value for complex EI (6 FP). You may encounter situations when the reverse could happen, and the complexity would have changed from medium to simple. In this situation, count the FP value for the simple category (3 FP).

- *CFP (Conversion FP):* Discussed earlier in this chapter. Any conversion of data during the maintenance activity is counted as conversion function points.
- *DEL (Delete FP):* The functions that were removed/deleted, if any, during maintenance activity are counted as Delete function points
- *VAFB-VAF before maintenance activity:* The value adjustment factor that existed before the maintenance activity was started
- *VAFA-VAF after maintenance activity:* The modified VAF after the maintenance activity is completed, if any, is taken into consideration here. Normally the VAF changes when there are substantial changes in functions of the application due to maintenance activity.

In actual maintenance activity estimations, not all the preceding components are applicable every time. For example, your application may not delete functions or the VAF value may not change.

It is important for the estimator and the maintenance team to take the FP counting activity to its full closure. After a maintenance activity has been completed, the revised FP count should be done immediately on the updated application and recorded accordingly. This process is known as the *application function point counting process* in the IFPUG FPA method.

NOTE The discussions for estimating maintenance requests here are applicable to medium and large requests only. Minor requests requiring less than a day's effort are not applicable here.

Case Study—Maintenance Request

Consider the example of an Inventory Management System (IMS) that manages the raw material stores of a large manufacturing company. All materials required for daily product manufacturing are stored and managed through the IMS. Although the IMS is integrated with many other applications within the organization, for case study purposes, the discussion is limited to the IMS only. The main functions facilitated by the IMS are

- Material Inventory System
- Material Rate System
- Supplier Database
- Material Issue System
- Goods Received System
- Inventory Analysis Reports

The current system includes a provision to record the inventory balance in the bins for various stores, based on daily issue of materials to the production floor. In addition, the system tracks goods received through suppliers. But in order to keep track of the store inventory balance and ensure that the balance does not fall below a certain threshold limit, the present application requires the store's in-charge person to generate a daily inventory balance report. When materials are needed, the stores raise a request to the supplier through the Order Processing System. Because this is a manual system, occasionally the production floor faced the problem of non-availability of critical material, and that led to production delays. A user request was sent to the IMS maintenance team to automate the triggering of orders for inventory that falls below threshold level.

Another concern faced by the production planning department was that of being able to predict more accurate raw material requirements for the various product orders in hand over the next three months. The planning department put forward a request to the IMS maintenance team to enhance the application with the feature that helped them work out the detailed material planning based on product orders on hand. The need was to add a product and sub-assembly management system that would facilitate recording the raw material break-up information for every product and sub-assembly. Based on this information, the system could generate a raw material requirement report depending on the product orders on hand.

Looking at the possible changes and enhancements that need to be incorporated in the IMS will help you see how to do an estimation of the resultant maintenance FP count as per the IFPUG FPA method. This section does not go into the details of attribute-wise DET, RET, and FTR. This example assumes complexity and proceeds with calculating

Table 8.1 *Enhancement List*

Module Impacted	FPA Attribute	Action	Complexity Before	Complexity After	FP Count
Sub-Assembly System					
Menu Change	GSC				VAF
Data Entry Screen	EI	Add		Complex	6
Sub-Assembly Reports (2)	EO	Add		Medium	5×2
Files Introduced (2 Files)	ILF	Add		Simple	7×2
Material Inventory System					
Screen Modified	EI	Modify	Simple	Medium	4
Inventory File Modified	ILF	Modify	Medium	Medium	10
Converted Inventory Data	EI	CFP		Medium	4
Interface to Order Processing	EIF	Add		Simple	5

the FP count. Table 8.1 shows the various attributes of the application that has been affected. The resultant change in attribute complexity and the resultant FP count impacted is also shown. This is only an illustrative example. In actual situations the details may change.

Although a change in the menu has been made to include the sub-assembly module access, the VAF is assumed to have remained the same (VAF=1.05). The EFP can be calculated as

- EFP = [(ADD + CHGA + CFP) * VAFA] + (DEL * VAFB)
- EFP = [(((6+10+14+5) + (4+10) + (4)) * 1.05] + (0 * 1.05) = 56 FP

Complexity in Estimation of Request for Service

Although IFPUG does provide a fairly decent method for calculating the FP count for a maintenance activity, quite often it is not easy to identify the complete set of attributes like EI, EO, EQ, ILF, and EIF that are impacted during the initial impact analysis phase. Nevertheless, the FPA method does give the estimator a process to estimate, with the accuracy being dependent on the level of inputs provided.

Although the FP sizing of a maintenance activity can be done using the preceding method; the effort to execute the actual maintenance activities does not always remain uniform due to certain other environment factors. Consider some of the key factors that impact the way the maintenance activities like bug fixes and minor and major enhancements are actually executed and the variance in the effort taken to execute them.

Ratio between Enhancement and Application Size

> *Fixing a leak in the water pipe in your house is not the same as fixing major water pipe damage to the city water supply line. Fixing a crack in the wall of your house is not same as fixing a breach in the river dam.*

The estimator needs to understand the critical difference between maintenance activities that are smaller in scale as compared to those applied to large applications. Surprisingly, the FP count may not provide the real clue to these drastically different situations in maintenance project execution conditions.

The three case studies shown in Figure 8.6 give you a fair idea of the relationship between the size of the application and the size of the enhancement (maintenance). The size of application could be very large as compared to the size of enhancement, or, on the other hand, the size of the enhancement could be almost 60 to 70 percent of the application size. To assess the impact of these varieties of ratio between application size and enhancement size, recall the earlier discussion of the

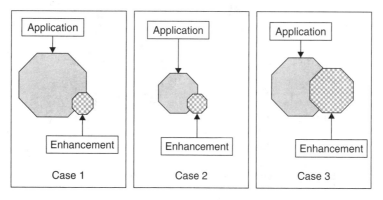

Figure 8.6 *Ratio between enhancement and application size.*

three main activities that are undertaken in a typical maintenance activity: impact analysis, coding, and testing.

- *Impact Analysis:* The time needed to do an impact analysis will vary among the three case studies. The effort will also depend upon the complexity of the maintenance request and will have another matrix with the complexity of the impact on various modules within the application.

- *Coding:* The coding and unit testing effort will also vary depending upon the complexity matrix between size of application and size of maintenance request as well as dependent upon the number of modules affected.

- *Testing:* The testing is an activity that cannot be negotiated for its completeness, whatever the impact of the maintenance request may be. Other than the usual tests like system test and integration test, quite often the user would be more comfortable if regression test and parallel tests also are conducted. This is done to ensure that the test results compare with the test results that were obtained before imparting the maintenance activity. As such, it is quite natural that the overall testing effort would remain the same, irrespective of the size of maintenance request. There could be exceptions if the maintenance activity is a simple bug fix.

The two types of enhancement are shown in Figure 8.7. A maintenance request may impact only a few modules of the application under the

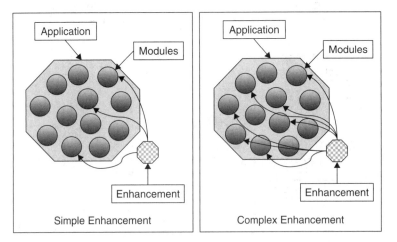

Figure 8.7 *Enhancement complexity.*

Table 8.2 *Variety of Maintenance Requests*

Module	FP Count	Function-1	Function-2	Function-3
Module-1	235	Yes	No	Yes
Module-2	460	No	No	Yes
Module-3	220	Yes	Yes	No
Module-4	640	No	No	Yes

simple enhancement category. On the other hand, when a similar size maintenance request impacts several modules, the enhancement could be called a complex one.

To summarize, the size of the maintenance request may not always lead to similar effort based on standard productivity. The effort may vary due to several additional reasons as discussed earlier. Perhaps there is a possibility of improving the accuracy of the size and effort estimations if you maintain more granular details of the application and its modules. Table 8.2 illustrates information that could be useful during estimations.

To illustrate with an example, first assume that the application has *n* modules. The data for the first four modules is provided in Table 8.2. The FP count for each module is also provided, along with the information on the basic business functions that exist in each of the modules. Now when a maintenance request is received, the following benefits could be obtained from the table:

- During the impact analysis stage, if you do a quick pre-impact analysis process through which you identify the list of modules that are affected, you can then get the total number of function points that need to be scanned for impact analysis. Through repeated data gathering during impact analysis activity, you can develop the productivity data per function point for impact analysis alone. This productivity can be used to arrive at the effort for impact analysis for a given FP size.

- Another benefit of the table will be to estimate the total testing effort. Based on previous testing productivity per function point, if you know the number of modules affected for a given maintenance request and hence the FP count of impacted modules, you can work out the testing effort based on the testing productivity of the maintenance team.

Conclusion

As essential as it is to understand all the nuances of a typical application development project, it is even more important that estimators understand and practice variations of the basic estimation methods under different varieties of project execution processes like maintenance, porting, reengineering, and migration. The difference lies in sizing as well as effort estimations. But estimators need to be aware of certain basic differentiators:

- FP sizing processes for different categories of projects like development, reengineering, maintenance, and migration are all different. Basically, however, the sizing processes are variants of the standard FPA estimation method.

- Productivity figures also vary for different categories of project execution

- The maintenance projects are the most complex from a sizing perspective. The FP count itself varies based on the impact of the maintenance activity. Also complex is the variety of maintenance effort due to a varying ratio between the size of the application and the size of the maintenance request

Normally the quality processes provide for collating data for all these varieties of project execution situations. It would be advantageous if the data collated is granular to the extent that the productivity figures for the various categories of projects discussed in this chapter can be evaluated in a flexible manner. The resultant size and effort calculated would be more accurate.

References

1.   International Function Point Users Group (IFPUG). *Function Point Counting Practices Manual (CPM) Release 4.2.*

CHAPTER 9

A Sense of Where You Are

On the Right Track, On Time

If you are running against time, it will be just a matter of time before time runs you out!

As important as it is to carefully plan your project, it is even more critical that you keep track of the project's progress at frequent intervals. Studies have shown that careful monitoring at predefined milestones helps in assessing and applying corrections early in the project. Projects that are monitored have less chance of failure or schedule slippage. But wait, when we say a "project," is this applicable only to a software project? No, in fact almost any work that has a defined set of activities to be performed in a given time with known deliverables can be called a project. Tracking and monitoring process is applicable to all kinds of projects.

Consider a few examples of successful project executions from the sports field. In particular, if you observe the project execution process followed by some world-class athletes, you will be able to see a pattern of careful tracking, monitoring, and correction applied throughout the project execution lifecycle. The style and type of corrections applied vary according to the game being played. For example,

- A long-distance runner has the complete race well planned. The race is divided into predefined milestones and the speed and time for each milestone is calculated well in advance. In consultation with the coach, the milestone strategy is rehearsed again and again. And finally when the race is actually in progress, a professional athlete sticks to the predefined strategy and thus increases the chance of success. During the race, if the athlete realizes that he or she is either behind or even ahead of schedule for a milestone or lap, the runner immediately makes appropriate correction to get back on course.

- A Formula 1 race car driver practices individual lap timings in consultation with the coach. During the actual race, the driver keeps track of the lap timings he or she is clocking. Based on the strategy planned earlier, the driver makes corrections in order to attain top honors.

- In a One-Day Cricket match, the team that has its strategy well-planned and manages to execute it as planned has a better chance of winning the match. While choosing to bat first, the run rate to be maintained during the first 10 overs, how to step up during the mid and end stages are all part of strategy. Similar strategy holds for the team that is fielding in the match. In either case, the team captain and the seniors track and monitor progress almost on every over basis and try their best to apply corrections.

The Sense of Where You Are

In his book, *The Sense of Where You Are*, John McPhee talks about Bill Bradley, an accomplished U.S. basketball player, and shows how a player on the field should use all senses to position himself exactly with respect to the match environment [1]. The following points summarize his ideas about the various guiding senses through which a player can be aware of the state of the environment:

- You need not look around frantically to know which side of the basketball court you occupy at the moment. Look at the markings on the floor, and you will know where you are.

- To differentiate between your teammate and the opponent, you need not stare at each and every player and make eye contact. Look at the shoes and socks of the various players around you and you can differentiate between your teammate and an opponent. If you take a quick glance at the images of the people moving around you on the court, you can possibly identify individual teammates based on their running styles and other body movements.

- Even when you are gauging where the ball is, you need not track the ball all the time. While concentrating on the movements of your opponents, you can look quickly at the referee, which enables you to position the movement of the ball as well.

- At times, playing defense, you are in front of your opponent. You sense the opponent's movements behind you through the touch of your hand.

- The roar of the crowd every time a basket is scored tells you who is winning as well as who is better supported by the spectators.

To recap, as a player participating in a crucial basketball match, you can tap various senses and signals around you to position yourself and the rest of your players in a dynamically moving scenario. A true professional basketball player uses this technique of sensing the environment through various sources of input and dynamically makes corrections to bring about the best possible performance.

Sensing Where You Are in Software Project Execution

You can use the technique from *The Sense of Where You Are* in the software project execution scenario and make corrections dynamically at every milestone or in other defined phases of the project. The source of input would vary and arise from different directions, To enumerate a few:

- Strategize the effort and elapsed time for each of the milestone stages. Continuously measuring and comparing progress with planned milestone metrics will help you know whether you are on track and on time.

- Assess the expected productivity of the team assembled to deliver your project. At every milestone, review and evaluate whether the desired productivity is being attained. If not, apply appropriate corrections.

- Evaluate the support, participation, and contribution from other stakeholders of the project (for example, the user/customer, the subject matter experts, the technical experts, and others). If the desired level of participation is not happening, discuss this with the stakeholders and make appropriate adjustments.

- Carefully collate quality metrics of the project. Gathering data about defects generated during coding, performance shortcomings, estimation blunders, and more, is critical to your project. Evaluate the impact this information has on the project schedule and make appropriate corrections.

Pervasive Estimations

*Even if you are on the right track, if you are sitting on it,
you will soon be run over by the train!*

Software projects and estimations are very tightly integrated entities. Success of the project depends a great deal on highly accurate estimations, among other parameters. Among the input you need to arrive at good estimations, the important pieces include

- The scope of the project that defines the functions that will be delivered by the end product
- The technology platform on which the software application is being developed
- Competency of the project team members
- The tools being used to develop the application
- The project management process being deployed
- Maturity of the quality processes that can control the quality of the product as well as the productivity of the project team
- Participation of subject matter experts in knowledge transition, who provide appropriate clarifications on various business functions being delivered through the project.
- The project execution environment in which the project team is working

Every project is unique. No matter how you evaluate them, you will rarely encounter two software projects that have these parameters with exactly the same degree of impact. On the other hand, estimations at the beginning of the project are based on certain assumptions because complete and accurate information pertaining to the parameters is not available.

IT organizations that have deployed mature quality and measurement processes have the comfort of analyzing historic data from a large number of projects executed in the past. And based on the analysis, the organization can predict its capability to deliver software projects in the future with a fairly well-defined level of quality and productivity parameters. These parameters include predictable competency on a given technology platform, quality of the product, number of defects, variance in estimation, and variance in delivery schedule.

As the project begins its first phase of capturing requirement specifications and analysis, the mode and quality of input may not meet the expectations of the requirements specifications team. In other words, the assumptions on the mode and quality of input during the requirements phase would not be met in the actual situation. Due to this change, project execution will be impacted two ways:

- The effort for the requirements phase will vary as compared to original estimates.

- The rest of the lifecycle phase activities are likely to be impacted possibly due to a change in requirements, and this almost always results in scope creep.

The Rippling Effect

A well-designed and well-planned software project will typically have its lifecycle phases well integrated. Based on the total scope of the project, the effort, schedule, resources, and the cost will be meticulously calculated and scheduled. Under these circumstances any noticeable change in the scope of any one of the lifecycle phase activities will immediately have a rippling effect on the other lifecycle phase activities. Normally the effect is seen more in the lifecycle activities on the downstream side and to a lesser degree on the upstream side.

For example, suppose that during the design stage, you find that the stringent performance needs from the application will require additional restructuring of the software architecture. This finding will have a rippling effect on the design, build, and test activities. The effort for all the three downstream phases is likely to increase. You will also need to modify the requirement specifications to map to the appropriate performance specifications. Basically a change in scope at any stage will

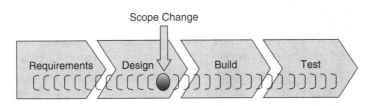

Figure 9.1 *Rippling effect.*

call for re-estimations of the rest of the lifecycle phases as well as some modifications to the upstream activities.

The estimation techniques in these situations must be nimble, with a built-in flexibility to re-estimate and revise the entire project schedule, effort, resource loading, and costs. Depending on the phase in which the change in scope happens, the rippling effect on all the project parameters will vary in intensity. The later the occurrence of a change in scope, the greater the rippling effect due to the fact that the rework will need to be done in all the preceding lifecycle phases as well as the remaining phases. And rework takes more effort than fresh development.

Change of scope is not the only reason to cause a rippling effect. Other reasons could include

- A decision to change the technology halfway through project execution
- A new version release of the product on which the application was being developed
- Key members of the project team have been pulled off for another project or have decided to leave the company
- A number of functional changes happened due to new business demands
- The project schedule was crunched due to severe competition in the market

How do you re-estimate under such situations? Which estimation method should you adopt?

Suppose that you are in the build stage of a project and now due to a change in scope, you need to re-estimate and calculate the overall impact on the project schedule, effort, and other parameters. Assessing and calculating the incremental change in effort in different lifecycle stages of the project due to the change in scope is quite a complex process. One possible solution to this problem is to re-estimate the total project size, effort, and other parameters and then redistribute the total effort into lifecycle phase-related effort. If you remove the actual effort already spent in the earlier lifecycle stages from the revised efforts, you will obtain the additional effort to be spent in various lifecycle stages that are already completed. For the lifecycle phases yet to be executed, the revised effort needs to be taken into consideration. The next section continues the discussion of this method.

Agile Software Projects

Question: How does a project get delayed?
Answer: One day at a time!
—Frederick P. Brooks, Jr. [2]

Among the analysis and findings of a variety of project failures, delays, and unsuccessful deployments reported in *The Chaos Report* [3], the most significant information is about the very low number of projects (<17%) that were finally delivered and deployed successfully. This is without a doubt an alarming finding, but it is doubtful that large software outsourcing service providers will agree to this data. With most outsourcing service providers boasting of highly mature software project execution and quality control processes in place, backed by SEI/CMMI Level 5 accreditation, the project delivery and deployment success rate is claimed to be more than 90 percent!

Without delving deeper into the debate of why and under what circumstances an IT organization can deliver a higher number of successful software projects, consider first the various complexities, uncertainties, and ambiguous situations that a typical project manager has to face in a fresh development project:

- *Scope:* Being able to get perfect, complete, and finally signed-off specifications for a development project will always be the dream of the development project team. But if you put yourself in the shoes of the user who has to sign-off on the final specification, things would look quite different and difficult indeed.

- *Design:* There are two kinds of design—application architecture and technical architecture—that are critical to an application being successfully delivered, deployed, and accepted by the user. Typically, early in the project execution stage is too early for a user to fully understand and approve these architectures. The result often is that changes in the application design occur at the build, test, and even acceptance stages.

- *Build and Test:* If defects due to improper design and bad coding exist, they are trapped during these phases. The test results throw up errors that could lead to review of coding and rework.

Also, if the test output does not conform to the expected output as desired by the customer, often it becomes necessary to revisit the design of the application and make appropriate modifications. This leads to additional work in other downstream activities of the project.

- *Acceptance Test:* Not all users have the luxury of actively participating in the entire project execution lifecycle phases. Normally, the key users, representing their user groups, participate early during the requirements phase and then on an as-needed basis in other phases. In situations where there is a lack of serious, early participation by the user it is observed that all the functional and non-functional (performance) defects and other shortcomings are finally trapped at this gate. The project team then has the arduous task of reworking the defects all the way from design to acceptance. This also means making appropriate corrections in the requirement specifications. The acceptance test phase has to once again go through the entire testing procedure until all the results are totally cleared and approved by the user.

Software development projects are likely to face one or more of the issues discussed here. Even if the outsourcing service provider is highly process-oriented, the client user team may not be in sync with the vendor processes.

In order to meet disruptions in project execution due to change in scope of work, planned or otherwise, it is essential that the project team be equipped with methods and techniques that help the manager quickly assess the impact and apply corrections immediately. These are the qualities of truly agile software projects. One of the key ingredients of an agile project is the capability of the team to correctly assess the impact on effort, schedule, resources, and costs across the entire project lifecycle and apply appropriate changes quickly.

Agility at Project Execution Milestones

Typically project managers take extreme caution and do all sorts of due diligence in preparing elaborate estimation data for the project being executed. But it is also commonly seen that once the formality of estimation is done, the information is carefully stored in a secure filing cabinet—very often, never ever to be opened again!

For a project to be truly agile it is considered a good practice to re-estimate project effort and schedule every time you encounter a change

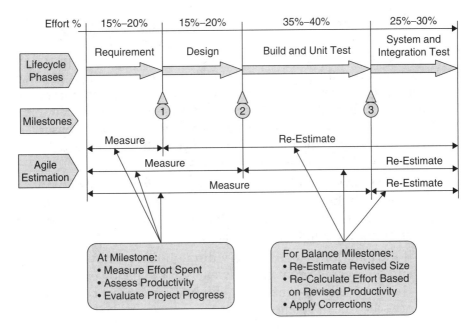

Figure 9.2 *Agile projects.*

in any project attribute, whether it is the scope, design, or even the skill level of the project team. Consider a few milestones of a typical development project to understand how re-estimation can lead to an agile project. This practice helps the project manager apply the "sense of where you are" concept.

Figure 9.2 provides insight into how reviews at different milestones can lead to the following:

*   Actual measure of the completed portion of lifecycle activities, from the beginning of the project through the current milestone. This measure will provide important input about the stability of project scope (through sizing) and actual productivity of the project team thus far.

*   The measure can be effectively used to evaluate change in scope, if any, and the difference in planned and actual productivity. Evaluating the productivity for a partly finished product may be complex but an approximate calculation, done by extrapolating the current productivity to the entire project lifecycle, should suffice for the time being.

- As you measure various parameters that include size, effort, productivity, and project progress up to a given milestone, there is every possibility that you will discover variations or slippage in one or more of the parameters. These variations are likely to have an impact on the rest of the project work. Evaluate the impact of the findings on the milestone phases that are yet to be executed. If there was a change in scope and also a change in productivity observed up to this point in the project, the balance of the milestone delivery schedule will likely be affected as follows:
    - Increase in size will increase effort to deliver the rest of lifecycle stage activities. For example, if you are reviewing the status at the end of the design phase, the change in size will affect the effort for the build and test phases.
    - If the milestone stage delivery through this point was delayed and the overall productivity was found to be lower than what was originally assumed, this will have an impact on the delivery schedule of balance milestones.

Case Study

An Order Processing System was being developed from scratch. Upon estimating the project delivery attributes, the estimator found the following information:

- Project Size: 450 Function Points (FP)
- Productivity: 12 hours per FP (J2EE Platform)
- Total Effort: 5400 hours (675 Person Days)
- Schedule: 5 months (110 Person Days)

The milestones of the project are given in Table 9.1.

At the end of design phase, a review of the project status was done and the data collected was compared with the original estimates. The project size was found to be 470 FP, and the milestones are shown in Table 9.2.

Based on the data collected as shown in Table 9.2, if you extrapolate the projected estimates for the balance phases of the project, the data looks like the following (the milestones are shown in Table 9.3):

- Revised Productivity: $801/470 = 13.6$ Hrs/FP
- Revised Schedule: $131/22 = 6$ Months

Table 9.1 *Case Study*

Milestone	% Time	Elapsed Time	# Resources	Effort
Requirements	14%	15 Days	3	45 P Days
Design	18%	20 Days	4	80 P Days
Build	45%	50 Days	8	400 P Days
Test	23%	25 Days	6	150 P Days
Total	100%	110 Days		675 P Days

Table 9.2 *Milestone Progress*

Milestone	% Time	Elapsed Time	# Resources	Effort
Requirements	14%	18 Days	3	51 P Days
Design	18%	24 Days	4	96 P Days
Total	32%	42 Days	*	160 P Days

*The number of resources allocated during a particular lifecycle stage varies depending on project size, lifecycle stage, etc. There is no concept of total resources but there can be a peak number of resources that generally occur during the build lifecycle stage of the project.

Table 9.3 *Milestone Re-Estimation*

Milestone	% Time	Elapsed Time	# Resources	Effort
Requirements	14%	18 Days	3	51 P Days
Design	18%	24 Days	4	96 P Days
Build	45%	60 Days	8	480 P Days
Test	23%	29 Days	6	174 P Days
Total	100%	131 Days		801 P Days

As you can see, the project schedule has shifted by almost one month. In order to apply correction at this stage, you have the following options:

- Increase resources for the build and test phases in order to increase effort in these phases and catch up with the original schedule of five months. If possible, bring the additional resources with high productivity and target reduced effort for the balance milestone activities.
- Negotiate reduction in project scope that can reduce the FP size and as a result, impact the overall effort for the balance phases.

This example illustrates the situation the at the end of design phase. You can follow the same process at the end of every milestone or at any stage there is a change in scope or any other disruption that calls for a re-estimate.

The Dream Project—Catch the Signals!

Remember the dream project that failed in Chapter 1? This section explores possible solutions to the problems faced by Sunil at various stages of the project execution and applies the "sense of where you are" technique.

Situation 1: Immediately after the big contract for the project was signed-off with the customer, Sunil decided to do a detailed evaluation of the scope and the derived effort and schedule estimations. He brought in a couple of seniors from the team and did an effort estimation based on the past experience of delivering similar projects. They had not sized a project of this magnitude before; nevertheless, having done smaller projects they thought they could do an extrapolation and arrive at a good guesstimate for the current project. They realized that it was indeed a very large project. After several rounds of deliberations, it was decided to fix the delivery schedule to 15 months with an average team size of 30 members. The team was aware that the customer had a tight deadline to meet and any further extension of schedule may not be allowed.

Solution 1: Without being aware of the higher level of risk attached to large projects, it was a wrong move to succumb to delivery schedule pressures from the customer. Sunil could have sought expert advice from experienced estimators as well as experienced project managers who had handled large projects in the past.

Situation 2: During discussions with customer on project execution strategy, the team realized the customer was quite inflexible on the delivery schedule of 10 months as was agreed upon during contract negotiations. Sunil had no option but to return to his drawing board and recalculate the project schedule and the related impact on other project delivery aspects. They had to do several rounds of review to arrive at the best possible project execution plan. The 30 percent reduction of the schedule (from 15 months to 10 months) had a direct impact on the average team size by a whopping 50 percent increase (from 30 members to 45 members). They also cut corners on some of the buffer that was built-in earlier. All the phases of the software project were very tightly planned with very little room to handle slippages.

Solution 2: IT organizations involved in frequent delivery of software projects should be well aware of any delivery limitations they may have. Limitations could be in different areas that include project members' competency, quality processes followed, ability to handle complex projects, and limitation on the maximum size of project delivery. If Sunil's organization had collated and published its limitation on executing large projects, Sunil could have surely looked at the alternatives that could be explored at this juncture:

- Negotiate reduction in the functionality that was originally planned, thus reducing the deliverable size. This might reduce the risk.
- Move the removed functionality to the next phase and plan to deliver the project in multiple iterations.
- Take an aggressive stance and insist that at least 50 percent of the development team be highly skilled. With improved productivity of the project team, the risk of failure is somewhat reduced.

Situation 3: During the requirements gathering phase, the scope was reviewed with the business users. It was then pointed out by business users that due to recent changes in government regulations, additional validation procedures needed to be embedded in the software application. This also meant a change in certain functional work-flow of activities. Sunil's team included all the relevant changes and did a quick re-estimation. It was found that the overall effort had gone up by another six percent. Once again, a negotiation with the customer to increase the schedule was turned down.

The result was an increase in team size by another three members. Sunil was worried about the possible impact and increased risk but was confident his team would deliver.

Solution 3: The project schedule was already at a high-risk level, so it would have been disastrous to accept more work, despite whatever additional resources were made available. Clearly, the option to be taken here is to negotiate and work on a trade-off between existing functionality and additional functionality such that the overall project size did not change significantly.

Situation 4: The first serious signs of problems surfaced during design phase. The software was being developed on a Java platform. The technology vendor had recently introduced a new product that would dramatically change the way the business workflow could be manipulated directly by the end users. Although it was a boon to the users, it meant two significant deviations to the project team: the team had to learn and understand features of the new product, and it also meant additional effort to include the new product into the revised architecture of the software application. Overall, the effort went up again. Sunil's team was rightly worried this time. The size of the project was ballooning, but the end date of delivery was not allowed to change!

Solution 4: Looking at the project execution stage and with almost no scope to stretch the project team any more, Sunil's reply should be a loud, "No!" Evaluating the benefits of the new product, and if they are accepted, making the appropriate architectural changes should be considered for the next iteration of product release. A re-estimation at this stage would give further credence to fact that suggested changes would involve a huge rework, leading to increased effort.

Situation 5: Sunil felt it was time to escalate the situation to his manager internally. His manager decided to do a complete review of the project status. There was another surprise waiting to be discovered. The project had already slipped by two weeks. The late changes in project scope and the last-minute changes due to the addition of a new product made its impact on schedule slippage. This was further aggravated when it was found that the new product was still in beta version and there were quite a number of bugs to be removed by the vendor. By now the team size had grown to 50 members and it looked almost impossible to meet the 10-month schedule.

Solution 5: By now it is almost too late to apply any corrections. A re-estimate at this stage would provide critical input on productivity of the project team, as well as a revised project size. Review and recalculation of the balance lifecycle phase activities based on revised productivity and size would indicate the possibility of project delivery getting delayed. The options available here would be to either negotiate for a project schedule extension or reduce some functionality.

Situation 6: During the coding stage, one of the key senior members fell ill and had to take two weeks leave. Two other developers decided to quit, thus compounding the problem. The early schedule slippage had a crunching impact on the duration provisioned for the coding phase. Despite Herculean efforts, it was found to be impossible to meet the original deadline. Sunil had no other option but to go back to the customer to negotiate more time.

Solution 6: Although it is considered a good practice to provide stand-bys for key resources, quite often resource shortages do not allow the luxury of stand-by resources for the project manager. Despite providing replacements, the productivity of the team is most likely to suffer. Re-estimate all project parameters and apply possible corrections.

During discussions with the customer, the criticality of the whole project emerged. The business users had planned for this project to be ready in 10 months in order to meet a possible window of business opportunity that would last only a few months. The team decided to work on weekends and also extended working hours to late nights. But during early tests, serious performance issues were detected. Also found were mismatch in coding standards followed by different groups within the project team. This again was a setback that had a direct impact on delivery schedule. It was now impossible to meet the deadline under any circumstances. The only option was to extend the delivery schedule by two months. The customer was aghast at the proposal. The matter was escalated to higher management and after couple of rounds of senior level meetings, it was decided by the customer to scrap the project.

What Really Did Go Wrong?

Large projects are risk prone (The term *large project* may be understood differently by different readers. Our definition of large project here is 10,000+ FP size or 500+ Person Months effort). For a successful project execution, the "sense of where you are" has to be applied in all its seriousness:

- Due diligence using this method needs to be applied after almost every month rather than after every milestone.

- The contract should include stringent clauses that strictly control project scope changes.

- Deeper participation by client experts throughout the project execution lifecycle would ensure better understanding between the user and the developer. This de-risking strategy would better control scope changes to the project.

Estimation Maturity

Although it is highly desirable that project teams apply agile estimation techniques in order to continuously monitor and apply corrections in projects being executed, an IT organization should also constantly measure the level of estimation accuracy and the results of software projects executed. Mature quality processes deployment does help in collating all kinds of metrics, including the contribution from good estimations. The variances in the delivered effort and variances in schedule adherence can be tracked and monitored. But in order to continuously improve the quality and accuracy of estimations, it is essential that IT organizations apply the "sense of where you are" technique to the estimation process improvement strategy.

It is quite normal for IT organizations involved in large-scale software project executions to adopt multiple types of estimation methods. The reasons for doing so are varied:

- Because there are various types of project executions, one estimation method does not suit all of them. For example, the function points estimation method may not be a good method to estimate embedded systems projects.

- The requirements specifications that have been prepared for a specific project, perhaps using the Use Case process, could be more suitable to the Use Case Points (UCP) estimation method

- The COCOMO II method would be well suited to projects that require schedule and cost estimations based on available inputs in the form of source lines of code (SLOC) or function points (FP)

- Many software projects do not conform to all the lifecycle stages of a typical software project. For example, there are projects that require an existing application to interface (connect) with another application or an external device. These types of projects consist of coding activities that are focused on work on platform internals. In these situations, the technology platform experts within the project team adopt what is known as the Simple, Medium, and Complex (SMC) estimation method. Here the effort for various design, code, and test activities is directly evaluated based on SMC complexity. There could be variety of SMC methods that are designed for specific varieties of project executions.

Figure 9.3 tries to capture the basic essence of the amount of fluctuation and variance that different estimation methods can bring when

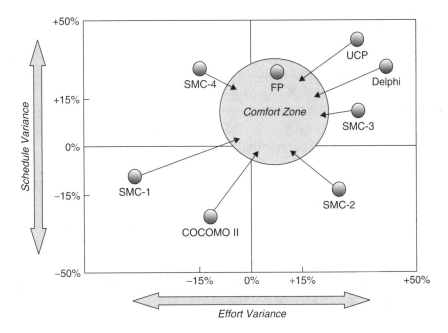

Figure 9.3 *Containing variance.*

compared to the desired level of zero tolerance on effort as well as schedule variances.

NOTE The estimation methods shown in Figure 9.3 are only illustrative and in no way indicate the real variances that occur due to their usage.

Each of the estimation methods has its own level of accuracy that leads to a range of variance in project effort, schedule, and costs. The IT organization management should try and eliminate possible estimation methods that can be replaced by established and more scientific estimation methods. Expecting a single estimation method to address all estimation needs of the IT organization is unrealistic, however. As such, estimators have to deal with multiple estimation methods.

Mentor and Monitor Estimation Methods

If an IT organization supports and maintains multiple estimation methods, keeping track of each of the methods and constant upgrades of its implementation methods would help bring better results during project executions. Mentoring and monitoring estimation methods requires a certain diligence in order to contain the variations between estimated and actual effort measured at the end of the project. The processes suggested are

- Collate various software projects being executed across your IT organization, analyze and evaluate them, and then decide on the top three or four estimation methods you intend to promote as well as monitor.
- Initiate a well-designed and planned measuring and monitoring process for each of the selected estimation methods. If possible, assign anchors for each initiative.
- Conduct an "as is" evaluation of each estimation method. Collate important and key information on usage and benefits of each method, including
  - Availability of a well-defined estimation process for the method identified.
  - Issues and concerns related to usage of the estimation method.
  - Output results of the use of the estimation method. The metrics could be variance in estimated versus actual effort and schedule variance.
  - Other pros and cons of usage of the estimation method.

- Define a "to be" state that you would want to achieve. Set targets for the "to be" that can be measured and monitored. The targets could include

  - The three key dimensions of successful deployment of the estimation method: Increase in usage, improvement in accuracy (variance), and clear process definition for the estimation method.

  - Set clear, phase-wise targets to achieve in each of the dimensions. Also indicate the level or quantifiable measure you would want to attain in each defined phase.

  - Define the evaluation process to assess progress on each of the estimation methods at each of the predefined phases.

- Deploy a continuous improvement cycle through which a core team of estimation specialists could mentor and monitor each of the identified estimation methods. The intention is to continuously improve the maturity of the identified estimation methods so that the estimated outputs attain the desired level of accuracy.

Bringing all estimation methods to the same level of maturity is not the goal here; in fact, this is not possible because of several environmental factors across the IT organization. Be realistic and set targets for the improvements and levels of maturity that can be attained for each of the identified estimation methods.

Conclusion

Estimation is the art of approximation to the nearest level of accuracy. If a project is re-estimated at appropriate stages of development, the probability of meeting estimated effort, schedule, and cost would improve as project execution moves toward the latter half of the lifecycle phase. As an illustration, based on experience across a large number of projects, the levels of estimation approximation that can be expected from an expert estimator are shown in Table 9.4.

The estimation variance percentage figures are the expected variance with respect to the effort and delivery schedule adherence. As the project progresses toward the last milestone, re-estimations

Table 9.4 *Milestone Progress Percentages*

Milestone	Estimation Variance
Requirements	20% to 30%
Design	15% to 25%
Build	10% to 15%
Test	5% to 10%

at these stages will yield accuracy within 5 to 10 percent of actual figures.

Beware of projects that are full of business process related bugs. It is likely that these bugs are found only during the final testing phase. Capers Jones says "… they [software projects] have so many bugs that the test cycle exceeds its planned duration by about 300 percent and this throws off everything else."

Being agile, nimble, and alert will keep the project execution disruptions under control. The agility should be backed by good re-estimation techniques that can clearly pinpoint the exact cause of disruption as well as provide the corrective measures that need to be applied to bring the project back on track. A good knowledge management process, if deployed in IT organizations, would facilitate reuse of past experiences. All estimation-related best practices, if recorded, would be of great help to future project teams.

References

1. McPhee, John. *A Sense of Where You Are*. Farrar, Straus and Giroux, 1999.

2. Brooks, Frederick P., Jr. *The Mythical Man-Month*. Addison-Wesley, 1975.

3. *The Chaos Report*. The Standish Group International, Inc., 1995.

Other Interesting Reading Material

Pfleeger Lawrence, Shari. "What Software Engineering Can Learn from Soccer." *IEEE Software,* November–December, 2002. Pp 64–65.

Kan, Stephen H. *Metrics and Models in Software Quality Engineering, Second Edition.* Addison-Wesley, 2003.

Jones, Capers. *Software Quality—Analysis and Guidelines for Success.* International Thomson Computer Press, 1997.

CHAPTER 10

Tips, Tricks, and Traps

Introduction

For every complex problem, there is an answer
that is short, simple, and wrong!
—H. L. Mencken

From time immemorial, gurus have passed on their experience to their disciples. The experiences could be in many forms like best practices, tools, tricks, do's, and don'ts. Traditionally, the knowledge sharing is done in two parts: First the basic skills training is provided and then the advanced or special skills are taught. In a very similar fashion, as you worked through the earlier chapters of this book, the knowledge sharing was the first step in building a solid foundation of basics of the subject of estimation. At the logical conclusion of the basic teaching, the guru delves into the many varieties of real-life situations and provides, through personal experience, the best of the solutions—also known as *best practices*—in the form of expert opinion.

I wouldn't call myself a guru on the estimation front. Nevertheless, drawing on my own experiences during project execution, interactions with my project managers, and the experiences of my colleagues at Infosys, I am able to present a collection of expert opinions in the form of tips, tricks, and traps.

Setting the Context

Often people tend to forget or maybe sometimes even ignore mentioning the context in which a particular discussion happens. This negligence could lead to incorrect assumptions regarding the context and the environment under which a particular tip, trick, or trap is being discussed. As such, I'm making certain basic assumptions about your experience level, including:

- Basic knowledge of estimations, either through previous experience or acquired insight by reading the earlier chapters of this book or other articles or texts on estimating
- Execution of at least a couple of software projects in the recent past
- Estimation of project efforts, schedule, and costs for at least a couple of projects
- Fairly decent exposure to quality procedures and processes

Additionally, keep in mind that the tips, tricks, and traps in this chapter have the following characteristics:

- The projects under consideration are medium or large sized projects.
- The project team resources are fairly skilled.

Expert: One who has made the maximum mistakes on the subject!

Tips

Estimate Invisible Overheads

While working on estimating the basic size, effort, schedule, and cost for a software development project, you make a number of inherent assumptions. These assumptions include

- The project team adopts the typical waterfall lifecycle execution process.
- The deliverables for the project are the usual artifacts, including requirement specifications, design document, code, test scripts, other documents, and manuals. Unusual requests, like developing a throw-away prototype of the application or early development of a proof-of-concept, are not included.
- The responsibility of the project team ends with testing and acceptance by the user group. Effort and cost beyond acceptance is not included.
- The project team size is normally small or mid-sized (between 3 and 12 members), depending on the effort and schedule for the project delivery.

This section provides tips related to situations that may occur during project execution that lead to unaccounted effort. It is not expected that these situations will occur in all medium or large projects, but one or more of the following situations may happen.

Even though size of an application can be well defined using the FP counting or other estimation methodology, when you convert size into effort, you should take extreme precaution. A variety of effort overheads exist that can occur in certain type of projects, and unless you are aware of these overheads, the overall effort figures might go awry. The intention here is not to delve into aspects of defining productivity parameters, but rather to highlight a number of project execution overheads that are normally ignored. This quite often can lead to unpredictable results.

Tip 1: Project Team Size

A number of overheads are directly associated with the size of the project team. Typically these are related to project management effort, configuration issues, and communication overheads.

For an average team size of 8 to 10 members, you typically assign one project manager. But if the team size increases to 15, 20, or greater than 30 it would be quite risky to manage the large team with just one project manager. A number of project management activities, quality control activities, and team dynamics will need closer monitoring. As such, it would be essential to provide additional team leads for every 8 to 10 team members and set up an organization structure accordingly. Alternatively, team leads could also be assigned to predefined groups of developers based on application modules or other project activities.

Setting up the configuration for large team sizes has its own complications, including version control, merging codes, multiple builds, simultaneous test facilities, and so on. Managing the configuration of large projects leads to assigning separate configuration controllers.

Communication among team members, for various reasons like design issues, coding or build issues, changes in codes, and version changes, are a common occurrence. As the team size increases, the communication channels between team members increase exponentially (see Table 10.1).

Table 10.1 *Team Size versus Communication Paths*

Team Size	2	3	4	5	10	15	25	50
Communication Paths	1	3	6	10	45	105	300	1225

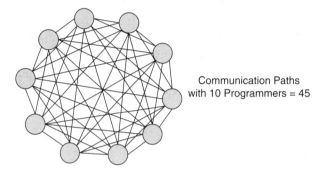

Communication Paths
with 10 Programmers = 45

Figure 10.1 *Communication paths.*

Figure 10.1 gives you an idea of how this phenomenon happens. As Steve McConnell, the author of *Rapid Development*, says, "The more communication paths you have, the more time you spend communicating and the more opportunities there are for communication mistakes" [1]. Ensure that you have accounted for these overheads while estimating final effort for the project.

Tip 2: Lifecycle Model

A common assumption among estimators is that the popular "waterfall" lifecycle model is adopted during project delivery. The IFPUG FPA method does not mention that the effort could vary depending on lifecycle model. This is so because the FP count (size) remains the same irrespective of the lifecycle model that is adopted.

Consider as an example the popular iterative lifecycle model. This model recommends that the project be broken down into multiple, iterative cycles with each cycle consisting of all the standard waterfall lifecycle phases (see Figure 10.2).

In a typical waterfall lifecycle model, each phase is assumed to be completed in all respects before moving to the next phase. As such, the effort estimation for each of the phases is clear cut and can be frozen.

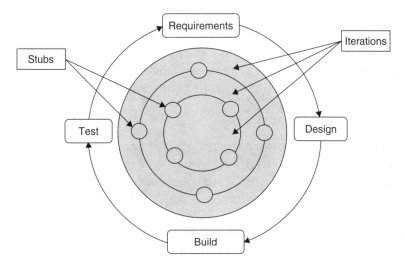

Figure 10.2 *Iterative lifecycle model.*

In an iterative lifecycle model, the execution process is quite different, as explained in the following points:

- The project is first divided into identifiable modules based on business functions that can be homogeneously identified. The modules identified are chosen such that effort for each module is comparable. Sometimes if the modules are small, two or more modules are combined. This ensures that each iteration is of decent lifecycle duration.

- During each iteration, starting from the base iteration, all the typical waterfall lifecycle phases are executed. It is expected that at the end of each iteration, the semi-finished application is in working condition and can be tested by the user.

- In order to ensure a smooth integration of modules introduced in successive iterations, appropriate stubs (dummy links to future expansions) are provided in each module. Stubs are useful for plugging in the next module functionality with the least amount of rework.

- Testing the entire set of functionality developed in each iteration is done extensively. Because the functionality added in each iteration is an incremental extension of the previous iteration, testing is normally done on all the modules developed so far. This process demands a large effort for testing alone as compared to the typical waterfall model.

- Other activities that consume additional effort in the iterative lifecycle model are for version control of code during different iterations and a rippling effect due to defects found in earlier iterations.

The process discussed here for the iterative model is just one of the many alternatives used by professional developers. It is difficult to provide an exact percentage of overhead that could happen due to the iterative model, but a general increase of overall project effort between 5 and 10 percent, depending on project size, is a reasonable expectation.

Tip 3: Warranty Support

Outsourcing vendors provide warranty support after the application has been formally accepted and deployed into production. During warranty support, a fixed number of programmers are assigned to monitor and fix any bugs that are found during the initial stages of application deployment in production. IT organizations collect metrics on project execution aspects to define productivity on various platforms. Normally the metrics are taken until project delivery and acceptance.

If you are sizing a project using the Function Points method and then converting the size to effort using the productivity provided by your organization, be sure to check whether this productivity calculation includes the warranty support effort. Normally warranty support effort is not included, and if your project contract has a clause to support warranty, you need to add this effort separately.

Tip 4: Prototype

Large project development schedules are typically long, drawn-out efforts sometimes spanning across fiscal years. End users feel uncomfortable waiting for long periods in order to get a glimpse of the final product. In order to overcome this discomfort and also to reduce the amount of rework due to incorrect understanding of true user requirements, the project sponsor sometimes includes the development of a prototype in the project activities. The prototype will normally be a dummy set of screens and reports that reflect the final product in look and feel. But the prototype is typically not a working product. Developing a prototype requires considerable effort. The IFPUG sizing model does not provide for prototype activities. If you are following the FPA method, separately calculate the effort for the prototype. For other estimation methods, include the additional prototype effort as applicable. The FP method can be applied to the prototype phase itself.

Tip 5: Proof-of-Concept

The situation for proof-of-concept could be quite similar to the previous tip, but the activity here is quite different. While designing the architecture of large or complex applications, the designers are uncomfortable due to the fact that the actual test of their design will happen only at the last phase of the project during various tests. If serious flaws in the design are observed during system tests and integration tests, this may lead to large amounts of rework all the way from the design phase.

Project managers resort to a proof-of-concept (POC) method in order to overcome the risks due to improper design of the technical architecture of the application. Typically POC consists of a very light, but end-to-end, version of the application. The POC takes up just one small function of one of the modules and creates all the components that can address the functionality. The components typically include a data entry screen, an intermediate layer, and the back end database. When completed and tested, the POC confirms the quality of the design.

Most estimation methods do not normally include effort for POC. If your project involves developing a POC to test the design and hence the performance of the application, ensure that the effort for POC is separately included.

A word of caution here: In situations where the project team decides to first develop a POC (as opposed to the user/customer requesting it), you may include additional effort for the POC, but you may not be able to charge the customer for it because this would be an internal decision.

Tricks

Trick 1: Manipulating Project Costs

Quite often IT organizations are constrained by budget limitations. Due to the availability of limited budgets for projects of lesser importance, project teams are asked to come up with innovative ways to deliver at reduced costs. Whether the project team is from the internal IT organization or an external outsourcing service provider, the pressure to deliver under a scaled down budget is similar to both. Under these circumstances, smart managers constantly create innovative new methods to cut costs and grab project opportunities. Among many such innovations, the temptation to hide known project efforts and present a budget that fits the sponsor's purse is strong. Sometimes the idea behind this innovation is to extract the hidden costs later during actual project execution through a change management process. **Change management** typically involves keeping track of any change in scope as compared to the originally agreed scope and presenting a bill based on the impact on the project in terms of effort and schedule.

The suggestion: Do not push known, critical, or functional requirements of the project into "change requests" in order to reduce project cost over-runs. It might later bleed the customer to death! It is a good practice to make the customer aware of the total cost of the project up front.

Floppy: The state of your customer's wallet
after paying for the project!

Competitive situations during contract negotiations (Request for Proposal) provide opportunities for you to be creative. Vendors sometimes go overboard to grab the contract. You don't need to know rocket science in order to manipulate the proposal costs by deliberately moving some of the key functionalities out of the scope of the contract. The intention is to claim the removed functionalities as additional work (change requests) during project execution and sometimes even charge these heavily. Thus an unsuspecting customer ends up paying much more than the original contract price. Be aware that this trick does not improve your customer relationships. Very soon you will find yourself being eased out, not only from the current contract, but with a possibility of getting blacklisted too.

If you have to juggle project costs, make customers aware of the functionalities that might be lost and get their approval ahead of time. Provide ample reasons for doing so. If done correctly, this approach might get you the contract and even bring customer appreciation.

Trick 2: The Balancing Effect

While following the step-by-step IFPUG FPA estimation methodology, you will often come across situations wherein the attributes gathered by you are not very accurate and have been made more by gut feel. In particular, while defining DETs and RETs, there is always some amount of subjectivity, which makes the estimator somewhat uncomfortable. But you should not worry unduly and you can take comfort from the fact that normally the margin of error in arriving at DET/RET tends to happen both on the positive as well as the negative side. This eventually evens out.

If you keep one leg on a block of ice and the other leg on
a hot plate, overall you are bound to feel comfortable!

The matrix table that defines the complexity of various components of FP calculation, ILF/EIF/EI/EO/EQ all are based on a couple of major parameters; that is, DET, RET and FTR. At each level of complexity (for example, simple, average, and high), a range of DET and RET is defined. For example, 20 to 50 DET and 2 to 5 RET for an ILF/EIF makes it of average complexity. There is a possibility that while calculating the complexity of one ILF, you will find that the number of DETs is, say, 52. This means the complexity is fixed at high, although it is bordering on average. While calculating the complexity of another ILF, you may count the actual DETs at 19, setting the complexity at simple, even though it is bordering on average. There could be more such situations in FP counting process for one ILF/EI.

Estimators need not worry about such border ambiguities. On an average, such situations occur uniformly on both sides of the range (higher and lower), and thus the complexity factor also evens out.

Trick 3: User versus Developer View

Beauty lies in the eyes (I's) of the beholder!

While assessing the size, and as a result, the effort and cost of the application being developed, one must understand that there is a great deal of difference between the way the application components are viewed by the user and the software programmer (see Figure 10.3).

There are always two views of a software application. The business user views the application from the business value perspective and measures its capability by the business functionalities provided by the application. On the other hand, the programmer views the software from a technology and processes angle, and values or sizes the application from the perspective of the technology complexity, volume of code written, and other related features like files, reports, etc. The two views are almost radically opposed but they both are right in their own perspectives.

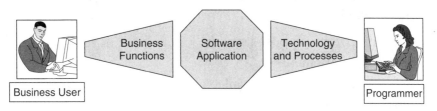

Figure 10.3 *Different views of software.*

As a professional software estimator, it makes good sense to orient yourself to the business user. In fact the IFPUG FPA method strongly supports this theory. There are several benefits:

- Better rapport with the user (and customer).
- Better understanding of the true business needs of the user.
- Key inputs to arriving at overall project effort, schedule, and costs.
- The project is most likely to have fewer problems during acceptance by the user due to the fact that the functionalities have been provided as per user view.

Periodic review of the project progress with the user further ensures better acceptance as there is early buy-in by the user.

Trick 4: Accuracy of Inputs to Estimation

As you sow, so shall you reap!

"How accurate are your estimates?" I was once asked by one of our clients. I replied, "If we set aside the variance in estimates due to limitations in an estimation method, the estimates otherwise are as accurate as the inputs to the estimates provided by the client."

The quality of the specification is the key to near accurate estimations. The specifications need to be complete, correct, and up-to-date for the calculation of sizing. The result of wrong size estimation will lead to incorrect projections, calculations, and planning because these activities are based on the size data.

Details of all the functionality required by the user at the time of project initiation may not be available, and this can lead to scope change later (also known as *scope creep*). The specifications should include the business data and reference data. But at the time of proposal (Statement of Work), the details of screen shots, data models, etc., may not be available. Function point sizing becomes more accurate when this input is available. Following are some of the points that need to be specified to ensure the quality of requirements specifications document:

- Objectives of the proposed system
- Business requirements
- Use case specifications (if available)
- Screens, reports
- External interfaces

- Operating environment (hardware, software, and network)
- Performance requirements
- Data migration and data retention
- Architectural requirements
- Consistency, reliability, traceability
- Testability

As Dick Fairley says in *Making Accurate Estimates*, "An estimate cannot be more accurate than the accuracy of the data used to develop the estimate" [2]. There have been situations when the input given by the client for estimating the size of applications to be maintained is in the magnitude of millions of lines of code. The statement of work says the application is 18 to 20 million LOC. Such input cannot lead to accurate estimates of application size, which is further used to calculate the number of resources needed to maintain the application (Full-Time Equivalents).

If you encounter a situation when the input you need for making the estimate is vague, get back to the user and obtain more details. And if you are unsuccessful in getting more details, provide an estimate in a specified range.

Traps

Trap 1: Estimation Tools

Using a good estimation tool does not guarantee that the output figures will be a perfect estimate! It all depends on what input you give to the tool. Do not expect the tool to do some magic and give you correct estimates.

A fool with a tool is still a fool!

Organizations wanting to set up their own internal measurement processes look at the option of procuring established tools available in the market. Most organizations are also aware that a combination of deploying the right quality processes supported by the right tools would make the initiative a success. But if this combination is not followed to completion, there is a possibility the initiative will fail.

A number of function point estimation tools and workbench products are available in the market. But procuring one of these tools is not enough for the FP estimation process to be implemented across the organization. The user may know how to use the tool but unless the tool has enough data from the past history of the organization, the tool by itself may not output the correct values. Also, it is essential that the user have a fairly good knowledge of the FP estimation methodology to be able to enter the right parameters for the tool. If not, the output will again be erroneous.

Garbage In = Garbage Out

Trap 2: Arbitrary Guesstimate

While working in a team that is responding to a project proposal, experienced managers sometimes tend to recommend a rough estimate. Often this estimate is a pure gut-feel figure based on certain environmental indicators that the senior managers feel they use to arrive at a good estimate. Avoid announcing arbitrary guesstimate figures. This has a psychological effect on the team and it may sometimes even lead to erroneous costing of the proposal itself.

Estimates tend to get stretched (or compressed)
to fit a predefined value!

Quite a few senior managers of internal IT departments take pride in hazarding a guesstimate effort/cost of a contract being prepared by their team. Typically these guesses are made with the assumption that the application size of the contract being drawn is very similar to one done in the recent past. Although the probability of the guess being right is low, it has an adverse impact on the team. Team members begin to mentally tally their estimates with the guessed figure, more so because the estimate has come from their manager.

Trap 3: GSC—The Killer

One of the key and critical attributes of IFPUG Function Point counting methodology is General System Characteristics (GSCs). The impact of the 14 GSCs on the total, unadjusted FP count can be as high as ±35%. For more about GSCs, see Chapter 6, "General System Characteristics."

Estimators are cautioned to take extreme care while arriving at the right attribute (Degree of Influence) for each of the GSCs. The following points explain why:

- There are 14 GSCs, and the degree of influence (DI) of each of the GSCs ranges between 0 and 5. If you consider the two extreme situations for each of the GSCs, the total DI would be either 0 ($14 \times 0 = 0$) or 70 ($14 \times 5 = 70$).

- The value adjustment factor (VAF) uses the formula VAF = (TDI × 0.01) + 0.65. And the Adjusted Function Point Count = Unadjusted FP Count × VAF.

- With every change in DI for any of the 14 GSCs, there is an equivalent change in the VAF and hence the adjusted FP count. This change is approximately 1 percent on the adjusted FP count, with a change in any DI by 1. For example, if the GSC Reuse had a DI of 2 earlier and was later changed to 3, the impact on the adjusted FP count will be about a 1 percent increase.

- The exact percentage change in adjusted FP count will vary depending on the base VAF value before change in DI. For example, if you compare two different situation of the TDI (30 to 31 and 40 to 41), the impact would be
  - Percent change –1 = (31 – 30)/((30 × 0.01) + 0.65) = 1.0%
  - Percent change –2 = (41 – 40)/((40 × 0.01) + 0.65) = 0.95%

- As such, every GSC needs to be evaluated carefully before fixing its DI value. Understand the impact of the GSC on the application as a whole and map it to the expectations of the user.

- It would be a good idea to be aware of future changes in the business scenario that would impact the application usage—such as performance, scalability, and availability—and increment the DI value of appropriate GSC. But remember that it is human to over-engineer. The technical architecture of the application is sometimes burdened excessively. This will lead to increased effort.

- It seems somewhat unusual but it is true that any change in DI value of any GSC has the same overall impact of nearly 1 percent on the overall FP count. For example, an increment in DI value for the GSC Facilitate Change has the same impact of about 1 percent on adjusted FP as it would if the DI for the GSC Distributed Processing is changed. We have not really come across an explanation for this.

Correct evaluation of GSC is a bit complex and requires a deeper knowledge of software engineering techniques. Due to this problem, IT organizations sometimes tend to completely skip the GSC evaluation procedure from the FPA method and try to adopt the unadjusted FP itself as the final FP count. All further calculations are then based in the unadjusted FP count. I would say this is a risky proposition. By skipping the impact of GSC on the final FP count, the final size may be different from the actual FP count by as much as 30 percent. The direct impact of this variance would be on the project team due to change in the overall effort and schedule that has been fixed by the manager.

Trap 4: Application Size and Delivery Schedule

Well-known analysts such as the Standish Group, Gartner, and others have been publishing IT industry performance reports periodically. Among many other analyses provided, the key information that stands out is the large number of projects that fail to get delivered year after year. Among the many known reasons a project may be shelved halfway through, one of the key factors is the failure of the IT managers to foresee a threat early in the game.

The reasons for failure of many critical projects include

- Unrealistic project schedules (Time-to-Market)
- Big-bang approach
- Disproportionate ratio of application size to project schedule

Typically the business users set up the requirement for an IT solution to meet their future business needs. The resulting application to be developed or enhanced has to meet a certain stringent deadline for delivery. Project managers, in their enthusiasm to take up challenging assignments, sometimes ignore the fact that projects of certain size can be delivered only in a given timeframe. This sometimes leads to project schedule slippage and eventually being shelved altogether because the business need no longer exists.

IT organizations as well as outsourcing service providers should take care to know the delivery capability of their software programmer community. The capability can be defined based on several parameters:

- Project execution capability for a variety of project categories, including development, reengineering, and maintenance
- Competency of their programmers on a variety of technologies, languages, and databases
- Managing large and complex projects with a project team of 100+ developers on a single project
- A proven past record of delivering projects within 5 percent of budgeted time and costs

While estimating the size, effort, schedule, and cost of a software project, the project manager should take extreme care and do due diligence while evaluating the capability of his programmer team to deliver the project. After converting the size in function points to effort in person months using the productivity of the project team, the next step is to fit the effort into a deliverable schedule (elapsed time). The COCOMO II method does provide the solution that converts effort into schedule. But quite often the schedules are driven by the management or the business users due to business pressures. Under these circumstances, if your project is under pressure to deliver on an unrealistic schedule, check the capability of your IT organization and, only if found suitable, accept the schedule.

Beware: Accepting an impossible schedule can be disastrous for both the project team and the user.

Trap 5: Caution while Counting the FP of Existing Applications

Quite often you come across situations when you need to do a function point count of applications that are already in production. Reasons could be several, including the need to assign budgets and resources to maintain or enhance the application functionalities. But this section will not delve into the reasons. The estimator should take extreme care while identifying various components of the existing application that are being evaluated for FP count. Otherwise, the final FP count may be drastically different from the real count.

A huge difference exists between physical and logical views of an application being counted. In fact this phenomenon can be related to two different situations when an application FP count is being done. When the application is yet to be designed and developed, the estimator identifies various items like files, screens, reports, queries, and interfaces based on the requirements specified by the user. At this stage, the attributes can be assumed to be logical because these attributes are yet to go through the design phase. But once the design of the application is completed, the logical attributes are converted to physical attributes because these now provide the input to the build and test phases. As such the estimator, while counting the FP of an existing application, gets to view mostly the physical attributes. It requires some amount of ingenuity to convert the physical attributes to logical ones and then apply the FP counting processes. In other words, adopt the user view to get the right perspective. Here are some guidelines that are also provided in the IFPUG CPM 4.2 Manual. [3]

- One of the main areas of confusion arises during the identification of the right set of files (ILF) that meet the IFPUG FP counting conditions. Information about files in existing applications is normally available in the form of data models. If you directly take each file (or table) as an ILF, this may lead to wrong FP counts. For example, if an employee application has a need to maintain data about an employee, the person's dependents, and experience, there is a possibility that due to RDBMS design constraints the designer would have created them as three different tables (files): one each for employee, dependent, and experience. These files would have been linked through the employee number as the primary key. In this situation, if you go by the data model design that represents the physical representation of files, you have to count them as three ILFs. But if you view this from the user's perspective, it will actually be only one ILF with possibly three RETs. And this is the right FP count that is based on logical representations.

- The reverse could also be true in some situations. Sometimes in order to improve the performance of the application response time, the designers combine two or more logical files into one single physical file. Once again, view the contents of the file from the user's perspective and then identify the correct number of ILFs.

- At times, due to design constraints certain additional temporary storage files are created by the designer. There could be several reasons for doing so including performance improvement, multiple choices of data processing needs, and similar requirements. Be aware of such needs and do not include these files in the final FP count because they are not arising from the user's view.

- Look out for processing logic that tends to repeat across transactions within the same application. Duplicate usage (reuse) of such processing logic is not allowed to be counted multiple times as per the IFPUG rule. For example, if there is a need to provide a drop-down list box item to choose an employee name in multiple data entry screens, this should be counted only once during the first occurrence and then ignored in subsequent occurrences. The processing logic behind the drop-down list box to select an employee from an employee database is created only once and reused across screens.

Conclusion

Although you may understand the theory behind an estimation method through manuals or classroom training and feel comfortable and confident in being able to apply them, the real life situation is quite different.

As an estimator, you have to train your mind to apply the estimation basics that have been taught in a modified version according to situations on the field. You will never come across the ideal situation that has been taught to you in classroom sessions.

I would equate this to the situation when we as toddlers were taught by our parents to walk. And when we started walking we were also taught the basics of crossing a road, climbing stairs, and similar activities connected to using our hands, legs, and other body sensors. But as time passes, we come across a million varieties of situations when we have to improvise the walking process taught to us by our parents, and we keep applying variations on the basics we learned as toddlers. Isn't this a miracle in our lives?

The situation while applying estimation methods to applications in a real IT environment is no different. Each situation will be unique. The more you use the method, the more you learn. Do not expect to hit the right estimates the first, second, or even the third time you attempt them. The more mistakes you make, the more you learn, and the more you will be known as an expert!

References

1. McConnell, Steve. *Rapid Development.* Microsoft Press, 1996.

2. Fairley, Dick. "Making Accurate Estimates," *IEEE Software,* November–December, 2002.

3. International Function Point Users Group (IFPUG). *Function Point Counting Practices Manual (CPM) Release 4.2.*

Other Interesting Reading Material

McConnell, Steve. "Estimation Tips," in *Rapid Development.* Microsoft Press, 1996. Pp 177–179.

CHAPTER 11

Insourcing versus Outsourcing

Introduction

Although it is normal for businesses to set up their own in-house IT departments that cater to all the IT-related needs of the organization, lately the outsourcing bug seems to be biting a large number of organizations looking to cut IT budgets and at the same time increase business growth through their IT systems.

With the boom in outsourcing, vendors around the globe, particularly in India, are pitching their best wares to win more and more IT outsourcing deals. Tough and fierce competition among the outsourcing vendors has forced them to continuously improve their software project delivering capabilities. Mature quality processes, innovations in project execution methods, and deployment of a young and highly talented resource pool have converted the outsourcing service provider community to become highly advanced in the software technology area. On the other hand, the age-old insourcing practices in internal IT organizations have retained experienced and mature software professionals who also have tremendous background in the business domain in which they are deployed. This chapter focuses on the differences in the way software project execution take place in two varieties of the IT environment: insourcing and outsourcing. This chapter also covers the impact of estimations due to the difference in the competencies of these two approaches to software development.

Environment—The Differentiator

First consider the key environmental differences between insourcing and outsourcing. This will set the context of the discussion later in this chapter on the role the environment plays in the way software project estimations are done. The parameters that define the environment include

- Organization structure
- IT applications
- Hardware and technology platform
- People and organization culture
- Skills
- Quality processes

Each of these environment parameters plays a role in shaping the behavior of the IT organizations, including the project execution processes. This includes the estimation processes as well as the input to the estimations.

The Insourcing IT Organization

Most large businesses have their own internal IT organizations. As the business has evolved and grown, the IT organization likely started as a small group of software developers, grew gradually into an IT department, and then emerged into a large IT organization. This phenomenon brings up a number of interesting flavors to the various parameters that define the environment of an IT organization.

Organization Structure

The IT organization within the business is typically considered to be an important department that has the responsibility to maintain and constantly upgrade the IT systems. The functionality that needs to be delivered through the IT systems is controlled by the business users of the organization. The IT organization, in consultation with the business organization, works toward keeping the applications in sync with business needs.

The budget for IT operations is based on business maintenance and growth plans for the year, and the budgets are always under pressure.

IT Applications

Applications evolve as the organization and its business grows. Quite often functionalities are enhanced to cater to newer business functions as well as enhancements to existing applications. When the organization decides to add new services, it requires that new applications be freshly developed or purchased to service the functions of the new service. Mergers and acquisitions bring their own set of adoption needs for applications in both merging organizations; they are designed differently but service the same functionality overall.

Hardware

Organizations that have evolved their IT systems over several decades tend to accumulate a large variety of hardware, connected interfaces, and networking systems. Huge transformational costs deter the IT management from upgrading to newer hardware. At the same time, maintaining the legacy systems incur huge operational costs. Lack of budgets adds to the woes resulting in the IT organizations maintaining their hardware platforms from the dinosaur era through the current jet age. They all co-exist and even talk to each other through middleware.

Technology Platform

Similar to the issues faced in hardware platforms, the technology platforms also evolve at almost the same pace, sometimes faster, and bring similar challenges to the IT management. Often while upgrading the technology on which an application was originally developed, IT managers simultaneously decide to upgrade hardware platforms. This packaging saves transformational costs.

People

Like a mature, strong tree, the developer community in an internal IT organization grows along with the organization and has deep roots and strong branches that can easily sense every movement of the wind, water, and earth (IT environment) to make appropriate corrections. Having literally been soaked in the day-to-day business transactions of the organization, almost all of the IT community has good insight into how each of the software application services the business functions. Functional enhancements, technical changes, or problem fixes to existing applications are executed very comfortably by the programmers.

On the other hand, sometimes temporary hires or subcontractors deployed in internal IT groups weaken the collective strength of the IT teams because they are moved frequently. All the extensive efforts put in by senior IT professionals to train subcontractors are lost instantly when the subcontractors are moved due to internal or external decisions.

Skills

When it comes to the technology platform area, the senior programmer community tends to stick to legacy technologies. This is natural because seniors from the older generation of software professionals have spent considerable energy and time to master the legacy technology. Whereas the legacy platform has been in existence for very long time, is stable, and can deliver high performance outputs, it is in user interface area that the newer technology shines. In these situations, migrating the application (at least the client portion) to newer technology would require a huge amount of time for learning the new technology. This is sometimes complemented by hiring programmers from the younger generation who can adapt to newer technologies easily.

Quality Processes

Internal IT organizations have not been very strong in adopting international standard quality processes like those prescribed by SEI—Capability Maturity Models. Low priority to metrics measurement programs, lack of continuous improvement programs, and insufficient documentations sometimes cause considerable anguish to the project execution teams. Estimation methods are typically budget based or based on other in-house estimation models. Exceptions do exist, however, in which some the IT organizations have strong quality processes deployed across the organization.

The Outsourcing IT Organization

Quite unlike the internal IT organization that works and behaves like any other department within the main organization, the outsourcing service providers thrive in a highly competitive, business-oriented environment. The very survival of the outsourcing organization depends on how well it can attain customer satisfaction through high-quality deliverables at the lowest cost. Some of the organizational, personnel, and infrastructure related behaviors that emerge due to the competitive environment are discussed in the following sections.

The Organization Structure

Because IT is the main line of business, almost the entire organization, from the top management to the junior developer, is highly IT-oriented. Smaller organizations are compact in nature and typically serve customers directly on an individual assignment basis. Large organizations are structured quite differently. Often they have special focus on vertical industry business areas as well as on technology platforms. As such, the organizations are normally bifurcated into business units that focus on industry verticals and technology units (providing support to the business units) that focus on technologies. Additional support functions are provided for deploying quality processes and training activities.

The IT Applications

Applications typically developed and maintained within outsourcing service provider organizations are for internal use only. They are of an MIS nature and help internal functioning of the organization's business. The applications also help tracking customer project activities that include project management, quality management and other reporting, and billing needs. The role of internal applications is to automate the IT delivery environment without compromising the quality of deliverables.

Hardware

Outsourcing service providers typically do not own huge hardware inventories. Other than the state-of-art hardware platform that is required to maintain their internal IT applications, most customer projects are typically executed on the customer hardware environment. With ever increasing pressure from fellow outsourcing service providers, the focus in these organizations is to move as much work to offshore sources as the project execution model allows. Offshore locations typically are low-cost software delivery locations like India, China, and the Philippines. In offshore situations, the outsourcing organizations set up network connectivity with the customer environment in order to facilitate seamless software project execution activities.

Inability to replicate the customer hardware platform at offshore locations has a direct impact on the productivity of the project team (and hence estimations). Some of the critical integration tests cannot be fully replicated offshore and therefore are completed later at the customer's location.

Technology Platform

Unlike the internal IT organizations, the programmer communities in out-sourcing service provider organizations belong largely to the newer generation. Having graduated recently from top engineering and business schools, the programmers are mostly educated on state-of-art technology platforms. Lack of deep knowledge of legacy technology platforms is made up through extensive training and mentoring by seniors within the organization. With a constant demand from clients to migrate to newer technologies, outsourcing organizations develop specific solutions to address these transformational project requirements and keep their developers appropriately skilled.

People

Once again, the competitive environment among outsourcing vendors drives the process of hiring the best available talent. The average age of the young programmer is normally 24 to 26 years. Over and above the education on newer software technologies that they acquire in their colleges, these young programmers are eager to learn more and hone their skills on a wide variety of technologies and project execution capabilities. Add to this the willingness to work extra hard and spend late hours at work, and you have a truly dynamic workforce to utilize.

Skills

Whatever the educational background of the programmers may be, most outsourcing organizations provide additional, focused training on specific software engineering, quality, and technology platforms to ensure the fine-tuning of their skills. On top of this, the programmers get the opportunity of working on a variety of software projects on the technology for which they have been trained and mentored. This helps in strengthening their technology skills, making them experts on the identified technology platform.

Quality Processes

A good majority of outsourcing service providers have been accredited at SEI CMMI Level 4–5 on the quality processes deployed by them. These organizations also have invested in knowledge-sharing initiatives that promote exchange of best practices in software project execution activities. One of their major goals becomes the deployment of continuous improvement programs that help them achieve lower levels of delivered defects, lower variance in effort, and schedule and estimations that more accurately reflect actual results. Investments in many quality-related initiatives are significant.

Estimation Approach

Now that you understand the difference in the environment between insourcing and outsourcing organizations, this section explores the difference in estimation approaches that are adopted by these two organizations.

Insourcing Estimation

Decisions to execute projects are often budget driven. The CIO is allocated an overall budget for the fiscal year based on several factors, including the business growth of the parent organization, plans to upgrade hardware and technology platforms, and the mandate to meet additional fresh application development needs put forth by business users.

Based on priorities set by the IT organizations internally, the overall budget is further divided into critical needs, long-pending important upgrades and enhancements, and futuristic technologies.

At times when the actual budget allocated to a specific software project does not meet the actual need, alternative approaches are explored. If budgets are low, outsourcing to offshore service providers is an option. Another option is to reduce non-critical functionalities that were originally planned for development projects, resulting in reduced costs. Yet another option is to implement the functionality in a series of smaller projects over a period of time (incremental development).

Some large companies have large internal IT organizations that at any given time may have a wide variety of IT-related activities in progress. These activities include new software development, maintenance of existing applications, migration to newer technologies, and other infrastructure-related operations. Some organizations set up an internal design and control office to handle centrally all the technical and estimation-related activities for the entire IT organization.

Outsourcing Estimation

Estimation is a totally different story here. The outsourcing service provider organization is completely focused on acquiring the software project contract. The competitive environment further complicates the estimation process.

In order to maximize revenues by winning the maximum number of contracts at a decent margin, the outsourcing organization maintains a meticulously tabulated repository of critical information about the capabilities of the programmer community that helps in quick and accurate estimations. The information includes

- Productivity of the company's resources on various technology platforms
- Accuracy of various estimation methods used by the organization and the variance as compared to actual effort spent
- Metrics on quality of projects delivered like defects and schedule variance

Estimation Process

The standard estimation process typically adopted by outsourcing organizations include

- Obtaining inputs about the project through the specifications provided by the customer
- Applying the estimation method that is most appropriate based on the quality, input specifications, and project size
- Converting project size into total effort based on the technology platform on which the project is being executed. The productivity for the platform is obtained from the data repository to derive the total project effort.
- Transforming the effort into resource loading based on the execution model and the schedule agreed with the customer
- Lastly, converting the resource loading data to actual costs based on rates that the outsourcing vendor has fixed for various roles (project manager, module leader, architect, business analyst, and programmer)

This estimation process is normally adopted for development, reengineering, and similar projects. Beyond this, a number of other factors play a significant role in defining the estimations and establishing the way in which the figures vary based on the type of customer project being executed. The accuracy of estimations is also affected by certain other environmental parameters. Some of the environment characteristics including the domain, the project execution process (maintenance), and customer expectations are discussed in the following sections.

Domain

The business domain, including the knowledge of business process workflow, is one of the critical areas where the outsourcing vendors normally lack depth of understanding. And scientific estimation methods like function points depend heavily on domain functionality delivered through an application. In order to overcome this deficiency, the outsourcing organizations not only maintain a repository of domain-wise generic business workflow model information, but also insist on obtaining a maximum amount of business information on the software contracts under negotiation. Situations wherein the project teams have absolutely no knowledge of the domain on which the project is being executed call for special training through internal or external resources. The costs are sometimes added to the overall estimations, reducing the potential savings in outsourcing.

Maintenance Projects

Taking over an existing application in a maintenance contract requires that a number of contractual obligations be met by the outsourcing service provider. The important obligations among them are

- Service the requests from the users. The requests could be for bug fixes, minor enhancements, and major enhancements.
- Ensuring that the outputs delivered are defect-free, completed on time, and within the budgeted costs.
- In most contracts, the services are bound by service level agreements (SLA). The SLAs define the accepted level of variance in defects and delivery schedules while servicing a request from the user.

The health of the application being taken over for maintenance is another critical factor that the outsourcing vendor verifies with due diligence. Some health indicators include the age of the application, stability, number of recent bug fixes, and number of enhancement requests. These factors determine the additional effort that needs to be spent by the maintenance team. As such, appropriate effort is added to the overall estimations.

Customer

Another factor that affects project execution activities is the customer group's complementary capabilities on quality processes as well as technology. The customer group should be able to respond to queries, issues, and concerns raised by the outsourcing vendor that directly impact the quality parameters like performance and scalability as well issues on architecture and other technical design parameters. If this does not happen, the project progress may suffer. On occasion the vendor might have to make decisions that are seen as appropriate to the situation. In these situations, additional effort is spent by the project managers as well as the team. Occasionally, meetings of outsourcing vendors with end users are organized by IT managers to validate the understanding of user requirements.

Outsourcing vendors evaluate the customer on some of the parameters mentioned here and add appropriate effort to balance the shortcomings on quality and technical competencies, if needed.

Insourcing versus Outsourcing: Pros and Cons

Insourcing and outsourcing both have advantages as well as disadvantages. The best answer depends on the real need of the customer organization. IT organizations that are under considerable pressure to cut costs and at the same time maintain and upgrade existing IT infrastructure look toward outsourcing as a possible way to achieve these goals. This section explores the pros and cons of the two types of sourcing by looking at the following categories:

- Strategic
- Financial
- Technical
- Operations

Businesses use one or more of the preceding perspectives to decide whether to keep a project in-house or outsource.

Table 11.1 *Insourcing*

#	Pros	Cons
1	Provides continued opportunity for the internal IT community to grow within the organization.	Work pressure may provide little time to hone their skills through internal or external training programs.
2	Critical and sensitive projects that handle classified information are retained with internal IT organization.	Upgrades and maintenance of these critical applications may require an upgrade in IT staffing skills.
3	Experienced and senior IT staff are retained internally on existing assignments.	Skilled resources could have been better utilized in new developments as well as in higher roles within the organization.

Table 11.2 *Outsourcing*

#	Pros	Cons
1	Better project execution capabilities with proved quality of deliverables could be availed.	Requires closer monitoring of outsourcing vendor activities.
2	Internal IT folks could be freed to take up assignment on state-of-art technologies.	Requires experienced internal IT managers to manage outsourcing contracts better.
3	Easy to scale-up as well as scale-down based on business needs.	Quality of resources during quick ramp-ups may not always be consistent.

Strategic Considerations

Tables 11.1 and 11.2 compare the pros and cons of insourcing and outsourcing as they relate to strategic issues.

Impact: The productivity of internal IT folks would be higher because they will understand the business process and requirements better than the outsourcing vendor team. Mature project delivery processes supported by well-defined quality procedures help outsourcing teams make up the gap in the productivity, but only to a certain extent.

Table 11.3 *Insourcing*

#	Pros	Cons
1	Costs are controlled and consistent. Budgets are known upfront and all planning is done accordingly.	This may sometimes lead to cutting down some of the upgrades when cost overruns happen.
2	Infrastructure including software licensing costs are internal and upgrades are controllable.	Trying out newer technology would require investments at risk.
3	Vendor management overheads are avoided.	Granular level internal management sometimes adds extra burden on costs.

Table 11.4 *Outsourcing*

#	Pros	Cons
1	One of the main reasons to outsource is cost saving.	Requires strict contract management to avoid cost overruns from additional costs due to scope creep.
2	Predictable cash outflows based on well-defined outsourcing contracts.	Could lead to getting tied up with one vendor for long durations.
3	Lower costs due to off-shoring as well as skilled resources on newer technology.	Controlling offshore activities becomes difficult and risk on critical projects is high.

Financial Considerations

Tables 11.3 and 11.4 compare insourcing and outsourcing from a financial perspective.

Impact: Project delivery costs are typically lower when outsourced to low-cost offshore vendors in countries like India, China, and the Philippines. This happens despite lower productivity of offshore vendor teams in certain areas like the requirements phase.

Table 11.5 *Insourcing*

#	Pros	Cons
1	Opportunity to learn newer technologies keeps internal staff comfortable.	Reskilling senior staff on newer technologies takes considerable effort.
2	Transformation of applications to newer technology ensures easy retaining of business functions.	Transformation to newer technology may sometimes lead to injunction of newer technical bugs due to lack of skilled resources.
3	A central core team that controls enterprise level standardization of technology upgrades could reduce technology disparities.	Migration to standardized technologies might be costly.

Table 11.6 *Outsourcing*

#	Pros	Cons
1	Adopting the latest technologies is quite normal and comfortable to outsourcing organizations.	Internal IT organization staff also needs to be knowledgeable on newer technologies to manage technology upgrades.
2	Frequent technology-based migration assignments across customer organizations makes outsourcing vendors develop predefined solutions for quick transformations.	Although technology migrations are perfect, maintenance of business functions as per original applications needs to be carefully verified.

Technical Considerations

Tables 11.5 and 11.6 compare the technical issues involved in insourcing and outsourcing development projects.

Impact: There are no significant benefits of outsourcing to a low-cost, young programmer community if the application systems are of a legacy nature. But in situations where applications are being migrated to state-of-art technology platform, outsourcing does bring in larger benefits in cost savings due to the fact that typically outsourcing vendors in low-cost countries like India are well equipped to deliver on newer technologies.

Table 11.7 *Insourcing*

#	Pros	Cons
1	Skilled and experienced operations staff ensure continuity in IT infrastructure operations.	Over the years, the cost of operations tends to increase due to increased salaries of senior staff.
2	Production support operations are well understood by internal staff and are in sync with user needs.	Long absence of staff requires temporary backups and may lead to drop in quality of service.

Table 11.8 *Outsourcing*

#	Pros	Cons
1	Provide good cost benefits by moving some of the non-critical operations to offshore areas.	Needs closer monitoring by internal IT staff.
2	Ramping-up of operation staff is considered easy with outsourcing organizations due to high availability of local resources.	Might sometimes lead to drop in quality of service and even failure on some of the service level agreements.

Operations Considerations

Tables 11.7 and 11.8 compare the differences involved in operations for insourcing and outsourcing projects.

Impact: Of late, organizations have started offshoring infrastructure maintenance and operations to low-cost locations like India and China. The outsourcing vendors have started perfecting the process of remote infrastructure management through some of the well-established tools. Because operations are directly dependent on the number of resources deployed, any replacement of resources with low-cost offshore resources results in direct cost savings.

What do these comparisons have to do with estimations? A lot. Most of the factors, both for and against insourcing or outsourcing, have a direct impact on the final estimations. Whereas the size of the application under consideration might remain the same, the overhead and variations due to the various factors mentioned will impact the overall estimations of effort and cost.

Conclusion

Considerable debate exists in the IT industry on the business benefits of outsourcing as compared to retaining operations internally. Lost jobs and loss of control on some IT operations due to outsourcing has been a point of discussion. But this is greatly offset by cost benefits that are so huge that the operational efficiency and the improved economies of outsourcing organizations override other discomforts.

Business organizations have made use of outsourcing options effectively by adopting a judicious mix of insourcing and outsourcing services. Also, the outsourcing services have been often distributed among more than one outsourcing service provider in order to mitigate risks due to heavy dependence on one vendor.

On the other hand, not all outsourcing contracts have been success stories. According to Capers Jones, "About 5 percent of outsource contracts end up in court" [1].

References

1. Jones, Capers. "Conflict and Litigation between Software Clients and Developers." Software Productivity Research, 2004.

CHAPTER 12

Key Factors
in Software Contracts

Introduction

Quite similar to any other business transaction between two organizations, outsourced software projects require a formal contractual agreement between the buyer and the seller. Software contracts also include the usual sections such as scope of work, schedule, and deliverables, as well as other commercial terms and conditions common to contractual agreements. But what stands out in software contracts is the specific definition of the scope that describes the features and functions the user expects to be able to utilize.

As discussed in Chapter 1, because software is *soft*, defining exactly the scope of a software project is quite complex as compared to the manufacturing of a TV set. The most users can do is describe the requirements and their expectations and hope that the delivered product will meet their actual needs.

This chapter intends to limit the discussion to the impact on estimations and costs in a software contract based on variety of project execution types. Legal and other non-project related aspects of a typical contract are not within the scope of this chapter.

Types of Contracts

The two most popular types of contracts used between the customer and the vendor are the fixed price contract and the time and material contract. There are a number of other varieties of software contracts; some are variants of these two. The choice of contract type is normally driven by the customer, and there could be several reasons for software contracts to be of varied types. Fixed budgets, limited budgets, the risk factor of the work, time to market, and phase-wise upgrades are some of the common reasons customers request one type of contract over another.

The Fixed Price Contract

Based on detailed requirements provided by the customer, the outsourcing service vendor prepares a contract that describes the vendor's understanding of the scope, the project execution steps, schedule, and the deliverables. The contract price is provided as a fixed price.

To date I have not come across a software specification with the scope defined perfectly to map to the last line of code generated in the actual software. At best, the scope can define the size of the final software product with an estimated variance of ±20%. This philosophy extends to the software contract as well. When a fixed price software contract is being drawn for a project, both the customer and the outsourcing vendor are aware of the inherent risks built into the contract due to several factors:

- The top three items of concern are scope, scope, and scope. It is almost impossible for a user (subject matter expert) to define the business functions that are required to be delivered by the software application that is being negotiated under the contract completely and 100 percent accurately. This is a fact well known both to the customer as well as the vendor and each tries to mitigate this risk through appropriate clauses in the contract.
  - The user includes a condition that at the completion of the requirements definition phase, the user's sign-off is mandatory. Despite this condition the user is not sure whether the total scope can really be captured during the requirements phase. As such, the user may want a provision of perhaps 3 to 5 percent increase in scope during the rest of software project execution phases.

- The vendor on the other hand is equally anxious of the fact that the company offered a fixed price to develop the software with certain basic assumptions on scope. Due to pricing pressure from competitors, the profit margin is kept thin. This means any increase in scope would directly impact the company's profitability. To overcome this risk, the vendor introduces a section in the contract known as "change control." Every time a change in scope is envisaged, the vendor does an impact analysis of the change. If the change in functionality was not part of the original scope, the vendor does an effort, cost, and schedule impact analysis. This information is presented through the "change control" process. Upon sign-off from the user, the work is executed.

- The quality of the delivered application is another serious cause for concern to the customer. Because the term *quality* is used loosely to define the final product, it has several critical parameters that have to be fully understood both by the customer and the vendor before the contract can be considered executed to the total satisfaction of both the parties. These parameters include

  - Quality includes the "usability" aspects of the application. This means that the user interface (UI) as well as the navigational aspects of the application should meet the user's needs. Unless the contract clearly specifies the process of user interface design approval by the users, the risk of rework during the application acceptance phase is high. In large application development contracts, a prototype phase is included to overcome this risk.

  - Response time to user requests is another "quality" parameter that needs attention. Typically the user expects the response time to be high (response time less than one second). Quite often the limitations of the environment and platform on which the application is being deployed do not allow the expected response time. To some extent the project execution team overcomes this deficiency through fine-tuning the architecture and design of the software application. This often results in significant unaccounted effort.

  - The ability of the application to scale up to peak load demands in terms of either large number of transactions or large number of simultaneous users is a key "quality" factor. Often the user is not able to clearly define these parameters in advance. If the user tries to play it safe by demanding a highly scalable architecture, the increased effort on design and coding as well as unforeseen upgrades of the environment may escalate the costs upfront. On the other hand if a safe scalability figure is provided, when during peak loads the demand exceeds the scalable limit of the application, the application may crash. Usually, a trade-off is best.

- Another critical parameter that impacts fixed price contracts is the "testing and approval" of documents, artifacts, and the code during various lifecycle stages of the software project execution. The reasons could be several:

  - Ambiguity or incomplete definition of scope can lead to delays in the sign-off of requirement specification documents.

  - Delays in approving the architecture and design of the technology platform on which the application is being developed impact the project execution. In some situations, the customer IT organization may not have experts on a specific technology and depend on the vendor to provide assistance.

  - The final testing and acceptance phase is the most critical phase of the project execution. Once approved and accepted, any modifications later would lead to additional expenses. As such, the sponsor of the project makes best efforts to deploy the most experienced subject matter experts in order to ensure that all the functionality that is expected to be delivered by the application is fully tested and evaluated. Quite often many functional requirements that were not originally defined are found missing, thus leading to rework. Remember that rework at the acceptance phase involves the maximum amount of work.

The understanding between the customer and the vendor and the level of comfort and confidence in mutually resolving deviations from contracted conditions during actual project execution determines how the estimations are buffered by the vendor. The catch here is that if there is too much buffering, the estimates and, as a result, the escalated cost of contract might lead to the contract itself being lost. On the other hand, being pragmatic and expecting the deviations during project executions to be addressed through the "change control" process is dependent on trusted customer relations.

The Time and Material Contract

The time and material (T&M) contracts are typically adopted when the project effort is not clearly predictable. Application maintenance projects normally are contracted on a T&M basis. Unlike the fixed price software project contracts that focus more on scope of work as the basis of pricing, the T&M software contracts are more dependent on the resources deployed to execute a project. Resources include the software programmers and sometimes infrastructure resources that are included in the T&M contracts. The T&M contracts can be deployed in a variety of outsourcing situations. The next section discusses the application maintenance contract that is normally costed on a T&M basis.

Application Maintenance Contracts

The actual number of resources, also known as full-time persons (FTP) that are required to maintain one or more set of applications are determined based on several parameters. These parameters include

- The overall size of the application that is required to be maintained. The size could be in a function point count, lines of code, or any other unit of size measurement.
- The technology platform on which the applications are deployed.
- The historic data about the applications that can determine the resources required to maintain them. The historic information includes
  - Age of the applications
  - Their stability
  - Number of bugs reported and fixed during last couple of years
  - Complexity of the applications
  - Criticality of the applications (mission-critical?)
  - Projected new functional enhancements to existing applications. This is largely dependent on user community and organization business growth.
  - Stringent service level agreements (SLA) to be met

Based on these parameters, IT organizations, both insourcing as well as outsourcing service providers, have evolved estimation models that provide fairly accurate numbers on the actual number of FTP required to maintain the applications.

In situations where a sizeable number of applications are to be maintained by a group of resources (also known as a **portfolio of applications**), IT organizations have innovatively deployed resources that are shared across multiple applications. In these situations, because one programmer could be servicing maintenance activities for more than one application, the resources are termed **full time equivalents** (FTE). As such, the FTE deployed for a given application maintenance may not always be a whole number but could be a fraction—for example, 0.5 FTE. The FTE totals are then converted to FTP, which is always a whole number. The term FTE is also commonly used to express equivalence to a full-time person (FTP) but compensates for their vacations and holidays.

Whatever the method adopted to arrive at the final FTP, the resources are then structured into a project team consisting of various roles like project manager, technical lead, module leads, and developers. The rates for the roles are fixed in the same contract. The overall hourly costs are calculated based on the number of resources under different roles deployed for a project.

The outsourcing service providers further extend the project execution to the popularly known Global Delivery Model (GDM). This model typically evaluates the necessity of various resources that need to be positioned at the customer location and the rest at an offshore location where the benefit of low-cost resources can be availed.

Case Study

This section provides an example of an application maintenance contract being negotiated under the time and material basis. Based on assumed application parameters, the following calculations are envisaged:

- Application size = 2500 function points
- Historic info: Pretty stable, normal quota of bugs and fixes, average complexity, and a non-critical system
- FTP (FTE) estimated: 10 resources (assumed)
- Roles breakup: Project Manager = 1, Business Analyst = 2, Programmers = 7

A table can be created to provide rates for individual roles on an hourly basis. Based on the rates, the monthly billing as well as annual costs can be calculated. If the outsourcing service provider adopts the GDM model, rates for the resources deployed offshore are applied accordingly.

Using robust estimation methods to produce the optimum number of FTEs required to maintain an application (or a portfolio of applications) is critical for even winning the contract itself. Historic data about the application characteristics as well as about the vendor organization's execution capability helps to produce the best FTE estimates. Profit margins in T&M contracts are generally fixed and steady because these kinds of contracts are based on hourly resource rates.

The Flexible Contract

Unique project execution situations sometimes provide estimators with the opportunity to develop unique software project contracts. These unique situations are basically faced by the customer (user) due to various business or budget situations. The situations might include

- Undefined project scope
- Limited project budget
- Tight delivery schedule

Undefined Project Scope

The business users have envisioned a new software application that will address business opportunities they see in the near future. But the exact scope of the business functions to be addressed is unclear. In this situation the sponsor would want to have the flexibility of understanding the scope and hence the overall cost of the project. There could be several other similar reasons where the scope is not fully known in advance.

The software contract in this situation is split into two portions. The first phase is limited to requirements elicitation only. During this phase, the business analysts and senior members of the project team do a complete study of the requirements based on interviews and other data gathering activities. At the end of the phase, the project is sized and then the cost and schedule for the rest of the project lifecycle activities is calculated. Sometimes the customer takes the option of assigning the requirements phase to two vendors in order to cross-verify the results and recommendations.

The scope of the project itself is unknown and in fact it is the *scope* being evaluated here. Typically the resources (FTE) are assigned on a gut-feel estimate basis. The contract is ideally done on a T&M basis.

Limited Project Budget

Quite often the sponsoring manager is constrained by limited budgets. Under these situations the sponsor explores the possibility of defining a contract that provides the flexibility of choosing the project deliverables. Some of the flexible items could be

- Reduced frills in user interface
- Include only absolutely necessary functions
- Reduced documentation
- Reduced number of internal quality reviews (even if it means lower quality)

A willing outsourcing vendor might work out a low-budget contract that could fit the available budget based on cutting some of the non-critical project activities. This may lead to a risk of poor quality software. An upgrade phase at a later stage when more funds are available could help mitigate this risk. In some cases, the customer requests reduced testing cycles, thus reducing the overall effort and costs. A word of caution: This may not be a good practice because it might lead to significant risks of application failure later.

The estimation method here is modified to accommodate revised productivity due to the modified project execution method discussed above. All changes in scope that may occur during project execution are managed through change control process.

Tight Delivery Schedule

In situations where the software project is expected to specifically address a critical business need, it is essential that the project is completed and ready for deployment before the business opportunity period starts. If not, the whole exercise might go to waste. In some situations, the project might be unnecessary if the business opportunity has passed.

In a business-opportunity/high-risk situation, the business user is not ready to accept any flexibility in the project delivery schedule. As such, extreme care should be taken while the software project contract is being drawn. Some of the critical parameters that should be clearly described and discussed in detail are

- *Scope:* The outsourcing vendor should thoroughly understand the complete scope of the application, including the functionality that is expected to be provided.
- *Schedule:* The delivery schedule is equally critical. The project manager should ensure that the estimated effort to deliver the project can actually be completed within the proposed schedule.
- *Variable Contract:* In the event that the project does not progress as planned, the project team should have the option of revising the scope to remove some of the non-critical functions in order to be able to meet the delivery schedule.
- In certain situations even the acceptance processes are toned down in order to facilitate deployment of the application in production.
- If the project is business-critical, it is not unusual for the outsourced vendor to include additional costs to mitigate certain known risks as discussed above.

Project Execution Methods

Almost every software project is unique in some ways. The uniqueness occurs for a variety of reasons. In a software project context, there are several people who play roles in defining the specific project execution process, including:

- *The Project Sponsor:* The sponsor has the purse to pay for the project. But he or she also ensures that the project is a success at any cost. The priority would be the project execution lifecycle model that is time-tested and ensures confirmed delivery of the application at the agreed schedule.

- *The User:* The user has several items on his or her wish list. The user interface should be good, response time to be under one second, and the application should be able to take peak transactions and user loads without affecting the response time.

- *The Architect:* The architect wants to ensure that the design is tested early in the project execution lifecycle. This will avoid rework at a later stage if the design is found wanting during stringent performance tests.

There could be additional reasons that lead to a variation in the project execution method. For this reason, it is essential that while defining the contract, the outsourcing service provider should understand the unique project execution needs and clearly spell out the project execution methodology in the contract. The following sections explore some of these variations in project execution methods.

Lifecycle Models

Do not assume that all projects are delivered using the standard waterfall lifecycle model. Different customer organizations may have different priorities on the project execution lifecycle model.

- *Waterfall Model:* Projects expected to be delivered under normal situations adopt this model. Compulsory review after completion of each phase is done. The final test and acceptance is done when the complete application is ready.

- *Iterative Model:* Serious business users depend on the application to facilitate improved business transactions. They understand the criticality of the project execution processes and its role in enhancing the application's ability to deliver the desired functionalities. Quite often users prefer the iterative lifecycle delivery model. This model ensures that the users get the benefit of reviewing the application after every iteration and test the functionality implemented so far.

- *The Big Bang Approach:* Normally users intending to save time and effort on reviews adopt the big bang approach. Once the requirements are frozen and signed-off, the user typically does not interfere in the project execution processes. Only at the completion of the testing activities does the user do an acceptance test of the entire application and other deliverables.

The software contract should include details on the lifecycle model being adopted. All the milestones applicable to the selected model should be identified along with deliverables at each milestone. The criteria required for the milestone to become acceptable should also be highlighted.

If estimates of project size are done using the function point method then you should be aware that the function point count (size) is independent of project execution lifecycle models. But the productivity for different lifecycle execution models does vary because such effort estimates for lifecycle models will also vary. The iterative model is likely to consume the highest effort for a given project FP size.

Product Quality

Applications that need to serve business-critical or mission-critical functionalities must meet stringent performance parameters. These performance parameters could be of different categories, including

- *Reliability:* The application (product) is reliable and its performance and output are consistent and uniform under all load conditions
- *Scalability:* The application can scale to peak loads of transactions or large number of users and continue to meet the same response time as seen under normal load
- *Availability:* The application design has been architected to be fault tolerant. The system is robust and its availability is high. Adequate backup, recovery, and stand-by facilities have been built-in to facilitate high availability.

If the software contract is for a critical application that has the requirement to meet one or more of the preceding product quality parameters, the design and test phases would have to be carefully planned to meet these requirements. These parameters are also known as **Quality of Services.**

Estimators using the function point estimation method will be aware of the 14 GSCs. These GSCs do provide for additional FP count through the value adjustment factor-based Quality of Services parameters that are applicable to a software project.

Project Specific Overheads

You learned about some of these topics in the estimation-related chapters, and heard more about them in "Tips, Tricks, and Traps" (Chapter 10). But while discussing the contract, it is essential to include sections that highlight some of these overhead activities because they directly impact the project costs as well the deliverables expected by the customer. The standard estimation methods typically address the application size and the standard project execution lifecycle activities starting from requirements and going through testing and acceptance. The estimated effort, schedule, resource loading, costs, and deliverables are all accordingly spelled out in the contract. But over and above the standard activities in project execution, a few other non-generic activities are requested by the user in specific situations, such as

- *Prototype:* Large and complex projects require special attention from several stakeholders in order to make the project a success. The stakeholders are not limited to the sponsor and the outsourcing vendor; they include the end users and business users. There have been situations wherein the internal IT team that is expected to take over the application after it is successfully delivered and deployed in production is also included as a stakeholder. In these situations it is a common practice to plan an early prototype phase in the project. The prototype will have the look and feel of the proposed end product except that the users will get only a demo version to review and it will not be a working model. This practice helps reduce the risk of project failure due to incorrect understanding of the requirements by the outsourcing vendor.

- *Proof-of-Concept:* Similar to the prototype situation, the stakeholders often request a proof-of-concept phase (POC). Unlike the prototype that has a focus on usability aspects of the product and displays various screens and other user interfaces, the POC has a focus on the architecture and the design of the product. The POC intends to test all the architectural layers of the application with lightweight but simulated real-time transactions. Without going into technical detail, imagine a project where the user interface is a web-based interface and the middle layer is an application server that facilitates transactions between the client user and the back-end database system. This is a three-tiered architecture. In order to validate the architecture, a small application module is developed on the exact platform in which the final product is being developed. This module, known as the POC, has a user interface screen that captures data from the user, transacts through the middle (app server) and back-end layer (RDBMS), and returns the requested information to the client (web screen). Thus the POC helps in validating the design and helps in fine-tuning any interface or finding shortcomings early in the project execution phase.

- *Large Projects:* Large projects need all planning to be done on a large scale. The team size is large, project activities are subdivided into smaller teams, and you need more than one manager to manage individual teams. On the other hand, the project sponsor also has to organize the team that interacts with and monitors the project progress at frequent intervals. Effort estimates are naturally affected and the overheads should be included in the overall project estimates. But from a contract negotiations perspective, the impact on both the sponsor as well as the vendor side should be discussed and highlighted. This will help reduce the risk in the project both from a cost as well as a project execution perspective.

- *Warranty:* As discussed in an earlier chapter, normal estimates do not provide for effort due to warranty-related obligations. Warranty stipulations vary from project to project and must be agreed upon in advance. The warranty phase kicks off immediately after the project is successfully accepted and deployed. The warranty period, number of resources deployed, and the service level agreements are some of the key factors that should be clearly highlighted in the contract.

An important issue that sometimes occurs with warranty-related contractual agreements concerns the actual start date of warranty period. Under normal circumstances it is expected that once the software project is completed in all respects and the final product is delivered to the customer, the product is deployed into production almost immediately after the acceptance phase is complete. The outsourcing vendor keeps resources ready to take over the warranty phase immediately after the product goes into production. But sometimes it happens that due to pre-planned release schedules, set up by the customer IT organization, or other similar reasons, the deployment of the product into production gets delayed. In these circumstances, the vendor faces the dilemma of holding the resources for a considerable time period and wait for the warranty period to kick in. You should be aware of this disconnect and ensure that appropriate clauses are incorporated in the software contract to mitigate losses due to unforeseen delays.

Estimators need to identify the project overheads applicable to their projects. Among the overhead items discussed, activities like prototype and POC can be estimated using a modified function point method. For other overhead activities, estimate the effort directly based on person hours that are likely to be spent.

Truncated/Partial Projects

It is not uncommon for the customer to offer software projects to outsourcing service providers that do not conform to typical, complete project execution phases. Indeed this situation could occur for the internal (insourcing) IT organizations as well. You may find several causes for truncated or partial projects:

- *Budgeting Purposes:* The user has a software project approved by the management in principle and has an immediate need to provide the budgeted costs for review and approval. The user creates a pilot project that consists of a high-level requirements gathering phase only. It is also expected that at the end of the requirements phase, the vendor will prepare a full proposal that provides the total cost of fully delivering the project itself. This cost, plus contingency costs, becomes the budget amount required to be submitted to the management for approval by the sponsor.

- *Partial Project:* Preparing the requirement specifications of complex business functions is not easy. The sponsors and the subject matter experts (SME) do not have the confidence that the outsourcing project team can do justification to the true functional requirement of the project and develop the perfect specifications. In these situations quite often the SME team themselves prepare the complete and detailed specifications. This specification is then contracted to outsourcing vendors.

Also upon completion of the requirements phase that provides the budgeted costs, it is not necessary that the user (sponsor) contract the same vendor to execute the balance of the project. The user may choose to hire another vendor to complete the rest of the project for which the requirements were developed by the previous vendor.

An extension of this situation occurs when the SME team has developed the requirements as well as high-level design of the application and expects the outsourcing vendor to complete the build and test phases (coding and testing).

Contracts for maintenance of applications typically consist of three major activities; bug fixes, minor enhancements, and major enhancements. Customers sometimes prefer to deploy more than one vendor on maintenance activities for the same set of applications. In this situation the bug fixes and minor enhancements are offered to one vendor and the major enhancements to another. This is sometimes seen as a vendor de-risking practice.

Bad and delayed project deliverables (defective) and non-process oriented project execution practices sometimes force the customer to terminate the contract with the incumbent vendor midway and hand it over to another outsourcing vendor. The project team that is taking over from the incumbent vendor team has to face a number of knowledge transition issues and hassles. Ensure that adequate provision is made in the contract to cover unforeseen take-over situations.

Provide for one or more of these project overhead phases clearly in the contract as applicable. Give details of impact on effort, schedule, and costs in the contract and ensure these aspects are discussed before the contract is actually signed-off. In situations where the customer IT organization also has to respond by providing review and monitoring support activities, calculate the impact on the availability of subject matter experts and the related costs to the sponsor and provide this information separately to the sponsor.

Integration Projects

Software projects that involve development or enhancement of new functionality in an existing IT organization are rarely of the stand-alone type. The application being developed normally has to integrate with one or more existing applications in the organization. Under these circumstances, the outsourcing vendor team has to get access to information regarding all other applications with which integration has to be provided. Quite often this integration activity causes delays in project completion due to incomplete or partial information being provided by the owners of other applications. The integration testing activities also require consent and collaboration from other application owners. It is essential that the software contract includes appropriate mention of assured participation from concerned groups within the IT organization.

Conclusion

Over and above the functional, technical, and commercial aspects of the software project that are covered in a software contract, it is essential that a number of non-specific and unique requirements of a software project are also clearly represented. I am not sure whether an absolutely perfect contract can be compiled that truly covers each and every aspect of the project. As such it will be in the interest of both the customer as well as the outsourcing vendor to develop a contract that can address the maximum number of known deviations in the project execution as compared to standard projects.

Sometimes mutual trust and long-standing relations between the customer and vendor help overcome deficiencies in the contracted obligations. Typically all contracts include a change management section that protects the vendor to be able to claim any deviations that have not been already specified in the contract. But taking undue advantage of this facility is not a good idea. On the other hand the outsourcing vendor has to take adequate precaution on termination of contracts midway due to various reasons. An exit clause with suitable claims on damages is normally included to take care of such situations. Additionally, software projects grow at a measured rate of two percent per calendar month. This growth has to be tracked and provision has to be made to manage this growth through the change management process [1].

References

1. Jones, Capers. "Conflict and Litigation between Software Clients and Developers." Software Productivity Research, 2004.

CHAPTER 13

Project Estimation and Costing

Introduction

Estimating the size of a software application is not the end of the estimation process but it is the means through which other project parameters can be further evaluated. Sizing the software by different units of measurement, including function points, source lines of code (LOC), and other measures, provides the basic information you can use to derive various project parameters. These parameters include the effort required to complete the project, the elapsed time required, the resources that need to be deployed during various stages of project execution, and finally, the overall cost of the project itself.

Business needs fuel IT growth in an organization but quite often budgets finally determine the fate of software projects. Costing of individual projects is critical due to the fact that the decision to go ahead with the project is based on available budgets as compared to the project costs.

Ingredients of Project Costs

This book has discussed various ingredients of project estimation including size, effort, resources, and costs. Each ingredient plays a key role in taking the calculations forward in a particular sequence. Figure 13.1 shows how the ingredients act in sequence to cumulatively determine project costs.

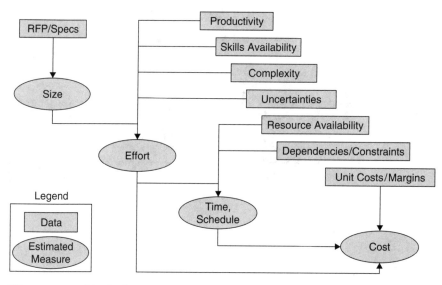

Figure 13.1 *Typical inputs to project estimates.*

Project Lifecycle Phases and Cost

You learned how project size is converted to effort, schedule, resource loading, and costs in Chapter 7. While calculating the various project parameters that led to the overall costing in that chapter, the example assumed an ideal environment where all the participants and resources were freely available and of desired quality and skills. But in real project execution situations, expecting the environment and the resources to be of ideal quality and quantity is unwise.

This chapter delves more deeply into various ingredients of a typical software project and shows how they impact the costing process. For each of the ingredients, there are variations in costing based on several environmental factors. This section follows the project execution lifecycle stages and discusses ingredients in these phases and how they affect costs.

Requirements Phase

Under ideal conditions, you can assume that the user has a good idea of the functionality of the product (project) and has all supporting documents for discussions. Also the subject matter experts are available and can spend considerable time with the project team. You also assume that the project team resources identified for the requirements phase have good previous experience of having done similar assignments in the past. But in real project situations, many of these assumptions may not be true.

The core of a software project is the functional requirements that are expected to be delivered by the finished product. All the remaining project phases depend directly on the requirements. Defects generated during the requirements phase that go undetected into the next lifecycle phases have higher fixing and reworking costs. The later in the lifecycle stages the defect is detected, the higher the fixing and reworking costs.

Consider a few key resources involved in the requirements phase and the impact they have on project costs due to incorrect or sub-optimal usage:

- *Subject Matter Expert* (SME): The SME is the most experienced and knowledgeable resource who can make a big difference in the project's success. For this reason, the SME is also in high demand to keep the current applications running. The SME is perhaps among the most expensive resource category as well.

  During the requirements phase in a project execution stage, it is essential that the SME play a key role in defining the project scope and help the project team thoroughly understand the project requirements. Unfortunately due to other project pressures, the SME is typically available for knowledge transition sessions for shorter durations only. The resulting impact is on the quality of requirements definition. Requirements defects tend to creep in and sometimes this is detected only during the testing and acceptance phase. The costs to fix the defects at the testing phase are quite high. On the other hand, if the project team is provided the support of the SME for longer and appropriate durations, many requirements-based defects and the resulting costs of rework could probably be saved.

- *Experienced Resources:* Demanding and obtaining full participation and support from the SME is not enough. It is equally important that the project team members who interact with the SME to obtain the accurate requirements are equally well-versed in the business domain and the functionalities that are required to be captured. A communication is said to be complete only when the receiver is able to fully understand and record the information provided by the sender. Deploying inexperienced resources in the project team for requirements capturing purposes will have even larger impact on project costs than non-availability of SME.

- *Requirements Capturing Processes:* The third component of the requirements phase that binds the SME and the expert resources is the well laid out process of requirements elicitation. In a structured process,

    - Templates and guidelines ensure that the right and the complete information are captured in a structured manner.

    - The validation process ensures early detection of defects, including missing information, and fixes them appropriately.

    - The testing process ensures those test scenarios are developed during the requirements phase. Through these test scenarios the business workflow could be evaluated for correctness of desired outputs.

Design Phase

Several factors feed into software architecture and design aspects. The user interface, transaction load, number of users, technology platform limitations, and other environmental factors are some of the contributors to the way design are done. But while estimating efforts and cost, estimators normally assume that the design created by the project team is perfect and suits project requirements. Quite often, the design is being modified to meet user requirements even during testing and acceptance phases.

Project costs can vary for several reasons, mainly due to imperfect design. The following list shows some of the common problems encountered during (or preceding) the design phase that have an impact on overall project effort and hence project costs.

- *Over-Engineered Requirements:* In the enthusiasm to exceed customer expectations, the project team sometimes tends to over-engineer the functions they promise to deliver through the application. This can lead to situations where the design team must bend the design rules to meet certain non-generic functional requirements. The associated increase in design efforts leading to increased coding efforts later add to overall costs.

- *Over-Architected Design:* Quite similar to the situation discussed previously, the technical experts in the project team sometimes tend to showcase their technical expertise. Unmindful of the actual needs of the end user, the technical architecture of the application is burdened with unwanted layers. This will have a direct impact on costs through increased design as well as coding efforts. It can also lead to the introduction of additional software in intermediate architecture layers that can increase costs significantly.

- *Poor Design:* Imperfect design can lead to the application's inability to meet stringent performance requirements. If the design validation process does not capture this deficiency, only during the performance testing phase are the defects trapped, thus leading to increased effort and costs due to extensive rework. Deploying unskilled (or under-skilled) technical resources could be one of the main reasons for design-related defects.

- *Interface with Other Systems:* IT organizations that have grown over several decades typically have a large portfolio of applications deployed on a wide variety of technology platforms. In these organizations, it is quite normal to expect the application being designed to interface with a few other existing applications. The technical experts involved in the design activities need to carefully evaluate all the interfacing requirements. The technical and functional designs of all other applications involved have to be fully understood before designing the interfaces. On many occasions the interface design deficiencies have surfaced only during the final system test and integration test phase. Fixing these interfacing defects sometimes requires changes in application design as well as significant changes in interface design parameters. The other impacts are on coding and retesting that further add to project costs.

Build and Test Phase

Having completed the requirements and design phases of the project successfully and reasonably on target, the project team moves on to the last major phase of the project: the build and test phase. Experienced project managers understand that despite the availability of two key inputs to this phase—requirements and design—things may not go as planned. There could be a number of environmental, technical, people, and operations-related issues that could derail the build and test phase. To resolve the issues and bring the project back on track might involve increased effort and cost. The following list presents some of these issues:

- *Environment Setup:* Project managers who take the lifecycle phases as they come and do not believe much in advance planning may face a large variety of issues during the build and test phase. Among them, the setup of the build and test environment is the most critical issue. The programmers start working on individual portions of the code assigned to them and when the time arrives to compile and test the modules, all the issues surface. These include

- Compiling issues due to improper setup of the environment
- Issues during the unit test of individual modules due to improper interfacing between various architectural layers
- Build and test failures due to improper setup of administrative parameters and access rights

Over and above the frustrations felt by the programmer team, considerable time is lost in setting the environment parameters mentioned above correctly. If the project team size is medium or large, the impact on lost hours due to environment issues is significant. A proof-of-concept test phase that actually tests the entire environment helps in containing these project effort and cost escalations.

- *Use of Tools:* Certainly there is considerable benefit from using tools during build and test phases. The productivity of the project team is certain to show noticeable improvements. A wide variety of tools is available on almost any technology platform. These tools could do the following:
  - Check coding standards
  - Verify codify style
  - Help develop online help documents automatically
  - Automate testing processes

While estimating effort for the build and test phases, the productivity that is considered for the project team does include the use of tools. But it is evident that use of tools saves costs during build and test phases. The more repetitive the activities in these phases, the greater the savings, if done with tools. For example, if the project team size is large and each module is developed by a group of programmers, the team needs to repeatedly test the functionality of the module. Testing tools facilitate recording the testing activities and allow automated repeat usage, thus saving considerable time with each test cycle.

Lifecycle Model

Adopting a specific lifecycle model has a direct impact on the effort and costs. Consider the two most popular lifecycle models:

- *Waterfall Model:* Although the waterfall model is the simpler of the two models, it has its own drawbacks. Once a particular phase is completed and project execution has moved forward, if there is a situation to move back to the previous phase, the overhead on various activities is heavy. While deciding on a waterfall model, project estimators should take into consideration the competency of the project team in various environmental factors that impact efforts. For example, if the technical experts in the team do not have adequate technical competency, there is every possibility that the design may have inherent deficiencies that will result in rework during the build and test phase. If this happens in a waterfall model project execution process, the costs will get escalated.

- *Iterative Model:* This model has built-in de-risking methods. Every iteration is a mini waterfall model in itself. The outcome of each iteration is a testable product. This means the product gets reviewed by the user progressively, thus gaining early acceptance by the user. But the flip side of this model is the increased effort due to repetition of some of the effort-consuming activities in each iteration. For example, the testing phase that happens after every iteration has to go through the test process that was executed for all the previous iterations as well. The costs due to the iterative model of project execution are usually higher than waterfall model.

Resource Allocations

Resources are one of the major cost consumers in a software project. Some of the best practices followed in resource allocations recommend allocation of the right resource with the appropriate competency to the right job. This will ensure cost optimization because resources cost differently for different levels of competency and experience.

While preparing the resource allocation chart, carefully identify the required competency at each lifecycle phase of the project and make allocations accordingly. Allocating the right resources at the right time is important, but it is equally important to release the resources when their roles are complete. Extended allocation (blocking) of key, high-cost resources in the project will have a direct impact on project costs. Project managers often are unwilling to release key resources anticipating unexpected emergencies during the deployment phase of the project.

Develop a Cost Matrix

As discussed in the previous sections of this chapter, a number of environmental parameters impact the overall project costs. Some of these

Table 13.1 *Cost Matrix*

Parameter Impact	Requirement	Design	Build and Test	Total Impact
Availability of SME	Yes		Yes	High
Domain experts	Yes			Medium
Technical experts		Yes	Yes	High
Poor design		Yes	Yes	Medium
Usage of tools	Yes	Yes	Yes	Medium
Environment setup		Yes	Yes	Medium
Lifecycle model	Yes	Yes	Yes	Low
Resource allocation			Yes	Low

parameters get included in the usual estimation processes, but most of them do not. For best results, develop a cost matrix table of your own and track costs due to various environmental and other factors. Table 13.1 provides an illustrative matrix for your reference.

Attach costs to each of the impacted project parameters and include these costs to the overall project costs. The table does not show the impact on additional software licenses due to over-architecting. You can add a column to show impact on software licenses and evaluate the additional costs they bring.

Estimation and TCO

While budgeting project costs, IT organizations view the overall costs that include many other expenses beyond the cost of developing the software application. This is necessary in order to provide for the costs that the IT organization has to budget for the current fiscal year as well as for future years. The total amount the IT organization can spend on a software application deployed in the organization—from the time the software was developed until it is retired—is known as the **Total Cost of Ownership** (TCO).

The following list introduces some of the key components of the TCO that are applicable to a typical software application in an IT organization.

Additionally, the list shows how and when they apply in the lifecycle of the application.

- *Application Development Costs:* The first-time conceptualization and development costs involved in the software project

- *Application Maintenance Costs:* Once the new software development phase is complete and the application is successfully tested, approved, and moved into production, it is time now to maintain the application. The software maintenance project involves all activities that include

  - Production support, including operations and online support to end users.

  - Fixing bugs that are detected by users during application usage.

  - Enhancing the application with functionalities as requested by users. The enhancements could be of the minor or major category.

- *Application Migration Costs:* At a certain stage in the life of the application, a need may arise for the application to be migrated to a newer technology platform. There could be several reasons to do this, including taking advantage of newer features in the target technology, better user interface needs, and higher performance requirements. Typically technology migration project assignments are not given to the existing maintenance team because it might impact maintenance activities. A separate project team is assigned to do the migration. The migration costs are incurred in these situations.

- *Application Retiring Costs:* There could be a couple of reasons to retire an existing application. Perhaps the functions delivered by the application no longer support the existing business functions, or the functions supported by the application are being transitioned and consolidated with another application. Whatever the reason, the retiring process involves a number of activities, including

  - Shutting down the application from production after all user communications have been completed.

  - Data that was being maintained by the application is moved to another application as required by the retirement plan.

  - Reverse engineering and reengineering into newer technology if the retirement plan requires it.

  - Designing, developing, and deploying the reengineered application into production.

All these activities involve costs that have to be taken into consideration as part of the TCO.

Estimating TCO Costs

While you are putting together the various components that constitute the TCO costs, you should be aware that the costs are not limited to application development, maintenance, and migration. Other costs include

- *Infrastructure Costs:* For the application to execute successfully in a production environment, it is essential that the entire supporting infrastructure also is set up. The infrastructure includes hardware and networking costs. Also included are other software licensing costs, including operating systems, database, and other integration software.

- *Operations Costs:* These are the costs of employees deployed to perform operations activities, including general administrative work, database management, and other production support activities.

Conclusion

Estimation methods normally are oriented toward sizing a software application. Very few estimation methods—for example, the COCOMO II method—provide a process of calculating the costs beyond software development costs. But the IT organization that intends to deploy and maintain the software application in production must address other expenses connected with each application. These additional costs could come from several places in the project:

- The project execution process adopted during the fresh development of the application
- The environment that has been set up during the application development as well as during application maintenance later
- Infrastructure costs
- Resource costs
- Operations costs
- Other recurring and incidental costs

The total costs towards application development, maintenance, and other operations costs are together known as **total cost of ownership.** But the TCO concept has a span across the lifetime of the application. Some of the costs occur during the first year and the rest are recurring costs.

Other Interesting Reading Material

Jones, Capers. *Estimating Software Costs.* McGraw Hill, 1998.

CHAPTER 14

Other Estimation Methods

Introduction

One estimation method doesn't fit all.

Software estimation and sizing concepts have been in existence almost as long as software itself. As software engineering, software technology, and software development processes evolved, a large variety of estimation methods also surfaced. Earlier chapters focused primarily on the function point estimation method. This chapter presents some of the popular estimation methods and their applicability in different project execution situations. The estimation methods discussed here are not an exhaustive list, but they represent some of the methods commonly practiced by project managers and estimators.

Estimation Methods

Over the past several decades, experts in software engineering have been evolving a wide variety of estimation methods based on years of personal experience as well as research and analysis of past software project data. As software project size grew in size and complexity, some of the rigid estimation methods could not keep pace with the scale, except for a few that kept improvising and managed to survive the increasing demands on software project estimations.

Estimation Approaches

The software experts adopted a variety of estimation approaches that derive the estimation method they conceptualized and developed. Most estimation methods can be classified into two major approaches to estimating software volume: *heuristic* and *parametric*.

- *Heuristic Approach:* Heuristic approaches by definition are the practices through which professionals experiment and find solutions to frequent problems. Software gurus, experts, and experienced professionals have developed estimation approaches that were evolved through extensive and repeated practice and experience. The practitioners of the heuristic approaches have experimented with various patterns of solving the software project estimating problem. Some of the commonly used heuristic approach-based estimation methods are the *expertise-based, analogy-based, bottom-up, top-down,* and *algorithm-based* methods:

  - *Expertise-Based:* Experts who believed in following their own past experience rather than using estimation methods developed by other experts adopted a variety of methods. "Expertise-based techniques are useful in the absence of quantified, empirical data" [1]. These methods were popular among a large community of software professionals.

  - *Analogy Method:* The analogy method uses the experience of past projects. This method compares the proposed project to previously completed, similar projects where actual project development information is known.

  - *Bottom-Up Method:* This method adopts the bottom-up approach by first identifying each and every component or activity at a very granular level. Then the method estimates each component of the software project separately and combines the results to produce an estimate of the entire project.

  - *Top-Down Method:* This method follows the top-down order of working through main modules, sub-modules, and the individual functions. This method is also referred to the Work-Breakdown Structure (WBS) method. There are other alternatives to this method that include the lifecycle-wise break-up of activities and estimation at activity level.

  - *Algorithmic Method:* Based on a certain pattern of data observed by the experts, the algorithmic method gets conceptualized. The pattern is further transformed into mathematical formulae that can be used to derive software estimates. But before the formulae are released to practice, the author of the estimation method validates the theory through a number of pilot trials and then through rigorous testing using historic data as well as other supporting research work.

- *Parametric Approach:* Well-known models like Rayleigh Model or other models devised by estimation experts were used to develop parametric approach-based estimation methods. Here the term *estimation* has been loosely used to cover application sizing as well as effort, schedule, and cost estimates. Some examples are

  - Larry Putnam's Software Life-cycle Model (SLIM) based on the Rayleigh Manpower Distribution Model
  - SEER-SEM by Galorath, Inc., based on the Jensen Model
  - SELECT Estimator based on the ObjectMetrix model developed by the Object Factory
  - COCOMO II based on the ingenious model developed by Barry Boehm
  - COSMIC-FFP based on the model developed by Common Software Measurement International Consortium (COSMIC)
  - Function Points based on the model developed by Allan Albrecht and later by International Function Point Users Group (IFPUG) [2]
  - Knowledge Plan from Software Productivity Research

Heuristic Approach

This section discusses some of the frequently used estimation methods that are heuristic-based. Experts and senior software professionals have developed these common-sense based estimation methods. These methods are not well documented, and the information that is available is of high level and includes loosely structured definitions. But these methods are easily and quickly understood by software professionals because they are naturally aligned to the way projects are actually executed.

Top-Down Estimation Approach

The process adopted in this method approaches the sizing of the application in a top-down fashion. Identify the topmost component of the application being sized and then drill down to lower levels until you reach an appropriate level of granularity. Next, estimate the effort to develop the component at the lowest level of granularity, aggregate the estimation data upward to obtain the overall estimate for the software project. Add overhead efforts as appropriate.

Several alternate approaches follow the top-down approach. Each one of these approaches is experience based and does not follow any predefined model. A few commonly used top-down estimation approaches include

- Work-Breakdown Structure (WBS) estimation
- Wideband Delphi method

The following sections explain each of these approaches.

Work-Breakdown Structure Estimation Method (WBS)

Originally developed by the U.S. Defense establishment during the early '90s, the WBS estimation method is described in Military Standard (MIL-STD) 881B as "a product-oriented family tree composed of hardware, software, services, data, and facilities." The WBS facilitates capturing all the activities that can possibly be involved in the entire project in an organized way. Typically, the WBS is shown graphically in a top-down hierarchical way, as shown in Figure 14.1.

The WBS method offers a number of alternative approaches to defining the top-down structure of the application system being estimated. Two examples are

- *Product-Centric:* The application is broken down into the main product, sub-product, modules, elements, and components. Actual estimated effort or cost for each component is evaluated and then aggregated upward.
- *Project Lifecycle-Centric:* The activities that are involved in the project execution are broken down lifecycle-wise (for example, requirements, design, build, and test). Each lifecycle phase is further broken down into individual activities. Estimates for individual activities are made and then aggregated upward.

Wideband Delphi Estimation Method

Originally the Delphi method was developed by the Rand Corporation in 1948. In the Delphi method, a small team of software experts come together and independently generate estimates for a given problem and through repeated iterations reach consensus on a mutually agreeable estimate.

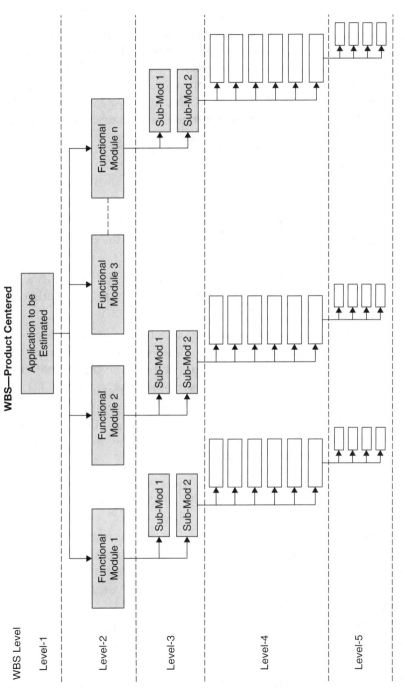

Figure 14.1 *Work-breakdown structure.*

The Wideband Delphi method was developed in 1970 when Barry Boehm designed this version jointly with the Rand Corporation. This method is a structured way of estimation based on collective expertise. Quite often the Wideband Delphi method is used to cross-validate estimations that have been done using other popular estimation methods. This is based on the recognition of the fact that when many experts independently arrive at the same estimate based on the same assumptions, the estimate is likely to be correct. "The consensus approach helps eliminate bias in estimates produced by self-proclaimed experts, inexperienced estimators or influential individuals who have hidden agendas or divergent objectives" [3].

The important steps followed in the Wideband Delphi method are as follows:

- A set of experienced software professionals are identified who have participated in estimation-related activities in the past. Also identified is an estimation moderator.

- A copy of the requirements is provided to all the estimators. Also provided is a well-structured form that can capture details of the estimation and other related attributes.

- A preliminary meeting is organized where all the estimators could meet, discuss, and exchange views, assumptions, and other parameters that are applicable to the project that is being estimated.

- The estimators make a list of tasks and other artefacts that are likely to be generated during the project execution. Along with each task, including documentation if any, the estimated effort is recorded. The data is entered in the form provided for the purpose. The filled form is then handed over to the moderator.

- The moderator tabulates the data from all forms provided by the estimators, analyses them, generates the results, and gives them to the experts.

- The experts meet again to discuss the results. In the meeting, the experts review the tasks they have considered for the estimate, refine their individual estimates, and give the revised data to the moderator. This is repeated until there is convergence on the estimates by the different estimators.

- Typically convergence happens after two to three iterations. The decision to go through further iterations is taken based on the gap between the lowest and the highest estimates.

- Once the gap is reduced to a level comfortable for all estimators, the group arrives at a consensus figure for the final value.

A moderator who facilitates the group meeting session runs the estimating process. The basic assumption is that no one knows the right answer. Everyone has a partial view; and the purpose of the Delphi process is to share those views. By encouraging the participants to discuss the project tasks, a skilled moderator can facilitate very informative discussions.

The Bottom-Up Approach

Unlike the top-down approach where the data about the application, its modules, and programs are vaguely known, the bottom-up approach requires the information about the components being estimated at the most granular level. This means that it is essential that a detailed requirement gathering and analysis phase be completed before the bottom-up estimation approach is attempted.

In this approach, the project work is first divided into major modules. Each module is further divided into programs. The programs are further classified as simple, medium, or complex and the estimated effort to build each program is done based on past experience of similar projects. This method estimates each component of the software project separately and then combines the results to produce an estimate of the entire project. The estimation is performed when the requirements are clear or have been approved. The bottom-up approach method has certain advantages, such as

- It provides a more detailed and accurate basis for estimation, because it deals with low-level components.
- It supports project tracking more directly than other methods because its estimates usually address each activity within each phase of the software development lifecycle.

Some known disadvantages of this method are

- Bottom-up estimates can be done only after the requirements and design phases have been completed. This could mean that almost 35 percent of the project execution has already been completed even before estimation begins.
- Estimating the components at the granular level consumes significant time.

Simple, Medium, Complex Method (SMC)

One of the most popular estimation methods among software programmers is the Simple, Medium, Complex (SMC) estimation method.

Perhaps the popularity and easy acceptance of this method is due to a few reasons: The method is easy to understand, has few rules to follow, and is flexible enough to be adapted to any estimation situation. The dissection of the project being estimated happens in a top-down approach, but once all the modules, sub-modules, programs, and the last level of objects are identified, the actual estimates are done in a bottom-up approach. Having estimated the effort required to code each module in the application at the granular level, the individual estimates are aggregated upward. The effort estimates at the program and object level are both for coding as well as unit level testing activities. Once the overall code and unit test (build) efforts are obtained for all the programs and modules of the application, the estimates for the other lifecycle phase activities including requirements, design, system, and integration tests are obtained by extrapolating the build efforts. Typically the effort ratio between build and other lifecycle phases are calculated based on historic data as applicable to your own IT organization.

The SMC estimation is generally done after requirements analysis, which includes the design of the application. At this stage details of the project are known and requirements are well understood. The project work is first divided into major programs (or units). Each program is classified as simple, medium, or complex, and the build effort for each program is directly estimated based on past experience of similar projects. The effort for other stages of the project is estimated using the effort distribution on similar projects. Guidelines for classifying programs into simple, medium, complex (S/M/C) are provided by the technology experts within the company. The main data source for estimation is the process database and the process-capability baselines. The procedure for estimation includes the following steps:

- Study the requirements and design of the application and, using the top-down approach, identify modules, sub-modules, programs, objects, classes, and other attributes including screens, reports, and interfaces that are encompassed in the coding and testing activities.

- Classify the attributes into three major categories as simple, medium, or complex (S/M/C). It is essential a predefined guideline exists to identify an attribute as simple, medium, or complex. Remember that the guideline may vary based on the technology platform and other environmental aspects.

- Take into consideration other impacting factors that include the skills of the programmers, the development environment, and the complexity of the coding language to further refine the build and unit test effort for each program in the SMC category.

- Add all the individual build effort to arrive at the total build effort for the entire project. Add any overhead interfacing or integration effort that might have been left out.

- Extrapolate the total build effort into efforts for other lifecycle phases of the project on a predefined ratio basis. IT organizations typically collate historical data from previous projects. This information would be quite useful to arrive at the ratio between different lifecycle stages. If none is available, use a gut feel ratio of 1:2.5 between build and overall project effort. In other words, it is assumed that in a typical project execution situation the programmers are fairly competent to develop and deliver the project. And in this situation the build effort is generally around 40 percent of the overall project effort. As a result, to extrapolate the 40 percent build effort into total project effort, multiply the build effort by 2.5 to get the total project effort.

- The SMC estimation process is based on the assumption that the project will execute smoothly without any hiccups or change in requirements, design, and other performance parameters. But this is only wishful thinking. Refine the total effort estimates based on project-specific factors. "Take special care to factor in project-specific factors like expected volatility of requirements, clarity of requirements, degree of willingness of the customer to work with you to generate clarity of the requirements, etc" [4]. Ensure that you document all the assumptions made during the estimation process.

Parametric Approach

"Parametric estimates approximate the software delivered volume using a predictor that can be more easily determined earlier in the software lifecycle, called a metric" [5]. Researchers go through extensive and rigorous analysis of historic data from past projects and develop parametric models that can predict desired outputs. Estimation models that are developed based on a parametric approach typically encompass the complete project execution lifecycle activities as a whole. Basically these estimation models assist in sizing or defining the volume of the project itself. The sizing could be in various alternative units of measurement that include source lines of code (SLOC), function point count, effort, or duration in person hours and other similar units.

The following sections discuss some of the popular parametric approach-based estimation models that include COCOMO Model, and COSMIC-FFP. The Function Points Analysis method is another popular estimation method that is parametric approach based. The FPA method has been discussed quite extensively in earlier chapters; therefore it is not repeated here.

COCOMO II Model

The COnstructive COst MOdel (COCOMO) was first proposed by Barry W. Boehm in his book *Software Engineering Economics* in 1981. The most fundamental calculation in the COCOMO model is the use of the Effort Equation to estimate the number of person-months required to execute a software project. The other COCOMO results, like estimates of person requirements and schedule, are derived from this quantity.

$$EFFORT = A \times (SIZE) B$$

In this equation, A is proportionally constant and B represents economy or diseconomy of scale. B depends on the development mode. The estimate of a project's size is in source lines of code (SLOC). SLOC is defined such that

- Only source lines of code that are delivered as part of the product are included; test drivers and other support software are excluded.
- Source lines are created by the project staff; code created by applications generators is excluded.
- One instruction is one line of code.
- Declarations are counted as instructions.
- Comments are not counted as instructions.

The development mode is one of the most important factors that contribute to a project's duration and cost. It affects the economy and diseconomy of scale. Every project is considered to be developed in one of the three modes:

- *Organic Mode:* The project is developed in a familiar, stable environment, and the product is similar to previously developed products. The product is relatively small and requires little innovation. A simple accounting system is a good example of organic mode.

- *Semi-Detached Mode:* The project's characteristics are intermediate between organic and embedded modes.

- *Embedded Mode:* The project is characterized by tight, inflexible constraints and interface requirements. An embedded mode project will require a great deal of innovation. A real-time system with timing constraints and customized hardware is an example of an embedded mode.

COCOMO is defined in terms of three different models: the basic model, the intermediate model, and the detailed model. The more complex models account for more factors that influence software projects, and make more accurate estimates.

COCOMO II takes software size and a set of factors as input and estimates effort in person-months. Estimates from the basic COCOMO II model can be made more accurate by taking into account other factors concerning the required characteristics of the software to be developed, the qualification and experience of the development team, and the software development environment.

This is an advanced version of the old COCOMO model, and it is still being developed. Two versions of the COCOMO model have been developed to be used in two stages of software development. They are the early design model and the post-architectural model. Both use the following basic equation:

$$PM = 2.45 \times EAF \times (Size)^B$$

In this equation, EAF is effort adjustment factor. EAF is a product of 7 effort multipliers in the early design model and 17 in the post-architecture model. Effort multipliers are rated in one of the following categories: very low, low, nominal, high, very high, and extra high. Numeric weights are assigned to them based on their effect on development effort.

B is a scaling factor (1.01 to 1.26), representing diseconomies of scale.

B is given by

$$B = 1.01 + \Sigma \cdot W_i$$

$\Sigma \cdot W_i$ is the sum of five components, which affect economy of scale. They are also rated, and weights (0.00 to 0.05) are assigned to them.

NOTE The COCOMO II model has been covered very briefly and at a very high level here. For full details of the model and its variants, please refer to the book *Software Engineering Economics* by Barry Boehm.

COSMIC-FFP Method

COSMIC Full Function Points (FFP) was developed by the Common Software Measurement International Consortium (COSMIC). The consortium started in 1998 and the core group consists of 12 expert members from seven nations in Europe, America, and Asia-Pacific.

The first version of its method, COSMIC-FFP v2.0, was published in October 1999, as the first, true second-generation functional size measurement (FSM) method [6]. Extensive and successful field trials were carried out over 2000 and 2001. COSMIC published its latest definition of the method, v2.2, in January 2003. Later, the COSMIC-FFP method of sizing the functional requirements of software was approved as an International Standard (ISO/IEC 19761:2003).

The COSMIC-FFP method considers the measurement of the functional size of software through two distinct phases (see Figure 14.2):

- The mapping phase consists of the following tasks:
  - Identify software layers
  - Identify boundary
  - Identify triggering events and functional processes
  - Identify data groups
- The measurement phase consists of these tasks:
  - Identify data movements
  - Assign size units
  - Aggregate results

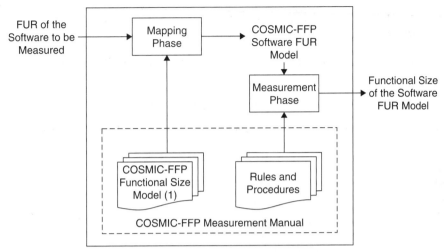

(1): *COSMIC-FFP functional size model includes concepts, definitions, and relationship of functional size attributes.*

Figure 14.2 *COSMIC-FFP: FUR.*

COSMIC-FFP method gives the size of software in terms of Cosmic Functional Size Unit (Cfsu). Use the productivity data for similar process types or projects to obtain the overall effort estimate. Overall effort estimate is the product of size (in Cfsu) and productivity (in person-hours/Cfsu).

A COSMIC-FFP data movement: moves one or more data attribute types belonging to a single data group type. There are four types of data movements:

- Entry
- Exit
- Read
- Write

An Entry (E) moves a data group type from a user across the boundary into the functional process type, where it is required.

An Exit (X) moves a data group type from a functional process across the boundary to the user that requires it.

A Read (R) moves a data group type from persistent storage within reach of the functional process that requires it.

A Write (W) moves a data group type inside a functional process to persistent storage.

A unit of measure is known as COSMIC Functional Size Unit = Cfsu.

The yardstick (by convention) to measure 1 Cfsu = 1 Data Movement.

Data movement types are: Entry (E), Exit (X), Read (R), and Write (W).

- Each added data movement receives 1 Cfsu.
- Each changed data movement receives 1 Cfsu.
- Each deleted data movement receives 1 Cfsu.

The size of a functional process is the sum of the number of data movements (Entries, Exits, and Reads, and Writes—see Figure 14.3).

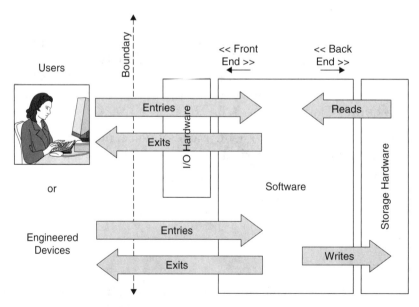

Figure 14.3 *COSMIC-FFP: Input/output identification.*

COSMIC-FFP is one simple model for both MIS and real-time software, in any layer or tier of a multi-tier architecture. This model can be applied at any time during the software development lifecycle. COSMIC-FFP is derived without reference to

- Effort
- Methods used
- Physical or technical components

COSMIC-FFP has not yet been designed to take into account the functional size of software or its parts, which are characterized by complex mathematical algorithms or other specialized and complex rules, such as those that may be found in

- Expert systems
- Simulation software
- Self-learning software
- Weather forecasting systems
- Processing of continuous variables, such as audio sounds or video images, etc.

NOTE The COSMIC-FFP model has been covered here only briefly and at a very high level. For full details of the model and its variants, please refer to the *Cosmic Measurement Manual* at www.cosmicon.com.

Estimation Models Pros and Cons

As discussed earlier in this chapter, different estimation models were designed by experts to meet estimation requirements. Different models also were developed in different time periods because software engineering itself was evolving. Table 14.1 provides a brief comparison enumerating the advantages and disadvantages of a few popular estimation methods.

Table 14.1 *Pros and Cons of Various Estimation Models*

Estimation Method	Applicable Stages	Advantages	Disadvantages
Function Point	Requirements to Testing	Confidence level of the estimate is higher. Estimate based on user perspective of the system. Function points are independent of the language, methodologies, or tools used for implementation. Non-technical users have a better understanding of what function points are measuring because function points are based on the user's external view of the system.	Depends on the subjective weight given by the estimator. Needs trained person to do it. Counting the function points needed for FPA remains largely a manual operation. Measuring rules and business logic is more complex.
COCOMO II	High Level Requirements	COCOMO II model not only can use source lines of code (SLOC), but also can use object points, unadjusted function points as metrics for sizing a project. Basic COCOMO II is good for quick, early, rough order of magnitude estimates of software costs.	Local calibration needed for accuracy. In early phase of system lifecycle, the size is estimated with great uncertainty value. Its accuracy is necessarily limited because of lack of factors that have a significant influence on software costs.

Table 14.1 *Pros and Cons of Various Estimation Models (Continued)*

Estimation Method	Applicable Stages	Advantages	Disadvantages
COSMIC-FFP	High Level Requirements	Usable for both MIS applications as well as real-time applications. Simple to use. No subjectivity in determining the model elements.	Benchmark data is not currently available. International acceptance is limited but growing.
Wideband Delphi Technique	Pre-requirements, Proposal	Useful in absence of quantified, empirical data. Can factor in differences between past project experiences and requirements of the proposed project. It has a high customization value specific to the organization taking reuse into account.	Estimate is only as good as the expert's opinion. Requires multiple experts to do the estimates. Hard to document the factors used by the experts and does not define a process for individuals to follow when estimating. It is a time-consuming process.
SMC (Simple, Medium, Complex Method)	End of Design	Easy to understand and use; program perspective. Can also be used for estimating enhancements and maintenance work.	The criteria and effort for SMC may not be consistent across users. Only experts on technology can do decent SMC estimates.

Conclusion

Software project estimation approaches and estimation models derived from various approaches have been in existence for several decades now. Different software project situations will require different estimation methods. Perhaps this is the point of contention—which estimation method should you use? My suggestions would be as follows:

- Ensure that you or your team identify an estimator who has a fairly good understanding of software engineering and software project execution processes.

- If you (the estimator) have not estimated software projects in the past, perhaps it would be a good idea to do a couple of estimation exercises, using simple estimation approaches like the SMC method. This will help you understand and fine-tune various aspects and attributes of the estimation process.

- Analyze estimation needs of your project team and your IT organization (if applicable) and classify them into typical software projects like development, maintenance, enhancement, reengineering, and migration.

- Obtain the assistance of an estimation expert to help you in identifying the right estimation model(s) to suit your software project estimation requirements.

- If possible, get your team trained on the selected estimation methods, through the help of the estimation expert or training vendors.

- Start with a couple of pilot estimations to fine-tune the estimation process. When you are comfortable, deploy the estimation method(s) for future projects.

While choosing an estimation method, explore the history of how the method evolved and how long it has been in existence. Look also at the support of the method by international committee or other bodies. Also check the kind of regression analysis that has been done on past project data before arriving at the selected model.

References

1.   Boehm, Barry W., Chris Abts, and Chulani Sunita. "Software Development Cost Estimation Approaches—A Survey." Barry Boehm, Chris Abts, University of Southern California, Los Angeles, CA

90089–0781 and Sunita Chulani, IBM Research, 650 Harry Road, San Jose, CA 95120.

2. International Function Point Users Group (IFPUG). *Function Point Counting Practices Manual (CPM) Release 4.2.*

3. Wiegers, Karl E. "Stop Promising Miracles." *Software Development*, Vol. 8, No. 2; February 2000. Pp. 49–54.

4. R. Agarwal, Manish Kumar, Yogesh, S. Mallick, R.M. Bharadwaj, and D. Anantwar. "Estimating Software Projects." Infosys Technologies Limited, IIM, *ACM SIGSOFT—Software Engineering Notes.* Vol. 24, No. 4; July 2001. Pg. 60.

5. Ibid.

6. COSMIC-FFP, Version 2. The Common Software Measurement International Consortium (COSMIC). www.cosmicon.com

Other Interesting Reading Material

McConnell, Steve. "Expert Judgment in Groups," in *Software Estimation—Demystifying the Black Art.* Microsoft Press, 2006. Pp. 149–155.

IFPUG. *IT Measurement: Practical Advice from the Experts.* Addison-Wesley, 2002.

Park, Robert E., et al. "Checklists and Criteria for Evaluating the Costs and Schedule Estimating Capabilities of Software Organizations." *Technical Report CMU/SEI 95-SR-005*; Software Engineering Institute; January 1995.

Putnam, Lawrence H. *Measures for Excellence.* Prentice Hall, 1992.

Putnam, Lawrence H., and Ware Myers. *Industrial Strength Software.* IEEE Press, 1997.

Roetzheim, William H., and Reyna A. Beasley. *Best Practices in Software Cost and Schedule Estimation.* Prentice Hall, 1998.

CHAPTER 15

Estimation Tools

Why Use Tools?

IT managers often expect a good estimation tool to solve their estimation deployment problems across the developer community. Simply acquiring a good software estimation tool does not guarantee good software estimates. If the quality of input to the estimation tool is poor, then poor estimates will result; this is what's known as the Garbage In = Garbage Out (GIGO) principle. You may have a high-powered Harley Davidson motorcycle, but unless you know how to drive it and you also know the roads, you may not be able to move any faster than you would if you were driving an ordinary motorcycle.

While discussing some popular estimation tools in her article, "Software Project Estimation," Kathleen Peters warns us to be alert to claims by software tool vendors. "No estimation tool is the 'silver bullet' for solving your estimation problems. They can be very useful items in your estimation toolkit, and you should seriously consider using one (or more), but their output is only as good as the inputs they are given and they require you to have an estimation and software development process in place to support them" [1].

Getting good estimates requires collecting, refining, and maintaining historical data from current and past projects to provide the necessary inputs required for the software estimation tools. An estimation tool will be a very handy tool to someone who knows how to estimate. If the estimator is experienced working with software engineering, domains, and technology, he or she would be able to extract maximum benefit even from a fairly decent estimation tool.

Evolution of Estimation Tools

For more than four decades now, experts on software engineering have been conceptualizing and developing early versions of estimation tools. The goal was to arrive at estimates of consistent accuracy through a better defined and more consistent software estimation process. These tools were developed based on historical data collated from several thousands of software projects, as well as research of critical components that feed into industry standards as well as proprietary estimation methods.

Lack of consistent and reliable historical data slowed down the progress of tools developed in the early '70s. As more data became available, however, estimation tools progressively improved, and they have continued to evolve. Most software estimation tools use algorithms based on reliable models, and some of the more advanced tools are rule-based or knowledge-based as well as interactive.

Ingredients of a Good Estimation Tool

If you intend to buy a good estimation tool from the market, make sure that you have done your homework thoroughly. Other than certain basic and mandatory estimation-related features, a large number of organization-specific requirements need to be met in an estimation tool. The tool evaluation procedure should cover these aspects.

Here are some of the key functional capabilities that should be considered when selecting a software estimation tool:

- *True Adoption of Estimation Method:* The estimation tool should truly adopt the estimation method that you intend to deploy in your organization. Localization and variation of the estimation method itself should not be allowed. For example, if you intend to procure a function point based or COCOMO II based estimation tool, ensure that the tool fully reflects all the processes as defined by the authors of the selected estimation method.

- *Customizable:* This feature will give the true flexibility of configuring the tool to suit your organization data with minimum data entry and manipulation overheads. The customization feature will help the estimator to define applicable input and map it to the estimation method-based data requirements. An important benefit would be the blending of the organization's historical data with current project data to generate software estimates. The SEI CMMI estimation process recommends estimation improvements through analysis of historic estimation data.

- *Facilitate Intelligent Estimates:* The tool should have built-in intelligence to be able to generate estimates early in the project lifecycle, even when data on project scope and technology platform is yet to be fully defined. As the project execution completes each lifecycle stage, the tool should allow the user to add or update data incrementally and thus provide updated estimates with a higher degree of accuracy. The project risks and probability of completing the rest of project lifecycle phases should be dynamically revised based on data fed up to that point.

- *End-to-End Estimates:* The tool should go beyond software sizing estimates. Based on input that includes resource rates and predefined resource loading patterns, the tool should be able to provide an overall project cost.

- *Estimates for Variety of Projects:* The tool should support the estimation needs for projects like maintenance, migrations, reengineering, and porting and package implementation over and above new development projects.

- *Maximum Utilization of Features:* Tools that brand themselves as having "mind-blowing features" are rarely fully utilized by the buyer. Out of a large variety of features provided by the tool, the user is only able to take advantage of an estimated 30 to 35 percent of the features. The rest of the features are not of interest to the user. On the other hand, the user may have a need for a different set of features that the tool does not provide.

  While evaluating the tool for features, do not forget to do a features-versus-needs match and also to watch for features that are not of use to you. Do not land yourself in a situation where you do half the work through the tool, do the rest manually, and then spend even more time connecting and analyzing the two outputs.

- *Good-to-Have Features:* The tool should have some of the basic features that would be expected in a good quality tool. These features include

  - Facilitate "what if" analysis based on different scenarios the user could provide as input
  - Provide good documentation
  - Provide multi-lingual support

- Facilitate interfacing with other tools and applications through some commonly used interface protocols like XML
- Facilitate ease of use through good GUI features and online help features

- *Officially Certified Tool:* If an organized body or a committee that owns the estimation method exists, verify that the tool is formally certified by this body. For example, if you are procuring a function point estimation tool, this should be certified by IFPUG [2].

The IT management should evaluate available tools in the market and choose the tool that best suits the IT environment in their organization. This section does not discuss the cost aspects of the tool because normally this is organization-specific and depends on the budgeting provided internally.

A few other critical parameters will help you assess estimation as well. These parameters are specific to the estimation process that has been approved and deployed in your IT organization. As an individual, you can choose the parameters with which you are most comfortable. Table 15.1 provides a closer look at the parameters involved in estimation.

Deploying Estimation Tools in IT Organizations

IT organizations are under constant pressure to improve the quality of software project executions and the output delivered. Typically, the IT management strategizes the process improvements in a phase-wise manner. If the IT organization has plans to implement the SEI-CMMI quality process, the phase-wise quality process improvements would be focused on achieving the next level of accreditation (Level 1 to Level 5). Improving estimation process is one of the key factors in these process improvement strategies. IT organizations sometimes decide to a procure a popular estimation tool from the market and deploy it across the organization in order to overcome the pressure to move to a higher level of quality processes implementation. Unless this move is backed with the appropriate level of maturity in measurement processes and also metrics collection and analysis processes in the organization, simply deploying an estimation tool may be a disaster.

Table 15.1 *Critical Parameters Desired in Estimation Tools*

Feature	*Description*	*Criticality*
Project Type Selection	Development, maintenance, enhancement, migration, porting, etc.	High
Calibration/ Standard	IFPUG, COCOMO II, NESMA, Parametric, Monte Carlo	High
Sizing Method	SLOC, Function Points, COCOMO II, UML Use Case, Object Points, etc.	High
Lifecycle Selection	Waterfall, iterative, etc.	Low
Programming Language Selection	At least 20+ popular languages	Medium
Maintaining Historic Data	Build repository of completed projects resulting in more accurate estimates	High
What-if Scenarios	Analyze different scenarios, such as whether to have a highly skilled team instead of a less experienced team, etc.	Medium
Track Scope Creep	Ability to track and flag changes in functional scope during project progress updates	Medium
Constraints and Priorities	Provision to identify constraints and priorities that map to project execution plan	Medium
Selection of Relevant Projects from Your History for Customized Estimates	Characteristics like efficiency, staffing, reliability, phase customization, etc., will be transferred to new estimate	Medium
Storage of Metrics and Data Analysis	Store quality metrics including effort and schedule variance, defects, and other overheads	Medium
Integrated Reporting	Flexible reporting features	Medium
Interface to Other Tools and Applications	Interface Microsoft Office and Web through protocols like XML for easy collaboration and sharing	Medium

Deployment of estimation practices supported by the right estimation tool should be a step-by-step process. Some of the critical steps to be followed include

- *As-Is Analysis:* The first step is to conduct an internal survey across all the IT groups, collating relevant information on project execution processes and estimation methods used. Analyze the information and identify key gaps that are estimation-related.

- *"To Be" Strategy:* In consultation with top management and other estimation and quality experts, define the To Be plan with respect to estimation deployment across the organization. This strategy should include key aspects such as

  - Setting up software measurement processes if not already done

  - Deployment of metrics collection processes

  - Training and enabling key software managers and estimators on some of the popular estimation methods as applicable to the IT organization

  - Process to evaluate and select the right estimation tool that suits the organization's IT environment

- *Pilot Project:* Once the IT organization is enabled on quality processes that include measurement and metrics collection processes, it is time to evaluate and choose a couple of tools from the market for pilot tests. Select a couple of project situations and pilot the tool.

- *Feedback and Analysis:* The feedback from the users of the estimation tool from the pilot projects, as well as the technical and feature evaluation done by estimation and quality experts within the IT organization would help determine tool procurement.

The pilot project test and the feedback will provide key insights into the probability of successful deployment of the estimation tool in the IT organization. More than testing the capabilities of the tool itself, the pilot process will test the deployment status of other quality processes. It will also help you understand the acceptance of estimation tools by the software community in your organization.

List of Tools

Table 15.2 provides a select list of tools that are popular in the software estimation community. Each tool has been designed with a specific estimation method and a specific output as an objective.

Table 15.2 *List of Popular Estimation Tools*

Tool	Features and Owner	Methods
Construx Estimate	Construx Estimate leverages a blend of proven estimation models to predict effort, budget, and schedule for software projects based on size estimates. The estimate comes calibrated with industry data, but is more effective when calibrated with your organization's data. http://www.construx.com/estimate/	Utilizes Monte Carlo simulation with two estimation models (Putnam Model and COCOMO)
Costar	Costar is a cost estimation tool that supports COCOMO II (and its variants), REVIC, and Ada. Costar is an interactive tool that permits managers to make trade-offs and what-if analyses to arrive at the optimal project plan. http://www.softstarsystems.com/	Parametric, COCOMO
Cost Xpert	Cost Xpert is a software cost estimating tool that integrates multiple estimating models into one tool to provide accurate and comprehensive estimates. It claims to be the only tool offering support for sophisticated modeling techniques, such as system dynamic modeling, knowledge-based modeling, both scholastic and deterministic modeling, and a variety of cost models including the latest release of COCOMO II. http://www.costxpert.com/	Parametric, Stochastic, System Dynamic, Knowledge-based, Database

(Continued)

Table 15.2 *List of Popular Estimation Tools (Continued)*

Tool	Features and Owner	Methods
Function Point WORKBENCH	Charismatek's Function Point WORKBENCH is a tool that expedites function point analysis by providing facilities to store, update, and analyze individual counts. FPW provides intuitive graphical support for the counting process of a base system or an enhancement to an existing application. http://www.charismatek.com.au/	Supports FP model by IFPUG and NESMA
KnowledgePLAN	SPR KnowledgePLAN provides a complete and rational view of all trade-offs among features, schedules, quality, and costs. You can explore the cost/value implications of additional resources, more powerful languages, development tools, improved methods, and other technical changes. You can also track milestones, schedules, resources, actual work effort, and defects found. http://www.spr.com/	Function Points by IFPUG
PRICE-S	True S and PRICE S estimate costs, resources, and schedules for software projects of all types—such as business systems, communications, command and control, avionics and space systems—and all sizes, from software components to extremely complex systems such as those deployed in mission-critical vehicles. http://www.pricesystems.com/	Function Points by IFPUG, Rigorous Monte Carlo or Latin Hypercube simulation for cost-risk analysis

Table 15.2 *List of Popular Estimation Tools (Continued)*

Tool	Features and Owner	Methods
SEER-SEM	Galorath's SEER-SEM is a decision-support tool that estimates the cost, labor, staffing, schedule, reliability, and risk for all types of software development and/or maintenance projects http://www.galorath.com/	Parametric
SLIM-Estimate	The Software Life-cycle Management (SLIM) tool for software cost estimating (SLIM-Estimate), provides features that include reliability modeling, schedule estimating, planning, tracking, and benchmarking. http://www.qsm.com/	Parametric

Conclusion

Tools are meant to improve the quality and productivity of any process. Estimation tools no doubt provide significant benefits to software project estimators. When used with the right input, the tools can provide a wide variety of output that can act as a decision support mechanism. There are many situations in IT organizations where estimation tools can bring immense value, including

- During software project proposal stage
- At the beginning of the project execution
- At every project execution milestone stage
- At every stage when changes in project scope or requirements occur
- At the completion of the project

As a general suggestion, however, I would caution you, as an estimator, not to jump into tool-based estimations too early in the game. Practice a few estimations manually first. Once you are comfortable with manual estimations, the next step is to develop your own estimation tool with some of the basic features. Tools like Microsoft Excel would be quite suitable for in-house estimation tool development. Once you are comfortable with the estimation process as well as the use of in-house tools, you can go for robust, tested, and market-approved tools.

References

1. Peters, Kathleen. *Software Project Estimation*. Software Productivity Centre Inc., Canada.

2. International Function Point Users Group (IFPUG). *Function Point Counting Practices Manual (CPM) Release 4.2*.

Other Interesting Reading Material

McConnell, Steve. "Software Estimation Tools," in *Software Estimation: Demystifying the Black Art*. Redmond, WA: Microsoft Press, 2006. Pp 157–164.

CHAPTER 16

Estimation Case Study

Introduction

The proof of the pudding is in the eating.

Estimators commonly attend professional training courses as a part of continuous enhancement of their skills in various areas. A professional trainer prepares well and ensures that the training sessions are conducted in a planned manner, perhaps following the pedagogic method of teaching. After the classes are over, estimators are thrilled to have acquired new knowledge through which they can go and conquer the world. But when they decide to try out the learning on a few immediate estimation assignments, the problems begin. I have often observed that while the instructor explains the tricks of the trade, it looks quite easy to understand. But when I am back at my desk and start working on a live problem using the same tricks taught by the instructor, all hell breaks loose!

This chapter has been developed keeping in mind the difficulties faced by estimators during live estimation situations. Though I do not claim to have answers for the entire spectrum of practical situations you may encounter, I have attempted to pick a variety of estimation problems and have worked out solutions for them.

Basic Assumptions

Before discussing the case study contents, I feel it would be appropriate to set the context for certain basic assumptions. These assumptions are generally applicable to all the exercises discussed here, unless a specific variation is mentioned.

- *Business Functions:* The different exercises here address a variety of business situations. A particular business workflow area in a large business industry may be selected, but the example will discuss only a very small component of the business. It should not be assumed that the example actually simulates the real-life business situation. When you attempt to capture business functions for a live case that you are working on, identify the right set of workflow procedures for the application you are counting.

- *Application Implementation Elements:* The number of (data entry) screens, reports, queries, and other implementation elements like the data model will be symbolically assumed. Also assumed will be the number of data elements (fields/columns) for each of the screens, reports, and tables. You may want to take your project requirement specifications as input for your counting purposes. Ensure that the specifications, including critical data elements, are actually verified and approved by the user.

- *Programmer Productivity:* Some examples here convert the size of the project in function points to effort in person months. An assumed productivity of the project team will be used for this conversion. This productivity may not be applicable to your organization. You may have to use data as applicable from your organization. If productivity data for your organization or project team does not exist, you may want to look at some of the industry standard productivity figures available in the public domain (www.isbsg.com).

- *Project Environment:* The standard project environment that includes the tools for coding, testing, and other project execution purposes is assumed to be available to the project team. Identify the tools and other environment complexities existing in your organization and accordingly adjust the productivity of the project team.

- *Application Performance Requirements:* Normal performance requirements are assumed for all applications unless otherwise specified. If there are instances of high performance needs in your project, this requirement may either be reflected in the calculations of general system characteristics (GSCs) or through a reduced productivity of the project team due to complex design, complex algorithms, extensive coding, and testing requirements.

Figure 16.1 provides a quick reference to various components of a function point counting process.

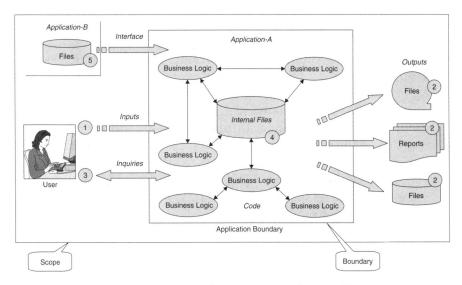

Figure 16.1 *Scope, boundary, and components of an application.*

Step-by-Step FP Counting Process (Development Projects)

Here are the main steps that you need to follow diligently if you want to obtain accurate FP sizing as well as derived effort and delivery schedule for software development projects.

- *Step 1:* Identify all the stakeholders, users, and other people who are likely to be either directly or indirectly associated with this module. This will help in better understanding the actual needs (requirements) of end users.

- *Step 2:* Identify the business entities. Based on the detailed specifications prepared earlier, determine the various category of information required to be stored, processed, and maintained through this module. Examples of information category could be the business functions, business entities, business processing rules, business workflow, and the input/output necessary for the software project under consideration (for example, Employee, Supplier, Customer, etc.).

- *Step 3:* Identify data items. Now convert the information to be processed into data items. Not all details of data items will be available in the specifications. It is the job of the designer to evaluate ingredients of the information that has to be processed and identify data items accordingly. For example, information regarding an entity "employee" may typically consist of data items (data elements) like employee number, employee name, personal details, professional experience details, educational qualification details, and dependent details.

- *Step 4:* Group data items into entities. Now comes the difficult step—grouping the data items into user identifiable business entities. Remember that each group of data items has to holistically encompass all information related to the identified business entity. The grouping has to be done with utmost care because this grouping will decide the identification of data files, Internal Logical File and External Interface File (ILF/EIF), as well as the Record Element Type (RET) within data files. (See items 4 and 5 in Figure 16.1. These items will be clear shortly when you learn about the business entities of the Invoice module.)

- *Step 5:* Identify the data functions (files, ILF/EIF, etc.) that are required to accommodate the groups of data items identified in Step 4. One or more groups of data items may together form one single data file. Also determine whether the data files thus identified are within the application boundary or external to the boundary. The findings can be explained as follows:

  - The data files identified within the boundary of the application are the ILF.

  - The data files outside the boundary are the EIF, and it will be assumed that these data files are maintained as ILF by another external application.

  - All the data items (fields/columns) are actually the Data Element Type (DET).

  - If more than one group of data items (DET) is identified within the same data file, these groups are identified as multiple record element type (RET).

  - Determine the number of DET and RET that exist in each of ILF/EIF by following the rules explained in Chapter 4.

  - Determine the complexity factor (low, average, and high) from Table 4.1 in Chapter 4, "Data Functions," based on number of DET and RET counted for each ILF/EIF.

  - Using the complexity factor, for each ILF, find the FP contribution (unadjusted FP count) from Table 4.2 in Chapter 4.

  - Using the complexity factor, for each EIF, find the FP contribution (unadjusted FP count) from Table 4.3 in Chapter 4.

  - Add FP contribution for all ILF and EIF to get the total unadjusted FP count for Data Transactions.

- *Step 6:* Identify the transaction functions (input/output transactions) that are required to input, process, output, and maintain information available in the data files that are associated with the application. Classify the transaction functions based on the type of information processing being done. The following steps explain the rules.
  - Ascertain that the identified transactions are outside the boundary of the application but within the scope of application. Figure 16.1 differentiates between application scope and application boundary.
  - The IFPUG FPA method recognizes three types of transactions: External Inputs (EI), External Outputs (EO) and External Inquiries (EQ). Refer to items 1, 2, and 3 in Figure 16.1. Determine whether the transaction is an EI, EO, or EQ based on the processing logic required by the user.
  - *External Input (EI):* This transaction function facilitates maintenance of data in internal data files (ILF). EI sometimes references (read-only) data from external interface files (EIF).
  - *External Output (EO):* This transaction function facilitates report generation based on information stored in internal data files (ILF) as well as external interface files (EIF).
  - *External Inquiry (EQ):* This transaction function facilitates user queries on the data stored in internal data files (ILF) as well as external interface files (EIF).
  - Determine the number of DET and FTR that exist in each of EI/EO/EQ by following the rules explained earlier in Chapter 5, "Transactional Functions".
  - Determine the complexity factor (simple, average, high) from Table 5.1 and Table 5.2 in Chapter 5, based on number of DET and FTR counted for each EI/EO/EQ.
  - Using the complexity factor, for each EI, find the FP contribution (unadjusted FP count) from Table 5.3 in Chapter 5.
  - Using the complexity factor, for each EO/EQ, find the FP contribution (unadjusted FP count) from Table 5.4 in Chapter 5.
  - Add FP contribution for all EI/EO/EQ to get the total unadjusted FP count for transactional functions.
- *Step 7:* Aggregate the data function FP count and the transaction function FP count to obtain the total unadjusted FP count.
- *Step 8:* Obtain the degree of influence rating for each of the 14 General System Characteristics (GSC) as explained in Chapter 6, "General

System Characteristics." Convert the total degree of influence value to Value Adjustment Factor (VAF). Multiply the unadjusted FP count with VAF to obtain the adjusted FP count.

- *Step 9:* Transform the adjusted FP count into the total effort required to execute the software project. This can be achieved by obtaining the delivery rate (productivity) of the project team and then multiplying the adjusted FP count with productivity. The effort thus obtained will encompass all the project execution lifecycle activities that include requirements, design, build (construction) and unit tests, and system and integration tests. The effort may or may not include project management effort, depending on the particular productivity baseline.

- *Step 10:* The total effort now needs to be adjusted to a project delivery schedule. There are methods available to do the conversion. COCOMO II is one such popular method. The delivery schedule (duration or elapsed time) obtained may sometimes need to be refined based on user needs.

- *Step 11:* Transform the total effort obtained in Step 9 into a resource loading chart. This step is significant in the sense that assigning the appropriate resource with the right skills for the appropriate lifecycle phase of the project is critical for the success of the project.

NOTE The various data elements that are being assumed in the following sections are for demonstration purposes only. Discussions on why certain data elements are required or not required are out of the scope of this book. You may want to identify your actual data elements and other project parameters based on actual requirements approved by the user. It is also assumed here that the requirements have already been done in consultation with the user and detailed specification (or Use Cases) documents have been prepared.

Case Study 1: Invoicing System

Fast Cars is an automobile dealership. The dealer has been in business for the last 20+ years and has its headquarters in Paris (France) and dealerships in France as well as across the U.S. and Europe. Fast Cars has a history of strategic relationship with Speed Motors Company, the leading automobile manufacturer in Europe. The dealer has grown organically, from a single dealership outlet in France to outlets across Europe and the U.S. Over the years it has also added other services to customers that include

- After-sales service facilities
- Spare parts sales
- Facilitating bank loans to customers
- Used cars buy-back program

Having established itself as a trusted partner to its customers as well as Speed Motors, Fast Cars has a respectable presence in most locations. The company has created partnerships with local banks to provide soft loans to its customers. Figure 16.2 shows a high-level structure of various workflow processes that happen in the dealer's organization.

The management of Fast Cars has a need to freshly develop an automated invoicing application. The implementation of the invoicing application is envisioned as done in phases. As a pilot, only the main dealership office in central Paris has been identified for implementation. All processing will be limited only to one dealership center. In later phases this is planned to be extended to other dealers' offices across Europe and then the U.S.

The invoicing system needs to be structured functionally and the top-level modules that need to be developed must be identified. For each of

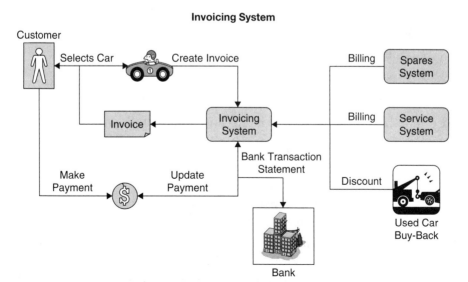

Figure 16.2 *Invoicing workflow.*

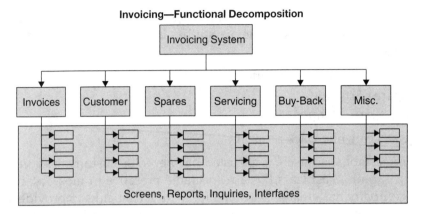

Figure 16.3 *Invoicing modules.*

the modules, you will then identify various inputs, outputs, inquiries, and data storage requirements that can then be evaluated for project sizing purposes.

The invoicing system will broadly have the following modules that have been envisioned based on the high-level business process workflow provided by the client. Figure 16.3 provides a high-level structure of the sub-modules.

- Invoices
- Customer
- Spares
- Servicing
- Buy-back
- Miscellaneous

The actual business workflow is explained in the following scenario:

- *Scenario 1: Buy a new car*
  - *Activity 1:* Customer (prospective car buyer) arrives at the dealer's showroom and identifies a car for possible purchase. The customer relationship process begins. The customer's personal details are recorded through the Customer module.
  - *Activity 2:* The sales executive prepares details of the costing for the car and other attachments/fittings. The details are provided to the accounts person, who in turn prepares the draft invoice for the car. The invoice is generated through the Invoices module.

- *Activity 3:* The sales executive determines whether the customer has an old car that the he or she may want to trade in order to receive a discount on the new car. If this is true, the price for the old car is negotiated. The details of the old car and the price negotiated are recorded through the Buy-Back module. Also the negotiated price is automatically updated in the draft Invoice against provision made for discounts.

- *Activity 4:* Customer makes payment toward the final deal. The payment received is updated in the above Invoice.

- *Scenario 2: Service a car*

  - *Activity 1:* Customer brings his or her car for servicing. The service attendant takes possession of the car, inspects the car, and prepares a service schedule using the Servicing module.

  - *Activity 2:* Upon completion of the servicing of the car, the service mechanic prepares the detailed list of servicing activities and use of spare parts, if any. The servicing invoice is then prepared using the Servicing module. Details of parts including the part number, unit rates, and quantity are all obtained from the Spares module.

  - *Activity 3:* The serviced car is delivered to the customer (owner). Payment is received and updated on the servicing Invoice.

Invoice Module

The Invoice module is the heart of this invoicing system. This module will facilitate some of the major invoicing, payment, and other related business functions for the Fast Cars automobile dealer. The list of business functions that are supported by the invoice module are

- *Invoicing:* Create, update, query, and delete invoices
- *Bank Advice:* Generate advice data to be sent to the bank
- *Reports:* Generate Invoice-related daily and periodic reports

This case study uses the Function Point Analysis estimation method. Based on the various input and output parameters shown in Figure 16.4 for the Invoice module, you can identify all five parameters of a typical FPA estimation method; EI, EO, EQ, ILF, and EIF. This section provides details of each of the sub-modules by evaluating the individual data elements that need to be maintained for an invoice.

You can use the FP counting steps described earlier in this chapter as a guide to arrive at the FP count, overall effort, and schedule, as well as resource loading details.

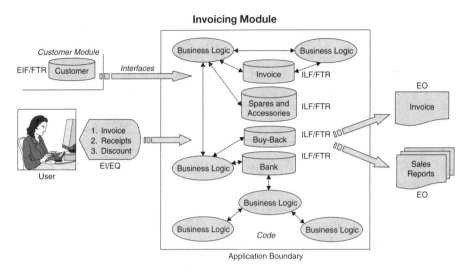

Figure 16.4 *Invoicing module attributes.*

Step 1: Identify Stakeholders

The stakeholders for the invoicing application can be broadly identified as follows:

- *Customer:* The buyer of the car and other accessories from the dealer.
- *Dealer:* The Fast Cars dealer who issues the invoice to the customer.
- *Accounts Department:* The accounts department requires information on assets (Car and Spares) sold against revenue earned.
- *Bank:* The bank to which the dealer sends the customer for possible financing of the car and also regular bank advice on daily payments received etc. is sent by the dealer.
- *Sales Executive:* The sales executives need to meet sales targets. The invoice data provides direct inputs to sales figures achieved.
- *Storekeeper:* The spares and accessories store personnel need to keep track of various spares and accessories sold to the customer.
- *Buy-Back Agency:* The buy-back agency (sometimes external) needs to incorporate their transactions into the invoicing application in order to adjust the discount offered to the customer who is trading the old automobile for the new purchase.

The process of identifying the stakeholders will help you begin visualizing the various pieces of information required to be maintained through the invoice application. Additionally, you will begin to understand the various transactions and reports that need to be incorporated into the application.

Steps 2 and 3: Identify Category of Information and Data Items

Having identified the stakeholders in Step 1, you can now work toward various categories of information that need to be processed through the invoice application. The requirement specification document will provide the key input. You can assume the following data items:

- *Invoice Information:* Details about the invoice that include
  - *Invoice Generic Information:* Invoice Number, Invoice Date, Customer Name, Customer Address (Door #, Street, Locality, State, Country, ZIP Code, Contact Numbers), Invoice Amount, Tax Percentage and Tax Amount, Discount Amount, Payment Date, Amount Received, and Payment Mode
  - *Invoice Items Information:* Item Code, Item Description, Item Category, Item Quantity, and Item Rate
  - *Customer Information:* Data items about the customer, including Customer Code, Customer Name, Customer Profession, Customer Address (Door #, Street, Locality, State, Country, ZIP Code, Contact Numbers), and Car Preferences (Cost, Capacity, and Color)
- *Dealer Information:* Data items about the automotive dealer, including Dealer Code, Dealer Location, Dealer Capacity (automobiles), Servicing Facilities, Spares and Accessories Capacity, and Sales Capacity (Revenue)
- *Accounts Information:* Account Code, Account Name, Amount, Transaction Date, and Transaction Type (Cr/Dr)
- *Bank Information:* Bank Code, Bank Name, Bank Address (Door #, Street, Locality, State, Country, ZIP Code, and Contact Numbers)
- *Sales Executive Information:* Data items about the sales executive include Sales Executive Code, Sales Executive Name, Sales Executive Designation, Sales Executive Address (Door #, Street, Locality, State, Country, ZIP Code, and Contact Numbers), Sales Executive Salary, Sales Target, Target Period, and Current Sales Status
- *Stores Information:* Store Code, Item Code, Item Name, Item Stock Quantity, Item Bin Code, and Item Re-order Level
- *Buy-Back Information:* This facility is not planned for the current development project. It is likely to be added as an enhancement later.

Steps 4 and 5: Identify Data Functions (Data Files: ILF/EIF)

Based on the broad categorization of information that is required to be stored, processed, and output through the invoice application (as specified in Steps 2 and 3), you can now identify various files (ILF/EIF) that are required to be designed for data input/output purposes.

- *Invoice Information:* Typically every invoice will consist of only one invoice header information record (generic information) and one or more invoice item records. Table 16.1 provides details about every data element (field) required in each of the files and further identifies record element type (RET) as appropriate.

Table 16.1 *Invoice Information DET and RET Count*

Information Item	Data Elements	DET Count
Invoice Generic Information (RET 1)	Invoice Number, Invoice Date, Customer Name, Customer Address (Door #, Street, Locality, State, Country, ZIP Code, Contact Numbers (2)), Dealer Code, Sales Executive Code, Invoice Amount	14
Invoice Items Information (RET 2)	Item Code, Item Description, Item Category, Item Quantity, Item Rate	5

- Follow IFPUG rules and determine whether each item in the preceding group is an ILF or EIF. The analysis of invoice information is given in Table 16.2.

Table 16.2 *Invoice Information ILF Identification*

ILF Identification Rule	Does the Rule Apply?
The group of data or control information is logical and user identifiable.	Yes. The complete data information of the Invoice together with Item details is user identifiable.
The group of data is maintained through an elementary process within the application boundary being counted.	Yes. The elementary process maintains the Invoice and Item Details data.

- Based on this analysis, the Invoice information, maintained within the boundary of the application being counted, is identified as an ILF.

- Note: Table 16.2 (taken from IFPUG CPM 4.2) will not be repeated again for the following ILF/EIF. This method will be used, however. Return to Table 16.2 to review as needed.

- The exact FP contribution for Invoice ILF can now be evaluated as shown in Table 16.3 using the contribution figures provided by IFPUG. Refer to Tables B.1 through B.7 in Appendix B, "Reference Tables: Data Function Points."

Table 16.3 *Invoice ILF Unadjusted FP Count*

Entity	File	RET	DET	Complexity	Unadjusted FP Count
Invoice	ILF	2	19 (14 + 5)	Average	10

- *Customer Information:* Two kinds of information need to be stored in the customer file: the customer personal information, and the customer preferences of cars and other special vehicles. Typically each set of customer information can have one or more car preferences. It is assumed that the Customer module exists as a separate application and it will now be integrated with the Invoice application. Table 16.4 provides more detail on the various data elements.

Table 16.4 *Customer Information DET and RET Count*

Information Item	Data Elements	DET Count
Customer Generic Information (RET 1)	Customer Code, Customer Name, Customer Profession, Customer Address (Door #, Street, Locality, State, Country, ZIP Code, Contact Numbers(2))	11
Car Preferences (RET 2)	Model, Color, Seating Capacity, Engine Capacity	4

- Follow IFPUG rules and determine whether each item in the preceding group is an ILF or EIF.

- Based on the analysis similar to the one shown in Table 16.2, the Customer information is not maintained within the boundary of the application being counted and cannot be identified as an ILF. Table 16.5 helps you evaluate whether this file can be identified as an EIF.

Table 16.5 *Customer Information EIF Identification*

EIF Identification Rule	Does the Rule Apply?
The group of data or control information is logical and user identifiable.	Yes. The complete data information of the Customer is user identifiable.
The group of data is referenced by, and external to, the application being counted.	Yes. The Customer data is referenced by and external to the Invoice application.
The group of data is not maintained by the application being counted.	Yes. The Customer data is not maintained by the Invoice application.
The group of data is maintained in an ILF of another application.	Yes. The data is maintained in the Customer application.

- Based on the analysis similar to the one shown in Table 16.5, the Customer information is maintained outside the boundary of the application being counted and can identified as an EIF.

- The exact FP contribution for Customer EIF can now be evaluated using the contribution figures provided by IFPUG. (Refer to Tables B.1 to B.7 in Appendix B.)

In order to arrive at the complexity level, you need to take into consideration the various DET identified in Table 16.4. Table 16.6 provides the details of DET, complexity and, as a result, the unadjusted function point count.

Table 16.6 *Customer EIF Unadjusted FP Count*

Entity	File	RET	DET	Complexity	Unadjusted FP Count
Customer	EIF	2	15 (11 + 4))	Low	5

- *Dealer Information:* Fast Cars Company has a network of dealers spread across the globe. The management intends to track various business growth indicators across its network of dealers. Various business measuring parameters, including Stock Capacity, Servicing Facilities, and Spares and Accessories capacity are required to be stored and tracked against each dealer. The file structure for the needs mentioned previously requires multiple sets of data elements, grouped together, that can have multiple records for each dealer. For example, a dealer in Germany may have the following capacity:

- Stocking capacity for 10 varieties of cars, trucks, and sports vehicles.
- Servicing capacity for 5 varieties of service for all vehicle models.
- The dealer can store all the spares and accessories for the variety of vehicles, including additional stock for older models.
- This analysis shows that each dealer record can have one or more stock capacity records, servicing facility records, and spares and accessories records. As such, the dealer file will have four record element types (RET) as shown in Table 16.7.

Table 16.7 *Dealer Information DET and RET Count*

Information Item	Data Elements	DET Count
Dealer Generic Information (RET 1)	Dealer Code, Location, Manager Name, Dealer Address (Door #, Street, Locality, State, Country, and Zip Code, Contact Numbers (2)), Sales Capacity, Messages	13
Dealer Stock Capacity (RET 2)	Model, Seating Capacity, Engine Capacity, Vehicle Category, Stock Count	5
Spares and Accessories (RET 3)	Spares Code, Capacity	2
Services (RET 4)	Service Code, Capacity	2

- Follow IFPUG rules and determine whether each of the items in the preceding group is an ILF or EIF.
- Based on the analysis similar to the one shown in Table 16.2, the dealer information maintained within the boundary of the application being counted is identified as an ILF.
- The exact FP contribution for Dealer ILF can now be evaluated as shown in Table 16.8 using the contribution figures provided by IFPUG.

Table 16.8 *Dealer ILF Unadjusted FP Count*

Entity	File	RET	DET	Complexity	Unadjusted FP Count
Dealer	ILF	4	22 (13 + 5 + 2 + 2)	Average	10

- *Spares and Accessories Information:* Each dealer needs to stock spares and accessories to meet servicing needs of the vehicles that the dealer is handling. A separate Spares and Accessories module will be needed (see Table 16.9).

Table 16.9 *Spares and Accessories Information DET and RET Count*

Information Item	Data Elements	DET Count
Spares and Accessories (RET 1)	Spares Code, Spares Category, Spares Description, Spares Unit, Spares Unit Rate, Spares Stock Count, Re-order Level	7

- Based on the analysis similar to the one shown in Table 16.2, the Spares and Accessories information, maintained within the boundary of the application being counted, is identified as an ILF.
- The exact FP contribution for Spares and Accessories ILF can now be evaluated as shown in Table 16.10 using the contribution figures provided by IFPUG.

Table 16.10 *Spares and Accessories ILF Unadjusted FP Count*

Entity	File	RET	DET	Complexity	Unadjusted FP Count
Spares and Accessories	ILF	1	7	Low	7

- *Servicing Facilities Information:* Each dealer needs to provide servicing facilities to meet the servicing needs of the vehicles that the dealer is handling. A separate Servicing Facilities module will be needed. Table 16.11 identifies the lone RET and various DET required.

Table 16.11 *Servicing Facilities Information DET and RET Count*

Information Item	Data Elements	DET Count
Servicing Facilities (RET 1)	Service Code, Service Category, Vehicle Category, Service Cost, Floor Capacity, Number of Technicians, Number of Vehicles	7

- Based on the analysis similar to the one shown in Table 16.2, the Servicing Facilities information maintained within the boundary of the application being counted is identified as an ILF.

- The exact FP contribution for Servicing Facilities ILF can now be evaluated as shown in Table 16.12 using the contribution figures provided by IFPUG.

Table 16.12 *Servicing Facilities ILF Unadjusted FP Count*

Entity	File	RET	DET	Complexity	Unadjusted FP Count
Servicing Facilities	ILF	1	7	Low	7

- *Accounts Information:* The accounts information here was required to record payment information against the specific account code that has been previously defined through the Accounts application. While designing the accounts information, developers observed that the accounts and payment information actually belongs to two different entities. As such, you need to identify two files, one each for accounts and payment. Table 16.13 identifies the lone RET and various DET required.

Table 16.13 *Accounts Information DET and RET Count*

Information Item	Data Elements	DET Count
Accounts Information (RET 1)	Account Code, Account Name, General Ledger Code, General Ledger Name	4

- Follow IFPUG rules and determine whether each item in the group is an ILF or EIF.

- Based on the analysis similar to the one shown in Table 16.2, the Accounts Data file is identified as an ILF.

- The exact FP contribution for Accounts EIF can now be evaluated as shown in Table 16.14 using the contribution figures provided by IFPUG.

Table 16.14 *Accounts ILF Unadjusted FP Count*

Entity	File	RET	DET	Complexity	Unadjusted FP Count
Accounts	ILF	1	4	Low	7

- *Payments Information:* The payments information is required to store details of amount received by the dealer against the car that was sold to the customer. Though the payment data will show on the invoice itself, internally this information is recorded in a separate file. Now find details of the payment file. Table 16.15 identifies the lone RET and various DET required.

Table 16.15 *Payments Information DET and RET Count*

Information Item	Data Elements	DET Count
Payments Information (RET 1)	Account Code*, Customer Code, Invoice Number, Amount, Discount, Transaction Date, Transaction Type (Cr/Dr), Payment Mode, Bank Code, Reference Number (Check #)	10

*Account Code is not counted in this table because it is treated as a reference key. In certain situations you can exclude Customer Code, Bank Code, and Invoice Number as reference keys.

- Follow IFPUG rules and determine whether each item in the preceding group is an ILF or EIF.
- Based on the analysis similar to the one shown in Table 16.2, the Payments Data file is identified as an ILF.
- The exact FP contribution for Payments ILF can now be evaluated as shown in Table 16.16 using the contribution figures provided by IFPUG.

Table 16.16 *Payments ILF Unadjusted FP Count*

Entity	File	RET	DET	Complexity	Unadjusted FP Count
Payments	ILF	1	10	Low	7

- *Bank Information:* The Bank information needs to be maintained in order to generate Bank Transactions at the end of day. A bank transaction statement is generated that includes all payment received data for the day, along with Account Code and Bank Code. This transaction statement is sent to the bank on daily basis. Table 16.17 identifies the lone RET and various DET required.

Table 16.17 *Bank Information DET and RET Count*

Information Item	Data Elements	DET Count
Bank Information (RET 1)	Bank Code, Bank Name, Bank Address (Door #, Street, Locality, State, Country, and Zip Code, Contact Numbers (2))	10

- Follow IFPUG rules and determine whether each item in the preceding group is an ILF or EIF.
- Based on the analysis similar to the one shown in Table 16.2, the Bank Data file is identified as an ILF.
- The exact FP contribution for Bank ILF can now be evaluated as shown in Table 16.18 using the contribution figures provided by IFPUG.

Table 16.18 *Bank ILF Unadjusted FP Count*

Entity	File	RET	DET	Complexity	Unadjusted FP Count
Bank	ILF	1	10	Low	7

- *Sales Executive Information:* The management of Fast Cars regularly tracks the targets set for each dealership. Information on sales is obtained through the daily sales achieved by the sales executives. Other personnel information for the sales executives, including salary data, is also required to be stored. Table 16.19 identifies the three RET and various DET required.

Table 16.19 *Sales Executive Information DET and RET Count*

Information Item	Data Elements	DET Count
Sales Executive Information (RET 1)	Sales Executive Code, Name, Designation, Address (Door #, Street, Locality, State, Country, and Zip Code, Contact Numbers (2)), Dealer Code	12
Salary Information (RET 2)	Sales Executive Code*, Sales Executive Salary, Salary Period	2
Sales Information (RET 3)	Sales Executive Code*, Sales Target, Target Period and Current Sales Status	3

* Sales Executive Code not counted.

- Follow IFPUG rules and determine whether each item in the preceding group is an ILF or EIF.
- Based on the analysis similar to the one shown in Table 16.2, the Sales Executive Data file is identified as an ILF.
- The exact FP contribution for Sales Executive ILF can now be evaluated as shown in Table 16.20 using the contribution figures provided by IFPUG.

Table 16.20 *Sales Executive ILF Unadjusted FP Count*

Entity	File	RET	DET	Complexity	Unadjusted FP Count
Sales Executive	ILF	3	17	Low	7

- *Stores Information:* All the necessary spares, accessories, and other extra fittings are stocked in the stores. Table 16.21 identifies the RET and various DET required.

Table 16.21 *Stores Information DET and RET Count*

Information Item	Data Elements	DET Count
Stores Information (RET 1)	Stores Code, Stores Name, Stores Location, Stores Manager	4

- Follow IFPUG rules and determine whether each item in the preceding group is an ILF or EIF.
- Based on the analysis similar to the one shown in Table 16.2, the Stores Data file is identified as an ILF.
- The exact FP contribution for Stores ILF can now be evaluated as shown in Table 16.22 using the contribution figures provided by IFPUG.

Table 16.22 *Stores ILF Unadjusted FP Count*

Entity	*File*	*RET*	*DET*	*Complexity*	*Unadjusted FP Count*
Stores	ILF	1	4	Low	7

- *Buy-Back Information:* This facility is not planned for the current development project. It is likely to be added as an enhancement later.

Step 6: Identify Transaction Functions (EI/EQ/EO)

Having identified the stakeholders in Step 1, you can now work toward various categories of information needed to be processed through the invoice application. The requirement specification document will provide the key input. For each of the business entities identified in Step 1, you can now identify various transaction functions that are required in order to facilitate business activities of Fast Cars dealers.

Typically there are three kinds (EI/EO/EQ) of transaction functions that are possible for each business entity. For the purpose of this case study, you can assume a variety of transaction functions that could possibly be applicable. For each of the transaction functions identified, you can then proceed with evaluating the function point count as per IFPUG CPM 4.2 guidelines.

Consider the rules for analysis of the three varieties of transactional functions (EI/EO/EQ) as shown in Tables 16.23 and 16.24. The tables cover the elementary process identification rules as well as the DET and FTR counting rules that generically apply to all varieties of transaction functions. Because you will evaluate these transaction functions for each business entity later in the chapter, these tables will be helpful in identifying the transaction function type (EI/EO/EQ) as well as its counting parameters DET and FTR.

Table 16.23 *Elementary Process Identification Rules*

Identification Rule	EI	EO	EQ
The process is the smallest unit of activity that is meaningful to the user.	Y	Y	Y
The process is self-contained and leaves the business of the application in a consistent state.	Y	Y	Y
The primary intent of an elementary process is to maintain an ILF or alter the behavior of the system.	Y	N	N
The processing logic of the elementary process contains at least one mathematical formula or calculation.	NA	Y	N
The processing logic of the elementary process alters the behavior of the system.	Y	Y/N	N
The primary intent of the elementary process is to present information to a user.	N	Y	Y
Is the data moving in from outside to inside (or vice versa) the application boundary?	Y	Y	Y
An ILF is maintained by the elementary process.	Y	Y/N	N

*NA = Not Applicable.

Table 16.24 provides guidelines on how to apply the DET and FTR counting rules for the three types of transaction functions: EI/EO/EQ.

Table 16.24 *DET and FTR Identification Rules*

Identification Rule	EI	EO	EQ
Count an FTR for each ILF maintained.	Y	Y	NA
Count an FTR for each EIF referenced.	Y	Y	Y
Count one DET for each user recognizable, non-repeated field that enters or exits the application boundary and is required to complete the input/output/query process.	Y	Y	Y
Count one DET for each message sent (Ex. Error/Confirmation Message).	Y	Y	Y
Count one DET for each action button.	Y	Y	Y

*NA = Not Applicable.

Taking each of the modules, analyze various transaction functions that are required to maintain the business transactions. You can also identify various DET/RET/FTR for each of the transaction functions.

- *Invoice Information:* The user has identified (assumed) the following variety of transactions, including input, output, and queries for the invoice entity as shown in Table 16.25.

Table 16.25 *Transactions for Invoice Module*

Transaction	Type	Comments
Create Invoice	EI	Invoice Data Entry provision
Invoice Query	EQ	Query on old Invoices
Print Invoice	EO	Print-out the final Invoice
Invoice Summary Report	EO	Summary Invoice Reports—Weekly/Quarterly
Receive Payments	EI	Payments (against Invoice) Data Entry
Payments Query	EQ	Query on old Payments
Invoice Aging Analysis	EO	Periodic Aging Analysis Report (Outstanding Payments)
Sales Reports	EO	Summary Sales Reports (Weekly, Quarterly, Yearly)

- You can now identify various DET and FTR for each of the transaction functions in the Invoice module. Table 16.26 identifies the various RET and DET required for each of the invoice transaction modules.
- *Customer Information:* It is assumed that the user has identified the following variety of transactions, including inputs, outputs, and inquiries for the customer entity as shown in Table 16.27. You can now identify various DET and FTR for each of the transaction functions in the Customer module.
- *Dealer Information:* It is assumed that the user has identified the following variety of transactions, including inputs, outputs, and inquiries for the dealer entity as shown in Table 16.28. You can now identify various DET and FTR for each of the transaction functions in the Dealer module.

Table 16.26 *DET and FTR Identification for Invoice Module*

Transaction	Type	DET/FTR	FP Count	Comments
Create Invoice	EI	Invoice Number, Invoice Date, Customer Name, Customer Address (Door #, Street, Locality, State, Country, and Zip Code, Contact Numbers (2)), Dealer Code, Sales Executive Code, Invoice Amount, Tax Percentage and Tax Amount, Click (Add, Edit, Delete and Save) Button, Error Messages (DET = 18) Item Code, Item Description, Item Category, Item Quantity, Item Rate (DET = 6) FTR: Invoice, Customer, Dealer, Sales Executive (Total: DET = 24, FTR = 4)	6 (High)	Data Entry Screen(s) for adding new Invoices
Modify Invoice	EI	All DETs/FTRs as identified for "Create Invoice" above) (Total: DET = 24, FTR = 4)	6 (High)	Data Entry Screen(s) for modifying existing Invoices
Delete Invoice	EI	All DETs/FTRs as identified for "Create Invoice" above) (Total: DET = 24, FTR = 4)	6 (High)	Data Entry Screen(s) for deleting Invoices. It is assumed that the user will require viewing all data before deleting.
Query Invoice	EQ	All DETs/FTRs as identified for "Create Invoice" above) (Total: DET = 24, FTR = 4)	6 (High)	Query and search Invoices on multiple DETs; Invoice #, Customer, etc.

Table 16.26 *DET and FTR Identification for Invoice Module (Continued)*

Transaction	Type	DET/FTR	FP Count	Comments
Print Invoice	EO	All DETs as identified for "Create Invoice" above except click button) + Invoice Total, Payment Received, Payment Date, Payment Mode, Balance Due FTR: All FTR from Create Invoice + Payments (Total: DET = 28, FTR = 5)	7 (High)	It is required to provide a hard copy of the final Invoice to the Customer.
Invoice Summary Report	EO	Invoice Number, Invoice Date, Customer Name, Invoice Amount, Tax Percentage and Tax Amount, Discount Amount, Payment Date, Amount Received, Payment Mode, Weekly Totals, Quarterly Totals (DET = 12) FTR: Invoice, Customer, Payment (Total: DET = 12, FTR = 3)	5 (Avg.)	Invoiced amount reports required by Dealers.
Receive Payments	EI	All DETs/FTRs as identified for "Create Invoice" above) + Payment Date, Amount Received, Payment Mode (Total: DET = 27, FTR = 3)	6 (High)	It is assumed here that in order to enter payment details, you also need to invoke Invoice details. Also you are allowed to modify payments in the same screen. Delete payments will automatically happen along with delete Invoice.

(Continued)

Table 16.26 *DET and FTR Identification for Invoice Module (Continued)*

Transaction	Type	DET/FTR	FP Count	Comments
Payments Query	EQ	All DETs/FTRs as identified for "Create Invoice" above) + Payment Date, Amount Received, Payment Mode (Total: DET = 27, FTR = 3)	6 (High)	
Invoice Aging Analysis	EO	Invoice Number, Invoice Date, Customer Name, Invoice Amount, Amount Received, Balance Due, Payment Pending Age (days), Ageing Totals (DET = 8) FTR: Invoice, Customer, Payment (Total: DET = 8, FTR = 3)	5 (Avg.)	Aging analysis for specified aging e.g., 30 days, 30–60 days, and 60 days and above. Sum totals for every category.
Sales Report by Sales Executive	EO	All DETs/FTRs as identified for "Invoice Aging Analysis" (Total: DET = 8, FTR = 3)	5 (Avg.)	Report sorted on Sales Executive Code
Sales Report by Dealer Code	EO	All DETs/FTRs as identified for "Invoice Aging Analysis" (Total: DET = 8, FTR = 3)	5 (Avg.)	Report sorted on Dealer Code
Sales Report by Location	EO	All DETs/FTRs as identified for "Invoice Aging Analysis" (Total: DET = 8, FTR = 3)	5 (Avg.)	Report sorted on Location Code
TOTAL		Unadjusted FP totals for entire Invoice Module (EI/EO/EQ)	68	

Table 16.27 *DET and FTR Identification for Customer Module*

Transaction	Type	DET/FTR	FP Count	Comments
Create Customer	EI	Customer Code, Customer Name, Customer Profession, Customer Address (Door #, Street, Locality, State, Country, and Zip Code, Contact Numbers(2)) (DET = 11) Car Preferences (Model, Cost, Capacity, Color) (DET = 4) FTR: Customer (Total: DET = 15, FTR = 1)	3 (Low)	Data Entry Screen(s) for adding new Customer
Modify Customer	EI	All DETs/FTRs as identified for "Create Customer" (Total: DET = 15, FTR = 1)	3 (Low)	Data Entry Screen(s) for modifying existing Customers
Delete Customer	EI	All DETs/FTRs as identified for "Create Customer" (Total: DET = 15, FTR = 1)	3 (Low)	Data Entry Screen(s) for deleting existing Customers
Customer Report	EQ	All DETs/FTRs as identified for "Create Customer" (Total: DET = 15, FTR = 1)	3 (Low)	This report is treated as EQ because there is no derived data.
TOTAL		Unadjusted FP totals for entire Customer Module (EI/EO/EQ)	12	

Table 16.28 *DET and FTR Identification for Dealer Module*

Transaction	Type	DET/FTR	FP Count	Comments
Create Dealer	EI	Dealer Code, Location, Manager Name, Dealer Address (Door #, Street, Locality, State, Country, and Zip Code, Contact Numbers (2)), Sales Capacity, Messages (DET = 13) Model, Seating Capacity, Engine Capacity, Vehicle Category, Stock Count (DET = 5) Spares Code, Capacity (DET = 2) Service Code, Capacity (DET = 2) FTR: Dealer, Vehicle Models, Spares, Service (Total: DET = 22, FTR = 4)	6 (High)	Data Entry Screen(s) for adding new Dealer
Modify Dealer	EI	All DETs/FTRs as identified for "Create Dealer" (Total: DET = 22, FTR = 4)	6 (High)	Data Entry Screen(s) for modifying existing Dealers
Delete Dealer	EI	All DETs/FTRs as identified for "Create Dealer" (Total: DET = 22, FTR = 4)	6 (High)	Data Entry Screen(s) for deleting existing Dealers
Dealer Report	EQ	All DETs/FTRs as identified for "Create Dealer" above) (Total: DET = 22, FTR = 4)	6 (High)	This report is treated as EQ since there is no derived data.
TOTAL		Unadjusted FP totals for entire Dealer Module (EI/EO/EQ)	24	

- *Spares and Accessories Information:* All information about all the spares and accessories that the dealer intends to stock will be maintained through the Spares and Accessories module. Table 16.29 identifies the various RET and DET required for the spares and accessories transaction modules.

Table 16.29 *DET and FTR Identification for Spares and Accessories Module*

Transaction	Type	DET/FTR	FP Count	Comments
Create Spares and Accessories Record	EI	Spares Code, Spares Category, Spares Description, Spares Unit, Spares Unit Rate, Spares Stock Count, Re-order Level (DET = 7) FTR: Spares and Accessories (Total: DET = 7, FTR = 1)	3 (Low)	Data Entry Screen(s) for adding new Spares and Accessories Record
Modify Spares and Accessories Record	EI	All DETs/FTRs as identified for "Create Spares and Accessories Record" (Total: DET = 7, FTR = 1)	3 (Low)	Data Entry Screen(s) for modifying existing Spares and Accessories Record
Delete Spares and Accessories Record	EI	All DETs/FTRs as identified for "Create Spares and Accessories Record" (Total: DET = 7, FTR = 1)	3 (Low)	Data Entry Screen(s) for deleting existing Spares & Accessories Record.
Spares and Accessories Report	EQ	All DETs/FTRs as identified for "Create Spares and Accessories Record" (Total: DET = 7, FTR = 1)	3 (Low)	This report is treated as EQ since there is no derived data.

(Continued)

Table 16.29 *DET and FTR Identification for Spares and Accessories Module (Continued)*

Transaction	Type	DET/FTR	FP Count	Comments
Spares and Accessories Billing	EO	All DETs/FTRs as identified for "Create Spares and Accessories Record" + Customer Code + Customer Name + Bill Total FTR: Spares and Accessories, Customer (Total: DET = 10, FTR = 2)	5 (Avg)	
TOTAL		Unadjusted FP totals for entire Spares & Accessories Module (EI/EO/EQ)	17	

- *Servicing Facilities Information:* All information about the servicing that the dealer intends to provide to clients will be maintained through the Servicing Facilities module. Table 16.30 identifies the various RET and DET required for each of the servicing transaction modules.

Table 16.30 *DET and FTR Identification for Servicing Facilities Module*

Transaction	Type	DET/FTR	FP Count	Comments
Create Servicing Facilities Record	EI	Service Code, Service Category, Vehicle Category, Service Cost, Floor Capacity, Number of Technicians, Number of Vehicles (DET = 7) FTR: Servicing Facilities (Total: DET = 7, FTR = 1)	3 (Low)	Data Entry Screen(s) for adding new Servicing Facilities Record

Table 16.30 *DET and FTR Identification for Servicing Facilities Module (Continued)*

Transaction	Type	DET/FTR	FP Count	Comments
Modify Servicing Facilities Record	EI	All DETs/FTRs as identified for "Create Servicing Facilities Record" (Total: DET = 7, FTR = 1)	3 (Low)	Data Entry Screen(s) for modifying existing Servicing Facilities Record
Delete Servicing Facilities Record	EI	All DETs/FTRs as identified for "Create Servicing Facilities Record" (Total: DET = 7, FTR = 1)	3 (Low)	Data Entry Screen(s) for deleting existing Servicing Facilities Record
Servicing Facilities Report	EQ	All DETs/FTRs as identified for "Create Servicing Facilities Record") (Total: DET = 7, FTR = 1)	3 (Low)	This report is treated as EQ since there is no derived data.
Servicing Billing	EO	All DETs/FTRs as identified for "Create Servicing Facilities Record" above) + Customer Code + Customer Name + Bill Total FTR: Servicing Facilities, Customer (Total: DET = 10, FTR = 2)	5 (Avg)	
TOTAL		Unadjusted FP totals for entire Servicing Facilities Module (EI/EO/EQ)	17	

- *Accounts Information:* All the financial transactions that happen at the dealer's office must be recorded against the appropriate account code. At present, a separate Accounts module does not exist. As such, the accounts information is maintained as another module. Table 16.31 identifies the various RET and DET required for each of the accounts transaction modules.

Table 16.31 *DET and FTR Identification Accounts Module*

Transaction	Type	DET/FTR	FP Count	Comments
Create Account Record	EI	(Account Code, Account Name, General Ledger Code, General Ledger (Name (DET = 4) FTR: Accounts (Total: DET = 4, FTR = 1)	3 (Low)	Data Entry Screen(s) for adding new Account Record
Modify Account Record	EI	All DETs/FTRs as identified for "Create Account Record" (Total: DET = 4, FTR = 1)	3 (Low)	Data Entry Screen(s) for modifying existing Accounts Record
Delete Account Record	EI	All DETs/FTRs as identified for "Create Account Record" (Total: DET = 4, FTR = 1)	3 (Low)	Data Entry Screen(s) for deleting existing Account Record
Accounts Report	EQ	All DETs/FTRs as identified for "Create Account Record" (Total: DET = 4, FTR = 1)	3 (Low)	This report is treated as EQ since there is no derived data.
TOTAL		Unadjusted FP totals for entire Accounts Module (EI/EO/EQ)	12	

- *Payments Information:* The payments information is required to store details of amount received by the dealer against the car that was sold to the customer. Though the payment data will show on the invoice itself, internally this information is recorded in a separate file. Table 16.32 identifies the various RET and DET required for each of the payment transaction modules.

Table 16.32 *DET and FTR Identification Payments Module*

Transaction	Type	DET/FTR	FP Count	Comments
Create Payment Record	EI	Account Code*, Customer Code, Invoice Number, Amount, Discount, Transaction Date, Transaction Type (Cr/Dr), Payment Mode, Bank Code, Reference Number (Check #) (DET = 10) FTR: Payments, Invoice (Total: DET = 10, FTR = 1)	3 (Low)	Data Entry Screen(s) for adding new Payment Record
Modify Payment Record	EI	All DETs/FTRs as identified for "Create Payment Record" (Total: DET = 10, FTR = 1)	3 (Low)	Data Entry Screen(s) for modifying existing Payment Record
Delete Payment Record	EI	All DETs/FTRs as identified for "Create Payment Record" (Total: DET = 10, FTR = 1)	3 (Low)	Data Entry Screen(s) for deleting existing Payment Record
Payments Report	EQ	All DETs/FTRs as identified for "Create Payment Record" (Total: DET = 10, FTR = 1)	3 (Low)	This report is treated as EQ since there is no derived data.
TOTAL		Unadjusted FP totals for entire Payments Module (EI/EO/EQ)	12	

*Account Code is not counted in this table because it is treated as a reference key. In certain situations, you can exclude Customer Code, Bank Code, and Invoice Number as reference keys.

- *Bank Information:* The Bank information needs to be maintained in order to generate Bank Transactions at the end of day. A bank transactions statement is generated that includes all payment received data for the day, along with Account Code and Bank code. This transaction statement is sent to the bank on a daily basis. Table 16.33 identifies the various RET and DET required for each of the Bank Transaction modules.

Table 16.33 *DET and FTR Identification Bank Module*

Transaction	Type	DET/FTR	FP Count	Comments
Create Bank Record	EI	Bank Code, Bank Name, Bank Address (Door #, Street, Locality, State, Country, and Zip Code, Contact Numbers (2)). (DET = 10) FTR: Bank (Total: DET = 10, FTR = 1)	3 (Low)	Data Entry Screen(s) for adding new Bank Record
Modify Bank Record	EI	All DETs/FTRs as identified for "Create Bank Record" (Total: DET = 10, FTR = 1)	3 (Low)	Data Entry Screen(s) for modifying existing Bank Record
Delete Bank Record	EI	All DETs/FTRs as identified for "Create Bank Record" (Total: DET = 10, FTR = 1)	3 (Low)	Data Entry Screen(s) for deleting existing Bank Record
Bank Report	EO	All DETs as identified for "Create Bank Record" above) + Account Code + Payment Amount + Payment Date + Payment Reference (Check #) + Total Amount FTR: Bank, Account, Payment (Total: DET = 15, FTR = 3)	5 (Avg)	This report is treated as a Bank transaction statement.
TOTAL		Unadjusted FP totals for entire Bank Module (EI/EO/EQ)	14	

- *Sales Executive Information:* It is assumed that the user has identified the following variety of transactions, including inputs, outputs, and inquiries for the sales executive entity as shown in Table 16.34. You can now identify various DET and FTR for each of the transaction functions in the Sales Executive module.

Table 16.34 *DET and FTR Identification for Sales Executive Module*

Transaction	Type	DET/FTR	FP Count	Comments
Create Sales Executive Code	EI	Sales Executive Code, Name, Designation, Address (Door #, Street, Locality, State, Country, and Zip Code, Contact Numbers (2)), Dealer Code, Sales Executive Salary, Salary Period, Sales Target, Target Period, Current Sales Status (DET = 17) FTR: Sales Executive, Dealer (Total: DET = 17, FTR = 2)	6 (High)	Data Entry Screen(s) for adding new Sales Executive Code
Modify Sales Executive Code	EI	All DETs/FTRs as identified for "Create Sales Executive Code" (Total: DET = 17, FTR = 2)	6 (High)	Data Entry Screen(s) for modifying existing Sales Executive Codes
Delete Sales Executive Code	EI	All DETs/FTRs as identified for "Create Sales Executive Code" (Total: DET = 17, FTR = 2)	6 (High)	Data Entry Screen(s) for deleting existing Sales Executive Codes
Sales Executive Report	EO	All DETs/FTRs as identified for "Create Sales Executive Code" above) + Current Sales Total + Target Total + Target Gap (Total: DET = 20, FTR = 2)	7 (High)	Sales Target vs. Actual report
TOTAL		Unadjusted FP totals for entire Sales Executive Module (EI/EO/EQ)	25	

- *Stores Information:* All the spares, accessories, and other extra fittings are stocked in the stores. Table 16.35 identifies the various RET and DET required for each of the stores transaction modules.

Table 16.35 *DET and FTR Identification for Stores Module*

Transaction	Trn. Type	DET/FTR	FP Count	Comments
Create Stores Code	EI	Stores Code, Stores Name, Stores Location, Stores Manager (DET = 4) FTR: Stores (Total: DET = 4, FTR = 1)	3 (Low)	Data Entry Screen(s) for adding new Stores Code
Modify Stores Code	EI	All DETs/FTRs as identified for "Create Sales Executive Code" (Total: DET = 4, FTR = 1)	3 (Low)	Data Entry Screen(s) for modifying existing Stores Codes
Delete Stores Code	EI	All DETs/FTRs as identified for "Create Stores Code" (Total: DET = 4, FTR = 1)	3 (Low)	Data Entry Screen(s) for deleting existing Stores Codes
Stores Report	EQ	All DETs/FTRs as identified for "Create Stores Code" (Total: DET = 4, FTR = 1)	3 (Low)	This report is treated as EQ since there is no derived data
TOTAL		Unadjusted FP totals for entire Stores Module (EI/EO/EQ)	12	

- *Buy-back Information:* This facility is not planned for the current development project. It is likely to be added as an enhancement later.

Step 7: Aggregate Data and Transaction Function (Unadjusted) FP Counts

Aggregate the data function FP count and the transaction function FP count to obtain the total Unadjusted FP Count.

Table 16.36 summarizes the overall data functions identified in Step 6 and also the total unadjusted function points for data functions only.

Table 16.36 *Total Data Function FP Count (Unadjusted)*

Data Function	Type	Complexity	Unadjusted FP Count
Invoice	ILF	Average	10
Customer	EIF	Low	5
Dealer	ILF	Average	10
Spares and Accessories	ILF	Low	7
Servicing Facilities	ILF	Low	7
Accounts	ILF	Low	7
Payments	ILF	Low	7
Bank	ILF	Low	7
Sales Executive	ILF	Low	7
Stores	ILF	Low	7
TOTAL			74

Table 16.37 summarizes the overall transaction functions identified in Step 6 and also shows the total unadjusted function points for transaction functions only.

- Total Unadjusted FP Count for the Invoice Application = 74 + 213 = 287.

Table 16.37 *Total Transaction Function FP Count (Unadjusted)*

Transaction Function	Type	Complexity	Unadjusted FP Count
Create Invoice	EI	High	6
Modify Invoice	EI	High	6
Delete Invoice	EI	High	6
Query Invoice	EQ	High	6
Print Invoice	EO	High	7
Invoice Summary Report	EO	Average	5
Receive Payments	EI	High	6
Payments Query	EQ	High	6
Invoice Aging Analysis	EO	Average	5
Sales Report by Sales Executive	EO	Average	5
Sales Report by Dealer Code	EO	Average	5
Sales Report by Location	EO	Average	5
Create Customer	EI	Low	3
Modify Customer	EI	Low	3
Delete Customer	EI	Low	3
Customer Report	EQ	Low	3
Create Dealer	EI	High	6
Modify Dealer	EI	High	6
Delete Dealer	EI	High	6
Dealer Report	EQ	High	6
Create Spares and Accessories	EI	Low	3
Modify Spares and Accessories	EI	Low	3
Delete Spares and Accessories	EI	Low	3
Spares and Accessories Report	EQ	Low	3
Spares and Accessories Billing	EO	Average	5
Create Servicing Facilities	EI	Low	3

Table 16.37 *Total Transaction Function FP Count (Unadjusted) (Continued)*

Transaction Function	Type	Complexity	Unadjusted FP Count
Modify Servicing Facilities	EI	Low	3
Delete Servicing Facilities	EI	Low	3
Servicing Facilities Report	EQ	Low	3
Servicing Facilities Billing	EO	Average	5
Create Account	EI	Low	3
Modify Account	EI	Low	3
Delete Account	EI	Low	3
Account Report	EQ	Low	3
Create Payment	EI	Low	3
Modify Payment	EI	Low	3
Delete Payment	EI	Low	3
Payment Report	EQ	Low	3
Create Bank Code	EI	Low	3
Modify Bank Code	EI	Low	3
Delete Bank Code	EI	Low	3
Bank Advice Report	EO	Average	5
Create Sales Executive Code	EI	High	6
Modify Sales Executive Code	EI	High	6
Delete Sales Executive Code	EI	High	6
Sales Executive Report	EO	High	7
Create Stores Code	EI	Low	3
Modify Stores Code	EI	Low	3
Delete Stores Code	EI	Low	3
Stores Report	EQ	Low	3
TOTAL			213

Step 8: Obtain GSC Values for Invoice Application

The next step is to obtain the degree of influence rating for each of the 14 general system characteristics (GSCs) as explained in Chapter 6. Table 16.38 evaluates the impact of each of the 14 GSCs on the invoice application. Convert the total degree of influence value to value adjustment factor (VAF). Multiply the Unadjusted FP Count with VAF to obtain the Adjusted FP Count.

Table 16.38 *Invoicing System—General System Characteristics*

GSC #	GSC Description	Degree of Influence	Comments
1	Data Communications	4	The application is online and supports at least one type of communication protocol.
2	Distributed Data	4	Distributed data processing and exchange is occurring in both directions; from corporate to dealers and vice versa.
3	Performance	3	Though performance requirements are not very stringent, the performance needs are business critical. Performance is not CPU-dependent.
4	Heavily Used	3	Limited operational Configuration constraint exists. Dedicated servers need to be set up for back-end processing.
5	Transaction Rate	3	Average transaction rates are expected. But during peak seasons (festive, etc.) the transaction rates are likely to shoot up.

Table 16.38 *Invoicing System—General System Characteristics (Continued)*

GSC #	GSC Description	Degree of Influence	Comments
6	Online Data Entry	5	More than 30 percent of transactions are expected to be interactive.
7	End-User Efficiency	5	More than six online functions are being implemented in the application.
8	Online Update	3	Online update of major internal logical files is designed. No specific built-in design for data loss envisaged.
9	Complex Processing	1	Limited processing complexity expected.
10	Reusability	3	At least 15 percent of code is expected to be reused across various modules of the application.
11	Installation Ease	3	The application (client portion) will be installed in multiple locations globally. The expectation is that the application installation is designed for this.
12	Operational Ease	3	Some of the standard requirements like automatic startup, backup, and recovery procedures as well as automating printer and other operational needs are being built-in.

(Continued)

Table 16.38 *Invoicing System—General System Characteristics (Continued)*

GSC #	GSC Description	Degree of Influence	Comments
13	Multiple Sites	4	Provision for installing at multiple locations and on varying hardware, supported by documentation, has to be made.
14	Facilitate Change	3	All variable/reference data has been kept out of code to facilitate easy modification by user.
	Total Degree of Influence (TDI)	47	
	Value Adjustment Factor	1.12	VAF = 0.65 + (TDI * 0.01)

Step 9: Transform the Adjusted FP Count into Total Effort

Transform the adjusted FP count into the total effort required to execute the software project. This can be achieved by obtaining the delivery rate (productivity) of the project team and then multiplying the adjusted FP count with productivity. The effort thus obtained will encompass all the project execution lifecycle activities that include requirements, design, build (construction) and unit test, and system and integration tests.

The following six steps take you through the sequence of converting the unadjusted function points count into adjusted function points and then to effort using assumed productivity. It then finally provides you with an option for adding the project management overhead efforts.

1. The Value Adjustment Factor (see Table 16.38) = 1.12
2. Final (adjusted) Function Points = 287 × 1.12 = 322
3. Assume the technology is J2EE and productivity for J2EE = 10 FP per Person Month
4. Engineering Effort required to develop the Invoice application = 322/10 = 32 PM

5. Additional Effort for Project Management and Configuration Management = 15%

6. Final Effort = 32 + 5 (15%) = 37 Person Months

Step 10: Transform the Total Effort into Delivery Schedule

The total effort now needs to be adjusted to a project delivery schedule. There are methods available to do the conversion, COCOMO II being one such popular method. The delivery schedule (duration or elapsed time) thus obtained may sometimes need to be refined based on user needs.

For simplicity's sake, assume that the customer has expressed a constraint in accepting any delivery schedule beyond five months. As such, you can assume the five months as delivery schedule (elapsed time) allowed from the start date of the project.

Step 11: Map the Resource Loading to Meet the Delivery Schedule

Transform the total effort obtained in Step 9 above into a resource loading chart. This step is significant in the sense that assigning the appropriate person with the right skills for the appropriate lifecycle phase of the project is critical for the project to be a success.

Table 16.39 shows the resource loading chart needed to meet the five-month schedule, as discussed in Step 10.

Table 16.39 *Resource Loading Chart (Illustrative Only)*

Lifecycle Phase ->	Req.	Design	Build		Test	
Month -> Resource Type	M1*	M2*	M3*	M4*	M5*	Total Person Months
Project Manager	1	1	1	1	1	5
Technical Architect		1	1	1		3
Business Analyst	2	2	2	2	1	9
Programmer/Tester		4	6	6	4	20
Total Effort (Person Months)	3	8	10	10	6	37

*M1 = Month 1.

The resource allocation for the various lifecycle phases of the project has been done with a certain assumption about the type of resources, resource numbers, and duration of allocation based on past experience of project execution. You may want to devise alternate resource loading methods based on your experience. Table 16.39 can now be converted to actual costs by

- Applying rate per day to each role (project manager, architect, analyst, and developer)
- Apply the rate for the assigned durations (person months)
- Add overheads like infrastructure, including servers, desktops, and software licenses as applicable
- Add other management overhead costs as applicable

Effort for the second and subsequent phase-wise expansions can be developed separately.

Case Study 2: Enhanced Invoicing System

Continuing the discussion on software development project(s) for our dear customer Fast Cars, an automobile dealer, the next phase involves improving the existing Invoice application by adding another important module. Consider this exercise an enhancement project.

Case Study 1 mentioned the Buy-Back module as one of the functions planned for development. This module was not included in the estimation process so that it could be introduced as an enhancement project. The next section discusses the estimation process as defined for enhancement projects in the IFPUG method [1].

Step-by-Step FP Counting Process (Enhancement Projects)

Here are the main steps that you need to follow diligently if you want to obtain accurate FP sizing as well as derived effort and delivery schedule for enhancement projects:

- *Step 1:* Ensure that you have all the information about the existing application with respect to the Function Points counting processes. The information should include following FP counting data:
    - # Internal Logical Files (ILF)
    - # External Interface Files (EIF)
    - # External Inputs (EI)
    - # External Outputs (EO)

- # External Inquiries (EI)
- # DET, # RET, and # FTR for each of the above attributes
- Degree of influence values for each of the 14 GSC
- Value adjustment factor

Verify the FP count by applying IFPUG counting method using the attribute data obtained as above. If for any reason you do not have the necessary information, you will have to follow the steps explained in Case Study 1 and obtain the required information. You may have to refer to the existing data model, input/output/query screens, interface to other applications, reports, and possibly portions of code in order to obtain a good picture of the application complexity. Without the required FP and its attribute information about the existing application, you cannot proceed with the IFPUG method of sizing estimation for enhancements. There are other alternatives to estimation of size and effort for enhancement projects but they are out of the scope of the discussions in this section.

- *Step 2:* Based on the detailed specifications prepared for the proposed enhancement module, determine the data functions and transaction functions as explained in Case Study 1 (Steps 3 through 6). The process of identifying these data and transaction functions should be done with the assumption that these functions are of a stand-alone nature.

- *Step 3:* The impact of the data and transaction functions of the enhancement module on the existing application have to be assessed next. Review all the data and transaction function attributes of the existing application and identify additions, modifications, and deletions, if any, to each of them.

- *Step 4:* Obtain the detailed information about the GSCs, their degree of influence value, and the final value adjustment factor figures of the existing application. Evaluate each of the GSC values for any possible change in the degree of influence due to enhancement data and transaction functions.

- *Step 5:* Evaluate the function point count for the enhancement project using the IFPUG method provided in CPM 4.2:
  - EFP = [(ADD + CHGA + CFP) * VAFA] + (DEL * VAFB)

NOTE For details on the EFP (Enhancement Function Point) formula, refer to Chapter 8, "Estimation Flavors."

- *Step 6:* Convert FP count into effort and schedule as done in Case Study 1.

Assessing the Impact of Enhancing the Invoice Application

You can now apply the preceding six steps to estimate the FP count for the Buy-Back module and then convert the FP count into effort.

- *Step 1:* Obtain the various FP counting parameters for the existing Invoice application. This has already been done in the Case Study 1. The details are available in Tables 16.36, 16.37, and 16.38.

- *Step 2:* Evaluate the data functions and transaction functions for the Buy-Back module enhancement project.

    - *Data Function Information:* Under the Buy-Back scheme, the dealer provides an opportunity for the customer to trade the old vehicle for a discounted cost against the new vehicle purchase. As a business strategy, Fast Cars does not encourage dealers to handle the Buy-Back business. This business is sub-contracted to external agents who specialize in handling purchase of used cars. The following DET and RET are expected to meet the requirements for the Buy-Back module.

        Table 16.40 identifies the RET and DET for data functions of Buy-Back Agent module.

Table 16.40 *Buy-Back Agent Data Function Information DET and RET Count*

Information Item	Data Elements	DET Count
Buy-Back Agent (RET 1)	Agent Code, Name, Designation, Address (Door #, Street, Locality, State, Country, and Zip Code, Contact Numbers (2)), Dealer Code	12

Table 16.41 identifies the RET and DET for data functions of the Buy-Back Cars module.

Table 16.41 *Buy-Back Cars Data Function Information DET and RET Count*

Information Item	Data Elements	DET Count
Buy-Back Cars (RET 1)	Customer Code, Car Category, Car Type, Engine Capacity, Seating Capacity, Color, Accessories, Manufacturing Year, Vehicle Condition, Vehicle Cost	10

- Based on the analysis similar to the one shown in Table 16.2, the Data Function for Agent and Cars, maintained within the boundary of the application being counted, are identified as an ILF.
- The exact FP contribution for Agent and Cars ILF can now be evaluated as shown in Table 16.42 using the contribution figures provided by IFPUG.

Table 16.42 *Spares and Accessories ILF Unadjusted FP Count*

Entity	File	RET	DET	Complexity	Unadjusted FP Count
Buy-Back Agent	ILF	1	12	Low	7
Buy-Back Cars	ILF	1	10	Low	7

- *Transaction Functions Information:* Provision has to be made to maintain data for Buy-Back Agents as well as Buy-Back Cars. Also required are a few reports to be generated to track the used cars business. These are evaluated in Tables 16.43 and 16.44.

Table 16.43 *DET and FTR Identification for Buy-Back Agent Module*

Transaction	Type	DET/FTR	FP Count	Comments
Create Buy-Back Agent	EI	Agent Code, Name, Designation, Address (Door #, Street, Locality, State, Country, ZIP Code, Contact Numbers (2)), Dealer Code (DET = 12) FTR: Buy-Back Agent, Dealer (Total: DET = 12, FTR = 2)	4 (Avg)	Data Entry Screen(s) for adding new Buy-Back Agent
Modify Buy-Back Agent	EI	All DETs/FTRs as identified for "Create Buy-Back Agent" (Total: DET = 10, FTR = 2)	4 (Avg)	Data Entry Screen(s) for modifying existing Buy-Back Agent Record

(Continued)

Table 16.43 *DET and FTR Identification for Buy-Back Agent Module (Continued)*

Transaction	Type	DET/FTR	FP Count	Comments
Delete Buy-Back Agent	EI	All DETs/FTRs as identified for "Create Buy-Back Agent" (Total: DET = 10, FTR = 2)	4 (Avg)	Data Entry Screen(s) for deleting existing Buy-Back Agent Record
Buy-Back Agent Report	EQ	All DETs/FTRs as identified for "Create Buy-Back Agent" (Total: DET = 10, FTR = 2)	4 (Avg)	This report is treated as EQ because there is no derived data.
TOTAL		Unadjusted FP totals for entire Buy-Back Agent Module (EI/EO/EQ)	16	

Table 16.44 *DET and FTR Identification for Buy-Back Cars Module*

Transaction	Type	DET/FTR	FP Count	Comments
Create Buy-Back Cars	EI	Customer Code, Car Category, Car Type, Engine Capacity, Seating Capacity, Color, Accessories, Manufacturing Year, Vehicle Condition, Vehicle Cost (DET = 10) FTR: Buy-Back Cars, Customer (Total: DET = 10, FTR = 2)	4 (Avg)	Data Entry Screen(s) for adding new Buy-Back Cars
Modify Buy-Back Cars	EI	All DETs/FTRs as identified for "Create Buy-Back Cars" (Total: DET = 10, FTR = 2)	4 (Avg)	Data Entry Screen(s) for modifying existing Buy-Back Cars Record

Table 16.44 *DET and FTR Identification for Buy-Back Cars Module (Continued)*

Transaction	Type	DET/FTR	FP Count	Comments
Delete Buy-Back Cars	EI	All DETs/FTRs as identified for "Create Buy-Back Cars" (Total: DET = 10, FTR = 2)	4 (Avg)	Data Entry Screen(s) for deleting existing Buy-Back Cars Record
Buy-Back Cars Report	EQ	All DETs/FTRs as identified for "Create Buy-Back Cars" (Total: DET = 10, FTR = 2)	4 (Avg)	This report is treated as EQ because there is no derived data.
TOTAL		Unadjusted FP totals for entire Buy-Back Cars Module (EI/EO/EQ)	16	

- *Step 3:* The impact of the data and transaction functions of the Buy-back Module on the existing Invoice application have to be assessed next. A review of the impact on the data and transaction function attributes of the existing Invoice application due to the enhancement module is done. The impacted data and *transaction* functions are discussed in Tables 16.45 and 16.46.

Table 16.45 *Modified Invoice Information DET and RET Count*

Information Item	Data Elements	DET Count
Invoice Generic Information (RET 1)	Invoice Number, Invoice Date, Customer Name, Customer Address (Door #, Street, Locality, State, Country, ZIP Code, Contact Numbers (2)) Dealer Code, Sales Executive Code, Invoice Amount, Buy Back Agent, Buy Back Amount	16
Invoice Items Information (RET 2)	Item Code, Item Description, Item Category, Item Quantity, Item Rate	6

Table 16.46 *Modified Invoice ILF Unadjusted FP Count*

Entity	File	RET	DET	Complexity	Unadjusted FP Count
Invoice	ILF	2	22 (16 + 6)	Average	10

- With the buy-back amount now being available for online processing, the Invoice module needs to be modified to include the buy-back data.
- The modifications to transaction functions related to the Invoice module are also counted. These are identified in Table 16.47.

Table 16.47 *DET and FTR Identification for Invoice Module*

Transaction	Type	DET/FTR	FP Count	Comments
Create Invoice	EI	Invoice Number, Invoice Date, Customer Name, Customer Address (Door #, Street, Locality, State, Country, ZIP Code, Contact Numbers (2)), Dealer Code, Sales Executive Code, Invoice Amount, Tax Percentage and Tax Amount, Buy-Back Amount (DET = 17) Item Code, Item Description, Item Category, Item Quantity, Item Rate (DET = 6) FTR: Invoice, Customer, Dealer, Sales Executive, Buy-Back Cars (Total: DET = 23, FTR = 5)	6 (High)	Data Entry Screen(s) for adding new Invoices
Modify Invoice	EI	All DETs/FTRs as identified for "Create Invoice" (Total: DET = 23, FTR = 5)	6 (High)	Data Entry Screen(s) for modifying existing Invoices

Table 16.47 *DET and FTR Identification for Invoice Module (Continued)*

Transaction	Type	DET/FTR	FP Count	Comments
Delete Invoice	EI	All DETs/FTRs as identified for "Create Invoice" (Total: DET = 23, FTR = 5)	6 (High)	Data Entry Screen(s) for deleting Invoices. It is assumed that the user will require viewing all data before deleting.
Query Invoice	EQ	All DETs/FTRs as identified for "Create Invoice" (Total: DET = 23, FTR = 5)	6 (High)	Query and search Invoices on multiple DETs; Invoice #, Customer, etc.
TOTAL			24	

- Consolidated list of data and transaction functions involved in the enhancement project are shown in Tables 16.48 and 16.49.

Table 16.48 *Total Data Function FP Count (Unadjusted)*

Data Function	Type	Complexity	Unadjusted FP Count	Comments
Invoice	ILF	Average	10	ILF Modified
Buy-Back Agent	ILF	Low	7	ILF Added
Buy-Back Cars	ILF	Low	7	ILF Added
TOTAL			24	

Table 16.49 *Total Transaction Function FP Count (Unadjusted)*

Transaction Function	Type	Complexity	Unadjusted FP Count	Comments
Create Invoice	EI	High	6	EI Modified
Modify Invoice	EI	High	6	EI Modified
Delete Invoice	EI	High	6	EI Modified
Query Invoice	EQ	High	6	EI Modified
Total			24	

- *Step 4:* Obtain the detailed information about the GSCs, their degree of influence value, and the final value adjustment factor figures of the existing application. Evaluate each of the GSC values for any possible change in the degree of influence due to enhancement data and transaction functions.

  A detailed review of the GSC Table 16.37 shows that there is no change in any of the degree of influence values for any of the 14 GSC. As such, the TDI remains 47 and the VAF value at 1.12. As such, VAFA and VAFB are of same value.

- *Step 5:* Evaluate the function point count for the enhancement project (EFP) using the IFPUG method provided in CPM 4.2:
  - EFP = [(ADD + CHGA + CFP) * VAFA] + (DEL * VAFB)
  - ADD FP = 14 (New ILF for Buy-Back Agent and Buy-Back Cars)
  - CHGA FP = 34 (Modified ILF Invoice + Modified EI/EQ for Invoice)
  - CFP FP = 0 (no conversions involved)
  - VAFA = 1.12 (same as VAF before enhancement)
  - DEL FP = 0 (no functions were deleted)
  - VAFB = 1.12 (as counted in Case Study 1)
  - FP = [(14 + 34 + 0) * 1.12] + (0 * 1.12) = 54 (rounded)

- *Step 6:* Convert FP count into effort and schedule as done in Case Study 1.
  - Assume the same productivity figures as done in Case Study 1; 10 FP per person month. Using this productivity, you get the total effort as

$$\text{Effort} = 54/10 = 5.4 \text{ person months}$$

- Add 10% for Project Management = 5.4 + 0.54 = 6 person months
- You can suggest a three member team working for two months to do the enhancement project.

This case study explains the process of estimating the FP count and derives the effort for an enhancement project. Other possible extensions of a typical enhancement project, like recalculation of the FP count of the upgraded application, are not covered here.

Conclusion

This entire chapter, dedicated to providing you with a very detailed case study, offers a specific focus on how to convert theory into practical implementation. Software sizing as well as effort and cost estimations are quite tricky when it comes to practical situations. Most estimation methods are designed to be a bit ambiguous in the sense that they allow flexibility in real-life implementation.

The two types of case studies provided in this chapter, development and enhancement, cover a large section of an estimator's needs. The intention here is to provide you with a process of applying the function point estimation method as well as other effort and resource loading processes.

References

1. International Function Point Users Group (IFPUG). *Function Point Counting Practices Manual (CPM) Release 4.2.*

Other Interesting Reading Material

Dreger, Brian J. "FPA Maintenance and Modification: Rules and On-line Parts System Example," in *Function Point Analysis*. Prentice Hall, 1989. Pp. 108–131.

APPENDIX A

Reference Tables: Transaction Function Counts

The following transaction function tabulation and calculation tables have been provided to facilitate easy processing of function point counts. You may want to create these tables in an Excel form to automate certain complexity, FP counts, and other sum totals.

Reference Table to Calculate ILF/EIF FP Count

Table A.1 *ILF/EIF FP Count Table (with Examples)*

File Name	*ILF/EIF*	*DET*	*RET*	*Complexity*	*FP Count*
File 1	ILF	12	1	Simple	7
File 2	ILF	26	3	Average	10
File 3	EIF	28	3	Average	7
Total					

Reference Table to Calculate EI/EO/EQ FP Count

Table A.2 *EI/EO/EQ FP Count Table (with Examples)*

File Name	EI/EO/EQ	DET	FTR	Complexity	FP Count
Data Entry Screen—1	EI	16	2	Average	4
Summary Weekly Report—1	EO	36	6	High	7
Query—1	EQ	12	2	Average	4
Total					

Reference Table to Calculate Total FP Count

Table A.3 *Total FP Count*

FP Attribute	Simple	Average	High	Total FP Count
ILF				
EIF				
EI				
EO				
EQ				
Total Unadjusted FP Count				

Reference Table to Calculate VAF from GSC—Total Degree of Influence

Table A.4 *General System Characteristics and VAF Table*

GSC #	GSC Description	Degree of Influence	Comments
1	Data Communications		
2	Distributed Data Processing		
3	Performance		
4	Heavily Used Configuration		
5	Transaction Rate		
6	Online Data Entry		
7	End-User Efficiency		
8	Online Update		
9	Complex Processing		
10	Reusability		
11	Installation Ease		
12	Operational Ease		
13	Multiple Sites		
14	Facilitate Change		
	Total Degree of Influence (TDI)		
	Value Adjustment Factor		VAF = 0.65 + (TDI * 0.01)

APPENDIX B

Reference Tables: Data Function Points

The following data function tabulation and calculation tables have been provided to facilitate easy processing of function point counts. You may want to recreate these tables in Excel to automate certain complexity, FP count, and other sum totals.

Internal Logical Files and External Interface Files

Table B.1 *ILF/EIF Complexity Factor*

Range	*1 to 19 DET*	*20 to 50 DET*	*51 or More DET*
1 RET	Low	Low	Average
2 to 5 RET	Low	Average	High
6 or more RET	Average	High	High

Once you decide the complexity of an ILF/EIF after referring to Table B.1, you then have to assign the actual FP contribution (count) to the ILF/EIF based on the complexity factor. Two separate tables, one each for ILF and EIF, provide the exact FP contribution for each category of complexity: simple, average, and high.

The contribution FP count table for ILF is shown in Table B.2.

Table B.2 *ILF FP Contribution*

Functional Complexity Rating	Unadjusted Function Points
Low	7
Average	10
High	15

The contribution FP count table for EIF is given in Table B.3.

Table B.3 *EIF FP Contribution*

Functional Complexity Rating	Unadjusted Function Points
Low	5
Average	7
High	10

External Inputs/External Outputs/External Inquiries

Table B.4 gives the reference matrix that can be used to determine the complexity factor of each EI.

Table B.4 *EI Complexity Factor*

Range	1 to 4 DET	5 to 15 DET	16 or More DET
0 to 1 FTR	Low	Low	Average
2 FTR	Low	Average	High
3 or more FTR	Average	High	High

Table B.5 gives the reference matrix that can be used to determine the complexity factor of each EO/EQ.

Table B.5 *EO/EQ Complexity Factor*

Range	1 to 5 DET	6 to 19 DET	20 or More DET
0 to 1 FTR	Low	Low	Average
2 to 3 FTR	Low	Average	High
4 or more FTR	Average	High	High

After you use the preceding table to decide the complexity of an EI/EO/EQ, you then have to assign the actual FP contribution (count) to the EI/EO/EQ based on the complexity factor. Two separate tables, one for EI/EQ and another for EO, provide the exact FP contribution for each category of complexity: simple, average, and high.

The contribution FP count table for EI/EQ is given in Table B.6, and the contribution FP count table for EO is shown in Table B.7.

Table B.6 *EI/EQ FP Contribution*

Functional Complexity Rating	Unadjusted Function Points
Low	3
Average	4
High	6

Table B.7 *EO FP Contribution*

Functional Complexity Rating	Unadjusted Function Points
Low	4
Average	5
High	7

BIBLIOGRAPHY

Agarwal, R. Manish Kumar, S. Mallick Yogesh, R. M. Bharadwaj, and D. Anantwar. "Estimating Software Projects." Infosys Technologies Limited, IIM, Calcutta, India. ACM SIGSOFT, *Software Engineering Notes*, Vol., No. 4. July 2001, p. 60.

Albrecht, Alan. The Function Point Analysis method was developed by Alan Albrecht and is now maintained by International Function Point Users Group. www.ifpug.org

Banker, R., R. Kauffman, and R. Kumar. "An Empirical Test of Object-Based Output Measurement Metrics in a Computer Aided Software Engineering (CASE) Environment," *Journal of Management Information System*, 1994.

Boehm, Barry W., and Richard E. Fairley. "Software Estimation Perspectives." *IEEE Software*, November/December, 2000.

Boehm, Barry W. *Software Engineering Economics*, Englewood Cliffs, NJ: Prentice Hall, 1981. Available online at: http://sunset.usc.edu/research/COCOMOII/index.html

Boehm, Barry W., Chris Abts, and Chulani Sunita. "Software Development Cost Estimation Approaches: A Survey." Barry Boehm and Chris Abts, University of Southern California, Los Angeles, CA 90089, and Sunita Chulani, IBM Research, 650 Harry Road, San Jose, CA 95120.

Boehm, Barry W. Delphi Method was originally developed by the Rand Corporation (1948) and improved into Wideband Delphi Method by Barry W. Boehm and colleagues in the 1970s.

Brooks, Frederick P., Jr., *The Mythical Man-Month*. Reading, MA: Addison-Wesley, 1975.

COSMIC-FFP, version 2.0. Copyright © 1999. The Common Software Measurement International Consortium (COSMIC). www.cosmicon.com

DeMarco, Tom. *Controlling Software Projects*. Englewood Cliffs, NJ: Prentice Hall, 1982.

Dreger, Brian J. *Function Point Analysis*. Englewood Cliffs, NJ: Prentice Hall, 1989.

Fairley, Dick. "Making Accurate Estimates." *IEEE Software*, November/ December, 2002.

Garmus, David, and David Herron. *Function Point Analysis*. Boston, MA: Addison-Wesley, 2004.

International Function Point Users Group (IFPUG). *Function Point Counting Practices Manual (CPM) Release 4.2*. http://www.ifpug.org/publications/manual.htm

International Function Point Users Group (IFPUG). *IT Measurement*, Boston, MA: Addison-Wesley, 2002.

Jones, Capers. Foreword to *Function Point Analysis* by Brian Dreger. Englewood Cliffs, NJ: Prentice Hall, 1989.

Jones, Capers. *Applied Software Measurement, Second Edition*. New York: McGraw-Hill, 1996.

Jones, Capers. *Software Quality*. Boston, MA: International Thomson Computer Press, 1997.

Jones, Capers. *Estimating Software Costs*. New York: McGraw-Hill, 1998.

Jones, Capers. "Conflict and Litigation between Software Clients and Developers," Software Productivity Research, Burlington, MA, 2004.

Jones, Capers. *Software Assessments, Benchmarks, and Best Practices*, Boston, MA: Addison-Wesley, 2000.

Jones, T. Capers. Feature Points developed by Capers Jones of Software Productivity, Inc., is a variant of IFPUG Function Point Analysis. www.spr.com/products/feature.shtm

Kan, Stephen H. *Metrics and Models in Software Quality Engineering, Second Edition*, Boston, MA: Addison-Wesley, 2003.

Kolathur, Somakumar, and Kingshuk Dasgupta. *Architecture Reference Model (ARM): Defining IT Architecture*. Infosys Technologies Ltd., 2001.

McConnell, Steve. *Rapid Development*. Redmond, WA: Microsoft Press, 1996.

McConnell, Steve. *Software Estimation: Demystifying the Black Art.* Redmond, WA: Microsoft Press, 2006.

McPhee, John. *A Sense of Where You Are*. New York: Farrar, Straus and Giroux, 1999.

Park, Robert E., et al. "Checklists and Criteria for Evaluating the Costs and Schedule Estimating Capabilities of Software Organizations," Technical Report CMU/SEI 95-SR-005; Software Engineering Institute, Pittsburgh, PA; January 1995.

Peters, Kathleen. "Software Project Estimation." Software Productivity Centre, Inc.

Pfleeger Lawrence, Shari. "What Software Engineering Can Learn from Soccer." *IEEE Software*, November/December 2002.

Putnam, Lawrence H. *Measures for Excellence*, Englewood Cliffs, NJ: Prentice Hall, 1992.

Putnam, Lawrence H., and Ware Myers. *Industrial Strength Software*, Los Alamitos, CA: IEEE Press, 1997.

Roetzheim, William H., and Reyna A. Beasley. *Best Practices in Software Cost and Schedule Estimation*, Upper Saddle River, NJ: Prentice Hall, 1998.

Robyn, Lawrie, and Paul Radford. "Using Function Points in Early Life Cycle Estimation." CHARISMATEK Software Metrics.

Ross, Mike. "Size Does Matter: Continuous Size Estimating and Tracking." Quantitative Software Management, Inc.

Schneider, Geri, and Jason Winters. *Applying Use Cases*. Reading, MA: Addison-Wesley, 1998.

Symons, Charles. *Software Sizing and Estimating*, Hoboken, NJ: John Wiley & Sons, 1991.

Software Engineering Institute (SEI). The Capability Maturity Model Integration (CMMI). Carnegie Mellon University. www.sei.cmu.edu/cmmi

The Standish Group International, Inc. "The Chaos Report." 1995.

Wiegers. E. Karl. "Stop Promising Miracles." *Software Development*, Vol. 8, No. 2. February 2000, pp. 49–54.

INDEX

A

Acceptance test phase, 200
Actual Effort (Person Hours),
    as estimation unit, 16
ADD (Added FP), 185, 188
Add elementary process, 79
Agile software projects
    case study, 202–204
    complex issues in, 199–200
    project milestones in, 200–202
Albrecht, Allan, 52–55, 100–102
Algorithm-based estimation approach,
    278–279
Analogy-based estimation approach, 278
Application maintenance contracts,
    253–254
Application servers, 140
Applications
    change management in, 171–172
    components of, 75–76
    estimating total cost of ownership,
        273–274
    estimation case study. *See* Invoicing
        system case study
    functional and non-functional
        requirements of, 122–123
    of insourcing IT environment, 235
    maintenance contracts for, 253–254
    in outsourcing IT environment, 237
    scope and boundary of, 64–65
Arbitrary guesstimates, 226
Architecture, IT, 257
    estimating efforts and costs, 268–269
    overview of, 138–140
    role of architect in project execution
        process, 257

As-is analysis, tool supporting, 302
Attributes, FPA, 55–57
Availability, software contract
    requirement, 258

B

Back tier, in IT architecture, 140
Big bang approach, in software contract,
    258
Boehm, Barry, 282, 286–288
Bottom-up estimation approach
    defining, 278
    overview of, 283
    Simple, Medium, and Complex
        method, 284–285
Boundaries, 57, 64–65
Bradley, Bill, 194–195
Budget estimates
    manipulating project costs, 221–222
    outsourcing, vs. insourcing, 239, 244–245
    project approval phase, 26–27
    project contract phase, 27–28
    in truncated/partial projects, 261
    using flexible contracts for limited,
        255–256
Bug fixes
    estimating FP count for, 185–186
    found only during final testing phase,
        212
    impacting maintenance projects, 183, 253
Build phase
    complex issues in, 199
    in failed dream project, 5
    impacting project costs, 269–270

373

G

U

THIS BOOK IS SAFARI ENABLED

INCLUDES FREE 45-DAY ACCESS TO THE ONLINE EDITION

The Safari® Enabled icon on the cover of your favorite technology book means the book is available through Safari Bookshelf. When you buy this book, you get free access to the online edition for 45 days.

Safari Bookshelf is an electronic reference library that lets you easily search thousands of technical books, find code samples, download chapters, and access technical information whenever and wherever you need it.

TO GAIN 45-DAY SAFARI ENABLED ACCESS TO THIS BOOK:

- Go to **http://www.awprofessional.com/safarienabled**
- Complete the brief registration form
- Enter the coupon code found in the front of this book on the "Copyright" page

If you have difficulty registering on Safari Bookshelf or accessing the online edition, please e-mail customer-service@safaribooksonline.com.

Addison
Wesley